*MEMOIRS
OF A
PRACTICAL DREAMER*

Memoirs
of a Practical Dreamer

FROM A RUSSIAN SHTETL
TO AN AMERICAN SUBURB

by Benjamin M. Laikin

Translated from the original Yiddish by
MURRAY KASS AND MOSHE STARKMAN

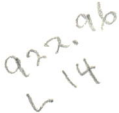

BLOCH PUBLISHING CO.   NEW YORK

Copyright © 1971 by Benjamin M. Laikin

Library of Congress Catalog Card No. 74-188371
SBN: 0-8197-0283-8

All rights reserved under international and Pan-American Copyright conventions.

Manufactured in the United States of America

IN MEMORY OF
MY BELOVED WIFE CHANA LEAH
WHO PASSED AWAY ON FEBRUARY 28, 1968
AND
IN MEMORY OF
MY MOTHER KREINA DEBORAH,
MY BROTHER SHOLEM,
HIS WIFE RIVKA,
AND THEIR CHILDREN MOSHE AND BASHE,
WHO WERE MURDERED BY THE NAZIS
ON THE FIRST DAY OF ROSH HASHANA
IN 1941

TABLE OF CONTENTS

INTRODUCTION 11
PREFACE 17

PART ONE
THE EARLY YEARS;
IN THE OLD COUNTRY

The Family and the Home 23
In Cheder—A One-Room School 26
Childhood Tragedies 30
A Jewish Town, Our "Shtetl" 37
Pogroms—Fear and Reality 40
In the Yeshivah 45
My Father Sharpens
   the Millstone and Brews Tea 48
Purpose and Hunger 50
Girls 54
At Home—And Away from Home 57
Commerce and Relatives 61
Grandfather's Inheritance 66
Self Education 68
A Boyhood Tragedy 70
An Orchard 72
At My Uncle's Mill 75

Hard Work 77
Some Thoughts on the Bellis Trial 79
Soldiering 80
New Hopes 83
We Steal Across the Border 84
In Galicia and Germany 86
On the Ship to America 90

PART TWO
IN AMERICA;
YEARS OF STRUGGLE

In America—A Greenhorn 95
A Mill and a Shop 98
Rags 100
Hatred of Yiddish 102
In Philadelphia 103
I Become a Peddler 105
War and the Troubles of a Greenhorn . . . 107
A New Name, A Revolt, and I Lose My Job . . 110
A New Home—A New Job 111
A Misfortune 114
Sick, Hungry and Out of Work 116
Difficult Days 117
I Become a Vegetarian 120
Thoughts about Death 121
Aimless 123
I Find Friends in Camden 125
In a New Place 129
In an Iron Foundry 133
Between Life and Death 142
The End of a Partnership 144
Labor Zionism and Freedom 146

Contents

I Become a Coal Miner 147
In Baltimore 149
Yiddish Schools 150
Crisis 152
I Get Married at a Bad Time 153
My Family Goes Hungry 157
An Enthusiast of Literature 159
Hard Work 160
I Travel Over the Country 169
My Trip to Japan 171
My Trip to Europe 172
A Bitter Disappointment 173
In Partnership 178
Difficult Days 181
Death Takes a Hand 184
On My Own 189
The National Recovery Act 196
A Letter Before the Supreme Court 198
I Become a Farmer 200
Up to This Point 202

PART THREE
COMMUNAL ACTIVITY;
FRUSTRATION AND FULFILLMENT

In the Struggle for a Jewish State 211
The Yiddish Book—
   Reproaches of a Devoted Reader 214
The Detroit Jewish Council 219
The American Jewish Congress 227
A Battle Against Communists
   and Their Fellow Travelers 229
Fund Raising 231

Zionist Activity	233
The Work of Zionist Council	236
Press and Radio	242
Mass Meetings and Labor Organizations	243
The Jewish Community Council	244
A Jewish Community Theater	248
Business—Caught in a Bureautic Maze	254
A Battle Against Bureaucracy and the Black Market	257
My Daughters	264
How the War and Its Outcome Affected Me	270
Creation of the State of Israel	275
The Hospital	281
Israel Bonds	284
A Summing Up	285
Personal and Business Problems	286
A Trip to Israel and Europe	290
Community Activity	297
A Former Nazi	300
Poale Zion, the Labor Zionists	305
The American Jewish Congress	308
Belonging to a Synagogue	310
Women's Rights	316
A Yiddish Writer and His Distorted Characters	322
Activities and Struggles	325
Other Campaigns	330
A Meeting with Sholem Asch	333
The Great Dictionary of the Yiddish Language	336
A Comment on Jewish Liberals and Radicals	339
A Visit to Israel	340
Family, Health and Children	347
Chana Leah, May She Rest in Peace	353

INTRODUCTION

THE REMINISCENCES OF BENJAMIN LAIKIN are a weighty and important contribution to Jewish memoir literature. They are especially significant because they trace the life story of an individual whose experiences, trials and tribulations symbolize the tragedies and triumphs of so many fine Jewish men and women from their early days in the now destroyed old country, the Jewish communities of Eastern Europe, to the time when they were able to establish themselves in their new homeland, the United States.

We have in Laikin's memoirs detailed descriptions of important periods in the history of the Jewish people in general and of Jewish life in America in particular. Laikin's pen included still another dimension. It shed light on corners of American Jewish life that remained largely dark and unknown. Most memoirs of Jews in the United States seem to dwell mainly on Jewish life in New York. Laikin takes his readers into the provinces, especially the bustling city of Detroit.

Laikin describes how Jewish immigrants who settled in the growing industrial cities of the middle west began slowly to play an important role in the economic life of the region and ultimately of the country itself. During this period of transplantation, they never once forgot from whence they came nor from whom. They established "tents of Jacob," so to speak, in the American milieu, planting social and cultural seeds to preserve their Yiddish heritage in the midst of a new and often strange civilization and culture.

Benjamin Laikin—his first name is the Anglicized version of the last part of his Hebrew-Yiddish name, Samuel Dov Ber—was born in 1896 in the small White Russian town of Pobolov. He studied in the traditional one-room cheder until his Bar Mitzvah and then for a short period, in a yeshivah in the provincial capital, Bobruisk. Mr. Laikin came to the United States in 1914, disembarking from an overcrowded immigrant ship in the city of Baltimore.

Two months later he arrived in Philadelphia where he made his home for some time on the benches of Fairmount Park. There seemed no bottom to the depths of his misery. He suffered all the torments of Gehenna, as did so many other Jewish immigrants.

From Philadelphia Laikin made his way to Gardner, Massachusetts, where he had at least the promise of a job. For five years he labored in a junk yard, earning barely enough to keep himself alive. He worked for a while in the coal mines of Pennsylvania, the only Jew in the area. He returned to Baltimore and there met Chana Leah Golomb whom he married in 1922. He tried to establish a business of his own but it didn't work out. He took a job as a travelling salesman for a rag firm and this gave him the opportunity to travel throughout the United States and Canada. He toured Europe, visiting no less than thirteen countries. He also made a trip to Japan.

In 1929, Laikin settled in Detroit where he established himself in business and raised a family of four daughters who

Introduction

married and presented him, in time, with eleven grandchildren, all of whom he has encouraged to follow in the ways of their ancestors.

Throughout a turbulent and busy lifetime, Mr. Laikin continued his studies; his thirst for knowledge knew no bounds. He helped to establish and support Yiddish language schools, helped finance the publication and distribution of Yiddish books and periodicals, and played an active role in Jewish cultural institutions. Perhaps his most gratifying and enduring contribution was his long years of work on behalf of the Zionist ideal, through the Poale Zion, the Zionist Organization of America and the Detroit Zionist Council.

Laikin's reminiscences remind us that not even the terrors of being a stranger in a strange land, nor the heartbreaking difficulties they faced in sinking economic and social roots in America, could extinguish the idealism that the Jewish immigrants brought to America with them. It was this idealism that led Laikin to the Poale Zion, to work for the American Jewish Congress, for Yiddish schools, literature and a host of cultural and national institutions and causes.

It was inevitable that a man of his devotion and ability should reach positions of leadership in the various organizations. To each activity, he contributed both time and money. Yet, he was not always blessed with the satisfaction of seeing his efforts come to fruition. Even so, his disappointments and frustrations did not hinder him from plunging into new projects which he considered important to the Jewish community.

Laikin believed passionately in perpetuating and strengthening Yiddish culture. He subsidized authors and helped publish their works. This is not to say, however, that he accepted everything that flowed from the pens of the Yiddish writers. He had little patience with stupidity and pomposity and frequently found himself in sharp disagreement with Yiddish authors, some of them prominent. The newer wave of authors who seemed to thrive on self-hatred he considered an abomination.

Jewish life in the towns of Eastern Europe has been depicted in great detail. Laikin, in his memoirs, reveals hitherto little-known aspects of shtetl life. He was part of and depicted what the late historian Jacob Shatzky, a close friend of Laikin's, described as "Jewish types and typical Jews." The descriptions will certainly evoke memories of similar experiences and similar characters among the aging generations of early twentieth century immigrants.

The difficult period of adjustment has also been described in searing detail by Laikin, sparing us neither the heartbreaks nor the betrayals. In this Laikin touches upon immigrant problems largely neglected by other memoirists. Laikin's early experiences in the old country, as a child and as a youth, his agonies of adjustment on arrival here and his deepening and strengthening roots in American life could well be included in the curricula and textbooks of our Jewish schools.

It would be good for the rising new generations here in the United States and also in Israel to learn what Jewish life was like in the old country and how young Jewish immigrants pioneered a new life in America. Such descriptions as can be found in Laikin's book could well be included in the source material for such a study.

The conditions and attitudes described by Laikin, reports of meetings and accounts of ideological struggles, provide an invaluable picture of Jewish social and communal life in America from the early nineteen twenties to the present. It is from these accounts that one begins to appreciate the efforts, in time, money and frustrations that went into each little advance in Jewish life. We also get a glimpse of the inexhaustible reservoir of Jewish idealism that impels men like Laikin to continue even in the face of disappointment and defeat.

If we learn in Laikin's accounts of incompetent leaders or of negative aspects of Jewish life, we also learn of the intense devotion of the masses of ordinary Jews to the loftiest aspirations of Judaism. These folkmasses, with Laikin frequently at their head, though pre-occupied with their own problems and worries, nevertheless gave time, effort and money to advance Jewish education, to support Jewish culture, to create and build the Jewish homeland, and to rally to the support of any cause devoted to the survival of the Jewish people.

In any autobiography the reader is always interested in the auther's family. It is well that Mr. Laikin devoted space to his late wife, Chana Leah, his four daughters, and his eleven grandchildren. One wishes that he would have written about them at greater length. Nevertheless, one learns from Laikin's account about the equally suffering and equally idealistic Jewish girls who subsequently became the Jewish mothers of the present generation; how they strived to make of their Jewish homes warm nests of human and spiritual values. One can also recognize his own experiences in trying to give his children a good Jewish education, often with inadequate facilities.

Many Yiddish writers and National Jewish leaders can testify to the warmth of the Laikin household. The Laikin house was, for many, home as well as the central bureau, the organization's headquarters of Detroit. Many fund raising campaigns were organized and conducted in Laikin's spacious basement "auditorium." Many lecturers educated and entertained their audiences in that basement meeting room. Many writers described their books and raised funds for their publication there. Some of his guests were destined to become leaders of the State or Israel.

Laikin possessed a wide store of knowledge, especially in Jewish life and thought. This was constantly enriched through the years by constant reading, attendance at lectures and association with Jewish intellectuals, many of whom came to Detroit in response to a personal invitation from Laikin. He also expanded his horizons by attending and taking part in national convocations of political and cultural organizations. In time Laikin became an influential speaker and lecturer in his own right. His own basically strong thought processes, cultivated and enriched by years of self-study and personal experiences, lent an air of authenticity and drama to his words.

Fortunately Laikin was on guard to avoid a recognizable literary style in his writings. He preferred to let the stark facts serve as their own descriptions. Thus, his memoirs have an honesty and an impact that might have been diluted by unnecessary embellishment.

In summation, Laikin's memoirs are a weighty contribution to Jewish reminiscence literature and a valuable addition to the history of Jewish communal life in America. One can only hope that this can serve as a measure of reward to Mr. Laikin for the many painful experiences and frustrations he suffered during so many years of effort to strengthen and enrich Jewish life in America.

My colleague, Murray Kass, and I are grateful for having had the opportunity to translate his autobiography into English.

—*Moshe Starkman*

PREFACE

EARLY IN THE 1940'S, I DECIDED TO REcord what I remembered of my life—in my home town in the old country, making my way to America and my life here. I was anxious to describe these events so that my daughters, my grandchildren and the generations to come will know something about one of their ancestors and what America was like for a Jewish immigrant in the first four decades of the twentieth century. To them and to the memory of my dear wife, Chana, I dedicate this book.

I ask the reader's forgiveness if my chronicle is sometimes repetitious or not in proper chronological order. After all, I am more a reader than a writer of books. Everything contained within these covers is the simple truth, without conscious omission or embellishment. So, I implore you, dear reader, to approach this feeble effort with understanding and compassion and not chastise me for my errors in details or judgement.

My good friend, Moshe Starkman, encouraged me to write these memoirs. Later he brought to me another friend, Murray Kass, and both took upon themselves the task of translating my memoirs into English. The original version, in Yiddish, was published in New York in 1970 and was favorably received by the literary critics of Hebrew and Yiddish publications, both in the United States and in Israel. Perhaps some of the literary lights of the English world will be equally kind.

—*Benjamin M. Laikin*
Southfield, Michigan

*MEMOIRS
OF A
PRACTICAL DREAMER*

Part One

The Early Years;
Life in the Old Country

THE FAMILY AND THE HOME

I WAS BORN ON THE FIRST DAY OF THE Jewish month MarCheshvan in the year 1896 in the small town of Pobolov in the Bobruisk region of the Province of Minsk in Russia. Although we were considered middle class my mother told me in later years that we were very poor at the time of my birth. At times there was not enough food in the house to feed the children properly.

All in all my mother gave birth to eleven children. Six of them died during their first month of life. I was the third eldest among those who escaped the clutches of the Angel of Death. Although this should have been a source of joy to my parents I came to realize as I grew up that my birth was not exactly a cause for great celebration.

My father's parents lived with us in what would ordinarily have been a fairly large house. But with so many of us, of varying ages and many demands, it seemed rather crowded. Grandmother died when I was still very young. I hardly remember her. I was told that she had been very pious. My grandfather had been a successful merchant in his younger years and had become quite wealthy, at least by the standards of our shtetl.

My grandfather and father built a mill to process buckwheat groats and that became our livelihood. It was a small mill, turned by horses. It served the peasants in the surrounding villages and for us it provided the necessities of life.

Grandfather was a pious Jew but he was not exactly a scholar. He was well versed in the Mishnah, the code of Jewish laws. He went to the synagogue every day to recite the prayers. He lived a long life and was active in business until about six months before he died.

My father was not a great scholar either. He had studied the five books of Moses, the Pentateuch, with the commentaries of Rashi; also the other books of the Bible and the Mishnah. Although father never said so openly, I always felt that he deeply regretted that he was not more learned. He was a clever man with a great ability to reason through a problem. But, unfortunately he was never able to throw off his small-town outlook on life.

Community affairs fascinated my father and few were more active than he. If he was unlearned in the Torah he was even more unlearned in the ways of his neighbors. For his sincere efforts he was frequently insulted and his well-thought out plans were often rejected. But father was not one to hold a grudge or fight back. He continued his efforts but made little progress.

My mother came from many generations of rabbis and scholars. Her own father died when she was only two years old. Her mother was very intelligent but strict. She too lived to a ripe old age.

In her younger days my mother was considered a beautiful woman. She was quite modern, well ahead of her time considering the small town we lived in. She was well read, in Russian as well as Yiddish literature, and perhaps for that reason her marriage was not a happy one. She and father came from different worlds.

With a small-town background and a small-town outlook, my father was content with the simple life. Food to him was merely fuel for energy. He had little interest in fancy foods or exotic dishes. My mother, on the other hand, was born for big city life. As for food she was always curious about different foods and new ways to prepare them. The smell of herring in oil made her ill.

My mother was a delicate woman, possibly because of her hard life. We had no servant girl and all the household tasks fell to my mother. They were too much for her. But she never complained.

I think she was more unhappy about her meager wardrobe than her housework. She longed for beautiful dresses and a fine coat. The few dresses she had were worn and not in the least attractive. Nevertheless, she retained much of her youth and beauty. In her late forties she was tall and slim and still a handsome woman. The streaks of gray that crept through her hair she carefully darkened.

Mother loved people but she was impatient with idle gossip and silly chatter. She longed for stimulating discussions and was especially happy when my older brother and sister would invite their friends. She took a lively part in their discussions and even in their games.

Unhappily, mother had no female friends. She had little in common with the small-town housewives. Still, many of the women came to her for advice. They valued her judgement and listened carefully to her words. Among those who sought her out were many unmarried young women from middle class and even well-to-do families. Alas, husbands she could not provide for them, but advice she could give them in abundance. On Saturdays she would read them selections from the Bible that were translated into Yiddish especially for housewives. Most of the women were uneducated and could not read.

IN CHEDER—A ONE-ROOM SCHOOL

CHEDER, THE TRADITIONAL ELEMENTARY school for Jewish studies, was situated in one medium size room, with a few benches for the students and a table of sorts that passed as a desk for the teacher. I was five and a half years old when I first set foot in the cheder. My first melamed (teacher) was called Feivel Shwebelnik. Hardly earning enough as a teacher to keep body and soul together, he also served as "Shammas" (beadle) in the little shul which was named appropriately enough "The Small Synagogue."

Of medium height and rather thin, he never had enough to eat to allow some fat to stick to his bones; his most prominent feature was a yellow goatee. On the surface he appeared to be a mild mannered person but somehow the simple act of punishing a disobedient or forgetful child aroused a passion in him. He would whip the children not out of anger but, it seemed, out of a firm conviction that it was the only way to teach children; the more he whipped the more they would learn.

For the most insignificant offense the melamed would order the boy to unbutton and lower his trousers. Using a wood twig he would come down lightly on the child's bare bottom two or three times, all the while humming a tune. The poor victims cried more of embarrassment than of pain. He never whipped me but the fear that he might do so, if

The Early Years; Life in the Old Country

not that day then the next or the one after that, kept me in a permanent state of fear.

For my second semester my father enrolled me in the class of the melamed Shmuel Hirsch. His specialty was teaching the children that the unstressed Hebrew vowel point "shvah" should not be pronounced like the vowel point "tzeyreh" (ey, like in grey).

Shmuel Hirsch was a bitter, morose man. His whippings were frightful; the children were terrified of his insane rages. He whipped in anger and as he whipped his anger grew and the angrier he became the harder he whipped. He would begin by grabbing the unlucky victim by the hair in back of his head and banging his forehead on the table. Then he would grab a stick, sometimes the bread paddle that stood near the oven, and beat the boy over the backside with it until he could no longer lift the paddle. Exhaustion alone was able to break the vicious cycle and save the luckless youth.

Fortunately I was spared the emotional and physical pain of beating at his, or the first melamed's hands. I always suspected that they never punished me because my father belonged to the upper stratum of the community and that he was no common workman or artisan as were the fathers of the other students.

Although I escaped a formal beating I still got my share of punishment. The melamed Shmuel Hirsch had a long thick strap which he held in his hand or kept nearby as he listened to the children recite. When a boy's mind wandered or if he did not answer quickly enough, a flick of the strap quickly brought the boy to his senses and, at least until the next time, he kept his eyes glued to the passage they were reading. This was not considered a whipping, however, only a reminder.

The strap was a hateful thing to the boys. Whatever pleasure there was in learning was destroyed by the cruelty of the melamdim. Surely those afflictions which we suffered at the tender age of six or seven were no less than those suffered by our ancestors in Egypt.

One boy, braver than the rest, determined to get rid of the strap. He stole it, not once but several times. Each time someone would find it—in the lake, in the tall grass, in the forest—and bring it back, for who was there that did not recognize Shmuel Hirsch's strap? The teacher was overjoyed when his missing strap reappeared and as if in celebration, he would let it sing and crack over our backs for the next week or two louder than ever.

One day the melamed let fly with his strap but instead of hitting the boy on the arm, hit him in the eye. The boy howled with pain. Even the "rebbe" was frightened. Later in the day, it was getting dark, the boy's older brother broke into the cheder and stole the strap. He turned the strap over to us and we boys gathered at the rear wall of the community bath house to hold a council of war. We were determined that the hateful instrument of torture should never again be resurrected from the dead.

We decided then and there that each boy would bite off a piece of the strap, spit it out, and that would be the end of it! Only two of the boys had teeth strong enough for the task. I was not one of them. I suggested that it might be better to bring a knife from our mill and cut the strap into little pieces. "Yes, yes," they shouted and off I ran to the mill. We quickly cut the strap into tiny pieces and threw them to the four winds.

At that point fear set in, but there was no turning back. Yet, we had committed a criminal act. We had destroyed our teacher's strap. True the strap had destroyed our morale—

but that apparently was no crime. To make sure that no one betrayed our secret we proclaimed a "herem," a ban, a taboo, worse than a curse, on anyone who would reveal our secret—even if he were subjected to the worst tortures. After all, what could possibly have been worse than the whippings and the strappings?

Since there were only eight of us, we included the old rabbi in the community in the ban, without his knowledge of course, and even the Lord of the Universe Himself! And so it was that no one found out what happened to the strap. Shmuel Hirsch was outraged and soon found a replacement for the old strap. But, somehow it did not have the same sting and to us it did not seem to hurt as much.

I studied under Shmuel Hirsch for two semesters. In the first semester I studied "Chumash," the five books of the Pentateuch. In the second semester I turned to the other parts of the Bible. Reb Shmuel Hirsch also taught me to write in Hebrew script.

Some years later when the overseer of the bath house died, Shmuel Hirsch was appointed to the job. And so the teaching career of Shmuel Hirsch came to a timely end.

My third melamed, Chaim Velyé taught the entire Bible. He also taught me to write Yiddish and Russian. Tall, with a greyish-black beard, he had a stately appearance. But, alas, he too believed that learning was a painful process. His specialty was grabbing a boy's ear and twisting it so that, as the saying goes, "one could see a vision of his great grandmother in the world above."

The afflicted boy, when he was able to catch his breath, was sure his ear had been wrenched from his head. He was both surprised and delighted to find that his ear was still there but considerably hotter than the untouched ear.

CHILDHOOD TRAGEDIES

ADULTS SOMEHOW GET OVER SUCH THINGS but for children the little childhood tragedies wound deeply and remain in one's memory for a lifetime. There was a tailor in our town who did work for the peasants in the surrounding villages. He was a "Cohen," a descendent of the high priests of Israel. This automatically gave his family exalted status.

Despite his priestly heritage the old man had a fondness for the fruit of the vine. He often became intoxicated and would sometimes even start fights in the synagogue. One such incident took place on Simchat Torah, the festival celebrating the completion of the public reading of the weekly portion of the Torah. The festival, which takes place at the onset of the fall season, concludes the feast of Succoth (Tabernacles).

The tailor had many children but I will confine my narrative to only three of the younger sons, Moshkeh, Zyameh, and Meir. Moshkeh was at that time about 17 or 18 years old. Zyameh was about 14 and Meir was 10. These three were an unholy group which bullied and terrorized all the other boys in our little town, our "shtetl."

I loved pocket knives and carried one with me at all times. I do so to this day. One day Moshkeh accosted me and took away my pocket knife. I started to cry but far from getting my knife back, I got a good thrashing instead. With a final blow he warned me not to tell anyone. Terrified, I remained silent.

This was only the first of a number of indignities I was to suffer at their hands. Moshkeh would watch for me and when he caught me he would demand my money. If I didn't have any he would beat me. I had already given him all the coins I had, my pocket comb, a knife and a mirror. Unhappily for me it was not enough. He demanded more and more.

To satisfy him—and to save myself from a beating—I began to steal money from the house. I stole a silver ruble and turned it over to him. My father became suspicious but since there were more than 40 silver rubles in the drawer, he wasn't entirely sure that one had been taken. I lived in fear of Moshkeh and in fear that I would be found out.

On another occasion I took 36 kopecks from my mother's pocket. She discovered her loss and surmised that it was I who had taken them but I stoutly denied it. Eventually it was my older brother who drew the secret out of me and told my mother, even though he had promised not to tell her that I had stolen the coins.

The following day when I came home from Cheder for lunch, my mother took me by the hand and led me back to school. We arrived while the melamed was still eating his lunch. Mother told him that I had stolen money from her pocket and that she wanted him to punish me. Without saying a word he took off his strap and started to unbutton my trousers. I was quite strong for my young years and tried to resist. Although he emerged victorious it was not a complete victory. All he succeeded in doing was to roll up my shirt and his strap fell only on my back, not my backside. My honor was saved! None of the other boys were there to exult in my shame. The "rebbe" himself said nothing to the children.

When mother left the teacher returned to the table to finish his lunch. He was still breathing heavily from the exertion.

"Why don't they leave me alone?" he sighed. I felt sorry for him. At home no one spoke of the incident. I was grateful. However, my troubles with Moshkeh continued. In fact they multiplied. He kept watch for me and pounced on me as soon as I emerged from the house. If I had no money, his beatings would become more and more severe. On the other hand, I was afraid to steal money from my parents. There seemed to be no solution or end to the problem.

One day he hit me so hard in the face that my cheek swelled up. Upon my return home my mother noticed the swollen cheek and became alarmed. She questioned me closely and it was not long before I began to cry and revealed the whole story. Mother was outraged and told my father and grandfather what the bully had been doing to me. Father and grandfather stood watch for Moshkeh and it was not long before they spied him taking up his usual post near my home waiting for me to come out. They caught him and dragged him into our yard. They must have put the fear of God Himself into the bully for he never bothered me again. I saw it all from the window, shaking with fear but relieved that at last my ordeal seemed to be over.

Some years later, Meir tried his brother's extortion trick on me but by then I was strong enough to fight back. I quickly put an end to Meir's little racket.

Around this time I attended Chaim Velye's cheder. I studied there for two semesters and it was during the second semester that I suffered an experience that left an indelible mark on me—a betrayal by my best friend.

I was one of the youngest boys in the cheder. One day I was notified by the "king" of the students (his name was Kaiser and had set himself up as leader of the class so naturally we called him the "king") that Yankel, son of the cobbler, had been declared a dog. I had never heard of such a thing! One boy, the oldest, and the strongest, proclaimed himself our ruler and whatever he said became law. Whatever he ordered the children had to obey. Otherwise the of-

THE AUTHOR

THE AUTHOR AND WIFE CHANA LEAH

My wife Chana Leah before we were married in 1922.

The Author Taken in 1913 in Russia.

My mother Kreina Dveira, sister Taible, father Moshe, brother Hayim and sister Rachel. Taken in Russia 1914.

Mother and Father, Russia, 1929, while I was there for a visit.

...ther, brother Sholom, his daughter Basha in his arms, sister Taible, sister Rachel, Rivka ...olom's wife), cousin Heshel. In front, Rachel's son and Sholom's son. Russia 1929. Parent's ...me in background.

Sister Rachel, brothers Hayim and Sholom. Standing, Yasha Kogan, Rachel's husba[nd]
Taken in Russia 1918.

Sister Rachel, Mother, sister Taible. Taken in Russia 1929.

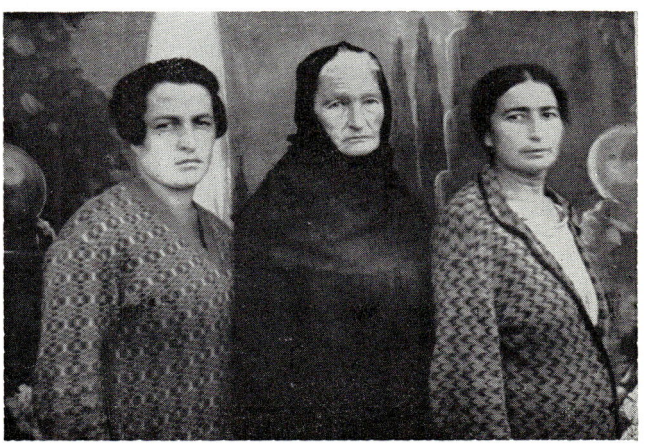

Sister Taible, Mother, sister Rachel. Taken in Russia 1932.

Daughters Pnina, Beth-Sheva, wife Chana Leah and daughter Shulamith.

fender would be declared a dog and would be ostracized. He would be placed under a ban and the other children would be forbidden to speak to him.

I had a friend Yankel who lived across the street from us. We played together as long as I can remember. So one can imagine how disturbing it was for me to be confronted suddenly with such a shattering "royal decree." My dearest friend had been turned into a dog!

When I came out to play I found Yankel sitting alone. The other boys were pointing in his direction and shouting, "dog, dog!"

That was more than I could bear. I defied the king and his royal decree. I went over to Yankel and said that I would play with him. He was overjoyed. One would have thought that I had saved his life.

We stole away to a secret hiding place and swore eternal friendship for each other.

Picture my astonishment then when on the very next day as I was coming out of cheder I was myself greeted with shouts of "dog, dog!" and who should be leading the pack but the very one who had sworn eternal friendship for me, Yankel. He had difficulty pronouncing the "r" so instead of Beryl, he called me "Beyl." And so he jumped up and down in front of me shouting "Beyl is a dog, Beyl is a dog!"

So deeply mortified was I by this betrayal that it affected my relationships with others throughout my life. This incident and another, similar, occurrence were so deeply burned into my consciousness that never from that time forward did I have any intimate friends. Always there was a slight reserve to guard against another betrayal.

I completed the last months in Chaim Velye's cheder without making up with the other boys. I was much too hurt by Yankel's treachery. I did become friendly with his older brother Reuven and often went to his home. But with Yankel I never exchanged another word.

Sixteen years later I returned from America to visit my parents who still lived in the old "shtetl." I also brought with me regards from the four sons of Beryl the cobbler who had also emigrated to the United States. Yankel was not one of them.

In due time I called on the cobbler to deliver the good wishes and the news of his four sons and was very warmly received. Yankel was there. I greeted him curtly. I could not get myself to converse with him. After all those years the wound was still painful.

My fourth "melamed" was Velye Kulyes. He was a real scholar, tall and thin, a small beard added dignity to his handsome face. Rebbe Velye was a Litvack, that is, he came from Lithuania. Of all my teachers he was the one I liked best. Never did I lose the feeling of affection and admiration that I felt for him.

His was an unfortunate marriage. His wife was totally deaf and a fool in the bargain. (May she in her Heavenly abode forgive me for my unkind words.) Velye Kulyes had three daughters. The oldest died in childbirth. Velye, who valued his son-in-law, a shochet (ritual slaughterer), and wished to keep him in the family, gave him his younger daughter in marriage. She was sixteen years of age. They went to another village to live and rarely visited Velye and his wife.

The third daughter was deaf. As a result, the sounds she uttered were completely incomprehensible. Communication with her was difficult, almost nonexistent. Today such people can be taught to speak and even to "hear" but not then and not in our small town. She was married off to a young man who was in hiding to avoid being drafted into the Czar's army. He taught cheder in another village and would leave his wife at home to return only during Passover and for Rosh Hashonah, the Jewish New Year. In his own home my dear teacher had no one to talk to.

Alas, when I returned from America in 1929 for a visit, my beloved teacher was no longer among the living. He had died only a few months before my arrival. And I had so much wanted to see him again, to greet him and thank him for his kindness, to tell him what a great influence he had on my life.

I studied at his cheder for five years; each year was divided into two semesters, with vacations only during the Jewish holidays. I started with the minor prophets and, at the age of nine, I began studying the Talmud.

Rebbe Velye's method of teaching was similar to that of the "melamdim" of old, only more thorough. He stressed the importance of pronunciation and drilled me endlessly in Hebrew grammar.

I was the only boy in town at the time who was so far advanced. Some years before there were several Talmud students, some from our town and some who came from nearby villages. But in my time I was the only Talmud student, which is probably why my teacher devoted so much time and effort to me. He would sit with me for hours expounding on the beauties of the Bible and discussing the commentaries of the sages.

At that time also, money was not too plentiful in our home. There was enough for food, to be sure, but not quite enough to clothe the entire family. It took a great deal of effort and scrounging to gather enough money to purchase clothing and shoes for the children. The one time of the year that we children got new shoes and clothing was on Passover.

My older brother was five years my senior. A sister was three years older. I had a brother three years younger. Unfortunately he was killed during the civil war in Russia after World War I. My youngest sister was still a baby and was suffering from rickets.

Until I became Bar Mitzvah I never wore a suit of clothes sewn especially for me. I always wore my brother's hand-me-downs but only when he outgrew them. They might have been too tight for him but they were too big for me. However, it was considered wasteful to shorten them. Besides, my mother said, I would grow into them soon enough and then they would fit me properly! And so, it was always my brother who got the new suit of clothes and I who inherited his castoffs.

I would clean the suit and take special care of it. I wore it only on the Sabbath and on holidays. Now, when my brother, who was equally proud and careful of his new suit, had to feed the horses and cows on Saturday, he had no intention of doing so in his new suit. So, back went my "new" suit for my brother to wear into the stable and the barn. I wept bitter tears and rebelled at the terrible injustice but my brother's heavy fists soon convinced me that the struggle was hopeless. Justice may have been on my side but my parents sided with my brother!

My brother was not overly fond of books. He seemed happier helping father in the business. One of his greatest joys was to hitch two horses to a sled, fill it with boys and girls and "haidah" off in the snow. He had a special affinity for me. As soon as I came near him he would give me a wallop, but so cunningly that no one would notice it. He also had a habit of punching me in the side and would hit me so hard that everything would turn black before my eyes.

Not all was sadness and beatings. There were many

good times. I enjoyed playing dominoes with my father. He was a good player and taught me the game when I was quite young. Even before I started my studies in cheder I was a better-than-fair player.

On one occasion, a "poritz," a wealthy non-Jewish landowner, who had come to see my father on business, sat me down on his knees to play with him. He was surprised and I was delighted—I won! I can still remember the moves each of us made that helped me to win.

Growing up in our town was not without a goodly measure of sorrow and joy.

A JEWISH TOWN, OUR "SHTETL"

THE YEAR WAS 1905. OF THE RUSSO-JAPANese War, I remember only that the Gentile soldiers worked hard at getting drunk. They came into Jewish homes to beg money for vodka. Often they would break windows if they didn't get drinking money, or, if they had already had their vodka and felt like showing their "manhood." It was so much easier to fight an unarmed Jew!

I have no recollection of the pogrom in Kishinev in 1903. I do have some memory of the pogrom in Homel but it is very vague.

Of the aborted Revolution of 1905 my memory is also dim. There were no factories in or near our town, so we had no proletariat, no working class. There were only some hired craftsmen: shoemakers, tailors, carpenters, and the like. I say there were only a few hired craftsmen because most of the craftsmen had their sons working for them and none was so busy that he had to have a large working force.

How did the town fare economically? The wealthiest

Jew in town was Abraham the miller. He leased the water mill. He was tall, with a sizable paunch, strong willed and shrewd. He was, naturally, fond of good food and drink. Somewhere along the way to his riches he managed to acquire some scholarly renown and was a more than fair cantor. He was not overly modest and was very much impressed with himself.

To disagree with him was to incur his mortal enmity. At dominoes he was not very good. When we played together I made sure he won. He would constantly correct his moves. I would permit him to change several moves at a time and, if even then he would find himself in danger of losing, I would allow him to rearrange his dominoes in such a way that he could not help winning.

There were three wealthy storekeepers and three small stores whose owners were not so wealthy. There was only one well-to-do craftsman among all the struggling ones, Beryl the cobbler. And why not? He had all of his seven sons working for him. On top of that he sometimes hired additional men. Beryl was the only craftsman considered to belong to the "balabatim," a member of the middle class. He led the congregation in the morning prayers and could interpret chapters of the post-Biblical Mishnah, the code of Jewish law.

There was one place where Beryl the cobbler could not gain admittance, and that was the rabbi's house on the Sabbath where in the late afternoon he would expound on the teachings of Hassidim. Only the homeowners, the middle class townsmen were privileged to attend.

There were four teachers in town, several religious functionaries, including two beadles (shammosim), since the town had two synagogues. The town contained a number of craftsmen, tailors, cobblers, and carpenters who would walk

The Early Years; Life in the Old Country

from village to village during the week to find work and return to their own town on the weekend. There were two teamsters and a blacksmith who had three loyal helpers, his sons.

In the summer many of the townspeople would rent orchards from the surrounding landowners. The orchards were small but the work was pleasant and there was plenty of fruit and an added profit at the end of the summer.

There were ninety Jewish homes and six non-Jewish homes in our town. Some of the more affluent families had servant girls but these were never Jewish girls. However, there were many Jewish girls from our town who hired themselves out as servants in the larger cities of Bobruisk and Rogachow. Our town had no market days but we did have two annual town fairs. Only some of the storekeepers profited from those fairs. The rest of us would have been happier without them.

Our town was several kilometers from the railroad station. This alone should indicate how small, poor and unimportant our town was.

We had our own radicals. They were socialists of sorts but we called them democrats. It was said that they would gather in the forest on Saturdays and desecrate the Sabbath by smoking cigarettes. They would also shout out to the surrounding trees such slogans as, "Down with dictatorship, down with the Czar!"

Leaders of the group were Reuven, son of Abraham Isaac the bath house attendant, and Archie the cobbler. Generally young men and women of the middle class did not participate in their activities, only those of the poorer families.

I do not recall in which year it happened but there was a rumor once that the socialists would demonstrate on the first of May. The local Jewish proprietors were worried. My grandfather threatened to split heads if any of the democrats showed up at the mill to persuade the worker to join in the demonstration. But, when on May 1st a committee of democrats showed up at the mill, it was grandfather himself who told the worker to go and join them. They went into the forest and held their meeting there. In the town there was no sign of anything unusual. The town was not at all affected by the Revolution!

POGROMS—FEAR AND REALITY

THE UNSUCCESSFUL REVOLUTION OF 1905 was followed by years of reaction. The peasants in the surrounding villages were restless, turbulent. It was a time of rising tensions and fears. There were no pogroms in our region but many times we felt the hot breath of violence nearby.

Once, it may have been in 1906 or 1907, there were rumors that our town had been marked for a pogrom. There were even some who swore that they had witnessed the arrival of peasants from far-off villages and that they were mobilizing in "The Village" as we called one particular village located about a mile away from our town of Pobolov.

Hastily the Jews organized a self-defense group. Our total arsenal consisted of a single revolver, owned by Archie the cobbler. Naturally it was he who took command of the defenders and led them out to the town line to face the marauders. Archie's was the first group. My father commanded a second group which took up positions on the mill street, not far from the town line. My older brother and my grandfather were part of my father's group.

My grandfather, an elderly man by then, took along the

"toolkatch," a heavy implement used to tamp the flour as it was poured into the sacks. He was determined to tamp out some punishment to the drunken ruffians.

My mother, sister, and younger brother and several women were hiding in the mill. I remained in the mill behind barred doors, standing guard with an iron bar in my hand. The night passed uneventfully. Even though nothing happened the incident has remained in my memory.

A permanent defense brigade was organized to guard against any future pogroms. We bought six revolvers, which were hidden in our house against the day when they would be needed. Every Saturday evening the defense committee would meet at our house. The committee consisted of three home owners and three of the "others," the so-called democrats. We might have had our political differences but we were all Jews nevertheless and I am sure the peasants would not have stopped to inquire about the political opinions of his victims before clouting them.

I never knew what took place at those meetings. Always the door would be bolted—from the inside. My mother tried to distract me. She told me they were trying to decide if a loaf of bread would be better if it was baked square instead of round. I found it very frustrating to be treated like a child. After all, I did stand guard in the mill!

We had a regular watchman in our town, a peasant. He was given a number of volunteers to assist him. Every night as the watchman made his rounds, he was accompanied by a two-man volunteer patrol, both armed with revolvers. There were quite a few volunteers and they took turns patrolling with the watchman. The volunteers came from different parts of town so they made sure that the entire town was patrolled.

The peasants became even more surly; or at least that is

what we thought. Drunken peasants would come into town on Sundays and frequently they would fight—with one another, never with the Jews. Even so, we were never free of the threat of violence.

My own life went along quietly. I continued my Bible studies. When the rebbe would ask me about a specific verse, I was able to tell him on what page he could find it, and recite it for him word for word.

For some reason the rebbe did not care much for the Book of Daniel. As a result I studied it by myself. His favorites were Isaiah and Jeremiah. Submerged in my studies I built a world of my own where I wove fanciful daydreams of events far removed from life at home and in the town. The Talmud played an important role in my make-believe world.

I was very much intrigued by the discussions of the sages about such questions as: what damages should be paid to the farmer whose cow was gored by an ox; how to divide a garment found by two people; the studies of the Talmud tractates Pesakhim (Passover offerings); Gettin (bills of divorcement), Khullin (matters dealing with dietary laws) ... and so on. All these were very much in my mind in my imaginary world. The rebbe never tried to relate these to the everyday world.

We all worked very hard at home and we got along. I helped out in my spare time. Mother's tasks somehow were heavier than those of the rest of the family. The male members took care of the horses but it was mother's job to take care of the cows, to feed them and milk them. The men in the family felt such work was beneath their dignity.

We always had lots of wood in the yard but, here again, it was not considered a man's job to haul wood into the house, so that too was mother's chore. In addition she had to do the cooking, the cleaning, dishwashing and the laundry. She also had to sew clothing for the younger children, repair the clothing of the older ones and, in her spare time, knit socks for the entire family.

During the winter months mother had to pluck feathers for pillows, prepare filling for the pillow cases for my sister's dowry, and also knit woolen gloves and woolen socks for the men in the family since it was very cold at the mill. She had other chores and was never surprised at the demands made of her.

One day my father came from the mill and said:

"Kraineh, I have just bought a wagon full of buckwheat and I need another 25 rubles."

Without a word, my mother put a kerchief on her head and went out to arrange a "Gemilut Khessed," a short-term, interest-free loan. With the exception of Abraham the miller and Hershel Leib the storekeeper, who never had need of such a service, everyone in town at various times made use of this practice. These loans were given to one another, freely and in good spirit. They were usually for one or two days, sometimes for a matter of hours. It was not unusual, for instance, to hear such a conversation:

"I can give you 50 rubles but I must have them back at 1 o'clock when I'll be leaving for Bobruisk."

"Very well, you shall have the money in time."

The loan was repaid on time. Where did the borrower get it? Probably a short-term loan from someone else. I can't recall a single instance when someone failed to return such a loan on time. Perhaps that is why they were given so freely and no one was embarrassed to ask for one. Even when Hershel Aryeh Nahum Yekels went into bankruptcy he returned the "Gemilut Khessed" money he had borrowed.

Life for me during this period was not easy. During the

summer months cheder would keep me occupied until it was time for evening prayers. During the winter months we studied until 9 o'clock at night. And when I came home I had to repeat the day's lesson in Talmud and grammar.

I had already started to help out in the mill, caring for the horses. It was then that I learned that it was my father's dream for me to become a rabbi. He insisted that I behave in a way fitting for a rabbi-to-be. This was a mixed blessing. I loved to play ball but that was not considered a fitting pastime for a future rabbi. For a future cobbler or a tailor yes, but not for a future rabbi.

So we would gather in the forest on Saturday afternoons to play ball until it was time for evening prayers. And before I could go to the synagogue I had to run home and tend to the horses, so Saturday was not much of a day of rest for me.

One Friday afternoon as I walked toward the synagogue I spied one of my friends tossing a ball around. He saw me and without thinking threw the ball to me. Automatically I caught it and threw it back to him. Unfortunately, my teacher, Velye Kulyes came along just then and witnessed the episode. He came over to me, gave me a sharp slap in the face and scolded me.

Adding to the monotony of life in a small town was the indignity of having to wear my brother's cast-off clothes, which were always too large for me, and the beatings I frequently suffered at his heavy hands. It is little wonder, then, that very early in my youth I had begun to think of escaping to the big cities and of a more practical future for myself than the rabbinate.

IN THE YESHIVAH

I WAS BAR MITZVAH ON THE FIRST DAY of Heshvan in 1909. It was in the fall, the holidays had passed and the leaves were turning brown. For the occasion I prepared and delivered a sermon on the problem: "Is a man who has lost his left arm permitted to wind the 'tfillin' around his right arm?" This is permitted only for those who are lefthanded.

Shortly after, I went off to Bobruisk where I enrolled in the Yeshivah, which was directed by the Rabbi of Chitofke. My father brought me to the city and took me directly to the yeshivah, which was located in the Butcher's Synagogue, so-called, logically enough, because it was established by the butchers and was attended by them.

My father arranged "eating days" for me in the homes of friends, that is, for every day but Wednesday. On those days, lacking a host, I had to scrounge for food or eat what I had been able to save from my previous meals. I slept in the community hostel near the synagogue together with some of the other students. The disorder and dirt were indescribable. But I was too excited and a little fearful of being away from home and so didn't mind the filth too much.

I was one of the youngest students—and terribly unprepared for such advanced studies. I could not understand the Talmud lesson at all and could not even repeat it to myself during the restudy period. The director came only for a few hours a day and during the few months that I was there never once asked me a single question; not once did he examine me on the lessons we were studying.

While I may not have been too quick to learn I always had a good memory. When I grasped something it remained with me; often though, I have to work hard at understanding it. Thus, what I lacked in speedy comprehension I made up by diligence.

Unfortunately, there was no one in the yeshivah to explain the lesson to me. The other students studied very little and wasted their time with play and pranks.

"Eating days" at the various homes was a painful and humiliating experience. I dreaded the coming of mealtimes. The richer the home, the worse it was for me. I had to wait for what seemed like hours before the mistress would order the servant girl to "give the boy some food."

Being of a practical nature even at that tender age, I realized that the yeshivah was not suitable for me. I could not study Talmud there and I could not study Russian as long as I slept in the community hostel. With a little hesitation and a great deal of apprehension, I sought out our town's teamster on his next regular trip to Bobruisk and persuaded him to take me home with him. I left without so much as a "good-bye" to the yeshivah people or the families who fed me, or should I say starved me.

Arriving home I had to do some fast explaining for such unexpected and unorthodox behavior. My father was terribly disappointed. He saw his great dream of me becoming a rabbi come to naught. Yet, strangely enough, he was the only one who did not reproach me. Mother nagged me and was sure that I would come to a no good end. My older sister agreed and so did my brother who harped at me and tormented me without letup.

In the meantime, it was decided that I would continue my studies with Velye Kulyes during the evening. During the day I was to sit in the synagogue and study by myself. And so it went. I enjoyed the arrangement very much, especially the evenings with rebbe Velye. He spoke to me as he would to an adult. The days began to pall on me. I disliked sitting there alone, but I did not dare go home. And so I sat there day in, day out, studying sometimes and thinking about my future the rest of the time.

My father, anxious to salvage something from his shattered dream, decided that I should become a public reader of the weekly Torah portion at Saturday morning services, to become a "Baal Kriyah," as it is called. But I, realizing that I was weak in remembering the traditional chant begged him to let me find some other path to righteousness; he was adamant.

And so I prepared for my first public reading. It was to be the portion called "Jethro" (Exodus XVIII-XX), which also includes the Ten Commandments (XX, 1-14). The dreaded sabbath finally arrived and I made by public debut. To my everlasting shame, it was worse than I had ever dreamed it could be. I was unable even to pronounce the words correctly; the chanting was awful. Fortunately I did not have to read it from the *Bimah,* that is, the elevated platform on which services are usually conducted. Instead I read it in the prayer room of the community house. My father was very charitable. He never mentioned that liturgical disaster and I was forever grateful to him.

Also about this time I had another searing experience. I had long suffered at the rough treatment of my older brother. I don't know which pained me more, the punches or the frustration. Anyhow, one day he gave me a particularly heavy blow. In a rage I drew myself up to my full height and shouted at him, "Enough, it's time to settle this once and for all!" I raised my fists and prepared to attack him but to my surprise he moved away without a word. Disbelieving, but relieved, I lowered my fists. From that moment on he never raised a hand to me again.

MY FATHER SHARPENS THE MILLSTONE AND BREWS TEA

WE HAD A GOOD WINTER. THE MILL DID well and food was plentiful. There was much to do but my father, grandfather and brother, Sholem, managed to get the work done without hiring additional help. They worked very hard. I helped too. I especially liked to help my father "smith" the millstone. Grandfather was too old for such work and my brother didn't like it. I enjoyed sitting up Saturday nights with my father punching at the millstone with a sharp hammer and etch little "teeth" into the stone so it would grind the buckwheat better.

My father, working along with me would hum a tune. He had a poor singing voice but that didn't stop him. I didn't mind the false notes at all. It was very pleasant. I felt very close to him on those occasions.

"Careful," he would caution me, "Not so hard, you'll break those little teeth."

Another time he would say, "Careful, careful. Don't be in such a hurry. Only the lazy are in a hurry. They're too anxious to get their work over with."

And so we sat facing each other, punching away at the millstone with our small sharp hammers. Sharpening a millstone was not just another task for my father. It was an art. He himself had built the mill. True, he did hire some laborers but he himself was the architect and the engineer. He couldn't stand a bungler. Everything had to be done right.

In the evenings, when he could spare the time, he would visit Abraham the miller for a game of dominoes. Otherwise, he would play with me. Always he admonished me, "Don't try to profit from someone else's mistake. If you see someone

The Early Years; Life in the Old Country

making a wrong move, tell him so. And if he wishes, let him retract it and move again."

Father went to the synagogue three times a day, for morning prayers, early evening prayers (Mincha) and evening prayers (Maariv). He would return home for a quick visit between Mincha and Maariv.

After the noon meal father would lie down for a brief rest. At three o'clock in the afternoon he would have his tea. Now, for ordinary people a cup, or glass, if you will—of tea, is a cup of tea. One drank it and that was that. But, with father drinking tea was a ritual.

First he lit the samovar, bringing the water to a boil. He then filled the teapot and added cold water to the samovar, thus reducing the boiling. He placed a piece of paper, with a hole cut in the center, over the chimney to slow the boiling still further. He poured some of the water out of the teapot, put fresh water in it and placed it on the samovar—so that it would draw out the essence of the tea slowly.

When the water in the samovar came to a boil again, father poured the water into six glasses and he himself drank from a seventh glass. Finishing the glass, father poured some essence of tea into each of the six glasses and then added water from another glass which he filled and refilled from the samovar. In this way he made sure that there was no sand residue on the bottom of the glass.

And so father drank the six glasses of tea, one after the other. For all six glasses he used only one lump of sugar. The glasses had to be thin and the tea had to have just the right color. He would hold it up to the light and if the tea was not the proper shade, he would pour it out and start afresh. He never added jam or sugar to the tea. He would seat himself at the table, place a yarmulke on his head, the one he wore to synagogue on the Sabbath, and proceed with the ceremony. On such occasions he would tolerate no interruption or noise until he was finished.

Father's spiritual pleasures were concentrated mostly on his Saturday visits to the rabbi's house to listen to him hold forth on the Talmud. The audience was restricted almost exclusively to homeowners. However, Beryl the cobbler, who was patronized by the homeowners and was included in their family celebrations, was tolerated but not for long.

When some of the "upper class" townsmen, those who were very conscious of their elevated status, remained away from the weekly sessions because of his presence, Beryl took the hint and stopped coming.

Father went to the rabbi's house during the week also on occasion but somehow they didn't seem to give him as much satisfaction as the Saturday sessions. He did not have the same radiant smile on his face that was always there when he returned home from the Saturday visits.

Sometimes the discussion took a little longer and the evening services were delayed. This would frequently evoke murmurs of annoyance from the artisans who were anxious to get to work when the evening prayers ended.

PURPOSE AND HUNGER

WINTER FINALLY CAME TO AN END. Through the white and freezing months I was beset by one problem which continued to plague me: to what purpose will I come? What am I to do? What does the future hold in store for me?

I did not want to remain in my father's mill for a number of reasons. First of all, he did not need me. My contribution would be neither important nor appreciated. Secondly,

I knew that quarrels between my brother and me would inevitably occur, which not only I, but father too would find painful. Thirdly, I did not think it was such a wonderful job to devote myself to until I would become eligible for military service. And after having completed my hitch, I thought, what then? My father was not a wealthy man and never would be one. So, if I wanted to do something about my secret and growing desires to go to America, it would be better to leave my family and make something of myself.

It was shortly after Pesach. A Jewish acquaintance from a village some eight kilometers distant paid us a visit. At one point during his visit he said to my father:

"Reb Moishe, I have heard that you have an amiable, accomplished boy. Give him to me. I need him to teach my children. He shall have everything he will need. We shall be good to him and treat him with the respect befitting him and we shall pay him 20 rubles a semester."

I was excited by the thought of being away from home, on my own, and, in a way, being a "melamed" myself. I looked forward to it. One day a short while later, my brother took me to the village where I was to become a teacher.

I found myself in a house with two rooms. The father, a cobbler, used one of the rooms as a workshop. He worked near the oven and at the end of the day would convert the room to a bedroom, sleeping there with his wife and my two pupils, two boys, one eleven and a half and the other nine. Working with the cobbler was an older son, about 20, and an apprentice, Reuben, with whom I had studied at one time. It was he who had recommended that I be hired as a teacher.

The second room was occupied by the cobbler's married daughter and her child. Her husband had gone to America and she waited for him to send for her. Also in that room were an older daughter of 30, a spinister, another daughter, in her twenties, a third daughter about seventeen or eighteen, the oldest son, the apprentice and I. I learned very quickly the art of undressing under the covers.

My daily routine was about as follows: At about 7 o'clock I would say my prayers and see to it that my two pupils would recite the morning benedictions. I then had a glass of tea and would begin my lessons. The younger boy I drilled in reading Hebrew, writing Yiddish and Russian, and arithmetic. The older one I taught the Pentateuch, but without Rashi's commentaries, the book of Samuel, writing, and arithmetic.

The studies lasted until Mincha and I was responsible for my pupils through the evening prayers. Everyone in the house called me "rebbe" and I had to act the part. Yet I was only thirteen and a half at the time! But I was called "rebbe" and so had to squelch my normal desires and try to behave like an adult.

At this house, for the first time in my life, I learned what it was to be hungry. The mistress of the house simply did not give us enough food. They were not poor. They had several thousand rubles in savings, they had two milk cows and every week they took the dairy products to town to be sold. During the week our meals consisted of sorrel (shchav) with "srovetkeh" (whey) and one slice of bread. The master would cut off the slices with his cobbler's knife and pass one to each member of the household. When the portions were distributed the bread was taken away from the table and hidden away.

Often in the evening I would go for a walk with Reuben, the apprentice. I asked him about the food and was told that it was always the same, too little. He said however, that things would improve somewhat when the fruits would

The Early Years; Life in the Old Country

ripen. Then there would be more to eat. What the mistress kept from us we could pick from the trees.

I did not complain about the food in my letters home. Most of my family were sure that I would not remain long anyhow. They did not have too much faith in me, especially after my flight home from the yeshivah in Bobruisk. So I hungered in silence. But when I noticed one day the cobbler's wife was feeding her children on the sly I was outraged. I told Reuben about my discovery and then and there we held a council of war. We decided to find out where the bread was hidden and simply steal extra portions to ease our hunger.

It did not take us long to discover that the bread was kept in the anteroom. The door was locked and the mistress kept the keys. However, we found that one could enter from the outside through a hole in the wall. Reuben would creep in while I stood watch and come out with his pockets and blouse bulging. We would then run off to the woods and have a feast. Looking back, I don't think I can recall ever having tasted any food as good as those pieces of dry bread we stole from the penurious cobbler's wife.

(Years later, in the United States, I had better and tastier meals. But, there were times of hunger, too. Once, after going without food for four days, I found myself picking crumbs out of garbage cans. And this was in America, where the streets were paved with gold.)

The cobbler's wife was not only miserly, she was miserable as well. She was tall, thin, dark, with thin, compressed lips, which rarely moved. She hardly uttered a word. The cobbler, on the other hand, was short and stocky and had a wide, bushy beard. He was quick to anger and had a vile temper.

Both were embittered people who found joy in nothing

and solace only in their rubles. A year before the older son had maimed himself in order to avoid military service. Someone informed on him and in the end he was not only drafted into the army but had been sentenced to serve in a disciplinary battalion. His letters were full of whining and complaints. Whenever they came the entire family would gather around the table to read them and weep.

GIRLS

THE OLDER DAUGHTER WAS NO BEAUTY. She had a loose mouth and a loose tongue. Both were always moving and she was well versed in the art of cursing. To me though, she was friendly, almost too much so. My relations with girls at that time were almost non-existent. I had never kissed a girl, had never even touched one.

Although I was but thirteen and a half I looked more like seventeen or eighteen. I grew more than a light fuzz on my face and began to shave. I even grew a mustache. Naturally I would not admit to being not yet fourteen. I passed for older. Apparently the older daughter believed it because she tried hard to entice me. Deterred by a combination of immaturity, inexperience and timidity I steered clear of her —much as I was tempted. The most she—or I—had gotten was a kiss, nothing more. Fear triumphed over temptation.

The second daughter, short and stocky, was a redhead and had a tongue as fiery as her hair. Her comments were invariably caustic, sarcastic—biting and offensive. I disliked her intensely and rarely exchanged more than a word with her.

The youngest daughter was eighteen years of age. Even so, she was treated like a child. She was even dressed like a little girl, possibly out of consideration for her two older sisters, both of whom were still unmarried.

There were three other Jewish families in the village, one was an innkeeper, a sickly man, and an impractical dreamer. Both in summertime and in wintertime he buried his head up to his bearded chin in a huge scarf. He coughed frequently, a short, sharp cough not unlike the bark of a startled dog. He considered himself a scholar of sorts and disdained to converse with ordinary mortals.

It was the innkeeper's wife, short and peppery, who was the breadwinner. There was a son who had married just that year and had leased a windmill. There was also a daughter of twenty, short, nicely rounded and with a beautiful face. She was a lovely person. But she would have none of me. I was non-existent, an unperson—something "to chew and spit out," she once said.

My employers though, had a low opinion of her and spread the rumor that she spent more time on mysterious visits to no one knows where than she did at home.

There was also a childless couple in the village. They lived in a small house. Everything in the house was tiny, except the wife. She was tall and a bit on the heavy side, a big woman all around. Her head brushed against the ceiling in spots and she had to stoop to get through the door. The husband was able to read and write but was helpless with simple arithmetic. The wife did not know how to read or write but somehow was talented with numbers. So she did the arithmetic and the husband wrote the figures down.

He often called on me for help. I found it most uncomfortable and so I was delighted when my employer ordered me not to go to the "berlinah" (barge) again. This was the nickname he had given the wife because she was large and bulky, like a barge. My employer didn't like the idea of me helping them while he was paying my salary—such as it was!

The fourth Jewish family consisted of my employer's sister and her husband, a diminutive man in his late sixties, A pauper, with little to recommend him, he was nevertheless and interesting person, a bit of a wag. He had a glib tongue and his witty barbs always reached their mark. His wife was blessed with a great talent for cursing and vituperation. This the husband would frequently defuse with a joke or a witticism. If someone gave him a glass of schnapps, he would reciprocate with a jig—despite the fact that one leg was ten inches shorter than the other—or, as he put it, "one foot is ten inches longer than the other." He was a glazier if he can be said to have had a trade.

Some time later a Jewish blacksmith settled in the village. Never had I seen a man as poor as he. There was not even a chair in his house, no bedding either. He had several black pots and some wooden spoons. His wife was a slut, incredibly ignorant and dirty. They had children as numerous as the sand on the beach, and with sand-colored faces. The blacksmith was deeply religious and was an exceptionally kind man. He could neither understand nor cope with the ways of the modern world, or his wife, so he withdrew into himself and his books.

The other families helped them as much as they could. They got him work on occasion and were overjoyed when he earned a few extra kopecks with which to feed his brood. The women joked about the wife. She would walk twelve miles to the town of Zhlabin to the "mikvah" and walk back again. I taught one of the sons for five rubles for the semester. My employer, however, took half of that as his share, why I still don't know. I do remember, however, how proudly and happily the blacksmith gave me the five rubles.

I enjoyed his good will and appreciated that more than his rubles.

AT HOME—AND AWAY FROM HOME

I RETURNED HOME AT THE END OF THE semester and was greeted with the deference due a melamed. Bearded Jews came over to me and said: "Sholom Aleichem." Apparently they had forgotten that I was only a year past my Bar Mitzvah. At the synagogue I stood at the eastern wall, most precious since it faced Jerusalem, and I did not go outside to chat and socialize with the young people when the weekly Torah portion was read. I remained seated inside with the elders, the scholars and the more pious Jews.

At home though I was still a boy, and that's how I was treated.

With the end of the summer I returned to my calling as a melamed. The winter months were not as pleasurable as the summer months. At my employer's home the second son had been drafted into the Czar's Army. The parents were morose. The evenings were long and unpleasant. There was nothing to do.

The older daughter, despairing of seducing me, treated me with contempt. Out of sheer boredom I sat down at the cobbler's bench, supposedly to help out. And so, gradually I learned the trade, not too well, I'm afraid, but I learned how to make a cobbler's thread, how to hammer nails into the shoes and even how to sew on a patch.

The winter dragged on and I was happy when the time came to return home for the Passover holiday. Shortly after I arrived home my old teacher, Velye Kulyes, came to see me. He had become a matzoh baker and wanted me to help him. He wanted me to be a "wheeler," to puncture holes in the dough so that the matzoh would not rise before being put into the oven. Actually I didn't want to take on the extra job but I couldn't refuse him. His former "wheeler" had left and since I had had experience in puncturing matzoh dough, he sought me out. I was paid thirty kopecks a day, a day which started at five o'clock in the morning and drew to a weary end at ten o'clock at night.

Since I had to bend over, the back of my neck soon became stiff and sore. To this day when I grow exceptionally tired, the bone in the back of my neck is the first part of my body to send out signals of fatigue.

After Passover I was again faced with the question, what shall I do? My father thought little of the teaching profession. My mother, on the contrary, regarded it very highly. Most of the men in her family were teachers when they were young. Somehow, in the growing up they changed their professions because all of them were well off and none of them remained a teacher.

Immediately after Passover, it was in 1911, I again sought a teaching position. I found one about fifteen kilometers from my home town. Stretching the truth by several years I told my employers that I was eighteen years old. Because of my father's prominence in the community I got the job. I was to teach five boys and was to receive forty-five rubles for the semester, with bed and board in a different home every five weeks.

One of my employers was a blacksmith, a pleasant, intelligent young man who was pious and scholarly. This was commendable but he soon began to intrude on me with endless questions on Rashi's commentaries, on various parts of the Midrash, and on the legendary comments of the Talmudic sages. He was not seeking answers. That I wouldn't have minded. What I resented was that he was testing me, trying to trick me into errors.

I had never studied the Midrash, it never occurred to me that I should. Still, it was an accepted fact that a melamed must have an answer for everything. The blacksmith's wife also put me to the test, but in a different way. She would often question me about handling children, about men and about family life. And I, despite my height, the stubble on my face and my pretensions to adulthood, was still but an inexperienced and unworldly stripling of fourteen!

Still they were tolerant. They treated me well. Food was plentiful. The mistress was afraid that someone might think that she was starving me and this would reflect unfavorably on her.

Later I had my room and board at the miller's house. Except for the Sabbath I rarely saw him. He was constantly at the mill. He was a hard worker and spoke little. Mama was the boss and he was content to have it that way. She was short and thin as a reed but what she lacked in substance she made up in words. They also had a daughter, in her twenties and quite beautiful. In time she met my older brother and fell in love with him.

The home consisted of one room. On one side of the everpresent oven were the beds of the husband and wife. They took up half the room. At the head of the room were two hard couches, a table, chair and two stools. This was the sum total of the furniture in the house. It should be noted that this was not exceptional for most Jewish homes in those impoverished villages were equally lacking in household goods—and, all too often, food as well.

My third employer was an idler. His wife, a dressmaker, was the breadwinner. He was in his sixties and she, his second wife, was in her early forties. She was an enterprising

"Breindeleh Kossack" and was not one to back away from a controversy. Once she came to me with a complaint against the miller's wife.

"She is a thief, rebbe," she charged.

I asked: "How can one say such a thing about a respectable Jewish woman?"

"Rebbe," she replied, "You don't believe me? Then you, too, are a thief!"

My fourth employer was an unusual man. He had been raised among gentile peasants and still retained many of their mannerisims. However, he married a very devout Jewish servant girl and it was she who turned him once again into an observant Jew. His Hebrew prayers sounded as if they came from a peasant's mouth, full of mispronunciations and faulty grammar. He spoke Yiddish like a non-Jew, if one can conceive of a Russian peasant taking the trouble to learn Yiddish.

He had previously been a cobbler. Now he was the owner of a store. When he had a few drinks in him he would regale his hearers with his experiences among the peasants, even describing the taste of such peasant dishes as pork in a bowl of milk. On such occasions the wife would get him off to bed and sleep as quickly as possible.

The former peasant was very much concerned about my own piety and watched me closely. He checked to see how long it took me to say my devotions and how long it took me to recite the Eighteen Benedictions ("Shimoneh Essray"). He was especially careful to see that I did not "waste" my time with girls. If I went out for a walk in the evening and failed to return when the cows came back from pasture, he would lock the door on me. I would have to knock on the door long and hard before he would let me in. On such occasions he would berate me adding that he did not want the girls in the village to bring my bastards into the world.

On hot summer nights we would sometimes sleep in the anteroom, where he kept the hay. When he was slightly drunk he would describe for me, in great detail, his exploits with the peasant girls. And each time he ended with the same warning: "But you rebbe, I will not let you commit such sins."

It was during that summer that grandfather became paralyzed. I was not told about it and didn't learn of it until I came home at the end of the summer. I was startled and deeply grieved to find my grandfather so helpless. He had been so strong—and now he could not even get off the bed. I wept bitterly.

COMMERCE AND RELATIVES

SUCCOTH MARKED THE END OF SUMMER and the beginning of a new season, a new semester. I suddenly decided I had had enough of the teaching profession. It was not for me. Instead of returning to my teaching post I remained at home helping my father in the mill.

My rebelliousness carried over into the mill and I had several arguments with my father. I tried to convince him that we should not confine our operation to the buckwheat brought in by the peasants for conversion into groats. For this they paid a tenth of the produce in lieu of money. The earnings were greater when the peasants paid a tenth of the buckwheat that was milled. If they paid in cash it came to five kopecks a "pood" (about 36 pounds). This netted us much less.

However, the season was unusually short—from Succoth to New Years (September to December) and from Passover to Shevuoth (April to June). But the horses had to be fed and grazed all year round, so in the end the horses ate up much of the profit.

I tried to persuade my father to buy the buckwheat in the surrounding villages and grind it into groats which we could then sell. Father argued that such an undertaking would require a large amount of capital. He didn't have that kind of money and he was reluctant to borrow such sums. If he did, he was afraid Chaim David, the money lender, would come every day to look into the pots and pans to make sure that his loan was not being eaten up or squandered.

According to my plan, we would increase production during the good season by working at night. We would grind our own flour and sell it immediately and realize ready cash. When the season ended we could expand instead of waiting until the end of the season to mill our own flour and then have to use it for ourselves and our horses.

My father was adamant. He said he had no desire to become wealthy. God had helped the family until then and would continue to do so in the future. My brother sided with father, but for a different reason. He feared that under my plan he would have to do more work. And so he would have!

Mother sided with me, and why not? Who could understand better the difficulty of feeding a family on seasonal earnings? A daughter was growing up and it was time to start accumulating a dowry for her. Nevertheless father rejected my plan. I determined to do something on my own. But what?

Father suggested that I open a store but that too was not for me. I knew that a storekeeper has most of his money tied up in merchandise that sits on his shelves. And in the register there are more records of debts than cash. And so,

The Early Years; Life in the Old Country

when the time would come for me to be drafted I would be without funds to buy my way out of military service or to leave the country. Obviously I had no wish to become a soldier in the Czar's army.

There was another reason why I did not want to become a storekeeper. However, I kept it to myself. The fact is that I could not operate a store by myself. I would have to make trips to the city to buy merchandise and someone would have to mind the store. In addition, I couldn't be in the store from early morning until late at night all alone. That meant that someone would have to be with me—someone from the family. And since I was only fourteen and a half, obviously anyone who would come to the store with me, being older, would naturally assume that he was my boss—and that I didn't want. I wanted something for myself not a family business with me as the very junior hired hand.

So, after some thought I decided to become a grain merchant. I had already gained considerable experience and was well qualified to judge the quality of the grain and barley. My plan was to make the rounds of the nearby villages buying up grain. The buckwheat I would give to father, the rye, oats and barley (there was no wheat in our region) I would transport to Bobruisk to sell there. Father was to supply the horse and wagon.

And so I became a grain merchant. Since it was unheard of in our part of the world for a child to pay for his food and lodging I was able to keep the money I had earned as a teacher. I had saved over 100 rubles, which I invested in my new enterprise. Soon I began to show a profit, particularly since I had virtually no expenses.

The winter of 1911-1912 was a good one. The harvest was rich. The prices were high and the peasants had enough grain to feed themselves and some left over to sell. Father's mill prospered. I had to remain home to help out. But I also had an opportunity to arrange a business deal for myself. However, one Friday night my venture into the business world collapsed, engulfing me suddenly, like a spring storm.

Before recounting the incident, however, I must retrace my steps to bring the reader up to date on some family matters. My father had two brothers and a sister. The older brother had emigrated to America, leaving at home a family consisting of a wife, five daughters, each one older than the next, and a son. Years before he had had a store but bad times forced him to give it up. With visions of gold in the streets my uncle left for America in 1903. He hoped to earn a modest fortune quickly and return to his home and his family.

Unfortunately my uncle had no more success in America than he did at home. He was unable to send his wife and children much money. Gradually they used up their savings and the income from the store. Soon they were left with nothing. A garden alongside the house and a cow provided my aunt and cousins with barely enough to keep them alive.

My aunt was a very proud and tight-lipped woman. No word of complaint came from her mouth. Nor would she permit her daughters to go to work. Her son, the same age as my older brother, about 19, also did not work. They refused offers of assistance and resented my parents' efforts to help them. But I knew that my brother Sholem would bring some grain to our aunt's house from time to time. And since Sholem was on good terms with the son and the older daughters, they accepted his offering with good grace. We younger children often visited our aunt but only auntie's younger children would come to our house.

My father's younger brother, who lived in Bobruisk, was,

at least by our terms, a wealthy man. He had leased a large, very modern water mill and, so it seemed, had no complaints against the world, God or his fellow man. Outwardly he and father were on good terms, but I could sense that their relationship was strained.

The reason? The mill had originally been leased to grandfather. My uncle, who had not yet been married, managed the mill for grandfather while grandfather took care of another mill in our home town. When it came time for my uncle to go into the army, grandfather spent thousands of rubles to buy him out. He was successful. Eventually there came a time when grandfather was pressed for finances and he asked my uncle for some money from the earnings of the second mill. Uncle gave grandfather 1,000 rubles but made grandfather sign a promissory note. He also went to the owner of the mill and persuaded him to change the lease over from grandfather's name to his. Grandfather was deeply hurt. So was father and relations between them ever since, while proper, were not very cordial.

Father's sister lived in Slabodka, a village right next to our town. Years before she had leased an inn which brought her a modest living. Her husband was an idler, more adept at producing progeny than running a business. They had five sons and three daughters. Most had left home. Two were still left, a boy my own age and a girl much older. One son lived in London; two sons and a daughter had gone to America.

One married daughter died leaving two young children. Another son, who had married, lived in Zhlobin; he was wealthy. My aunt had a hard time. She sold whiskey illicitly. She would carry sacks of potatoes and grain for miles, some of them weighing as much as a hundred pounds, which she collected from the peasants in payment for the whiskey.

For all her woes, my aunt was a kindly woman, not at all bitter. She visited us often since she admired my mother, her sister-in-law, very much.

GRANDFATHER'S INHERITANCE

GRANDFATHER DIED THAT WINTER. During shivah, the traditional seven days of mourning, we were still eating our Friday night meal when my uncle's daughter burst into the house bringing with her the local police chief who began to take an inventory of all of grandfather's belongings. He listed all the furniture, the household goods and even the jewelry that mother had received as wedding gifts.

They then went to the mill, counted and listed everything in sight and then locked and sealed the mill with a warning to my father that nothing was to be moved. We were thunderstruck. Aside from being outraged by the vulgar and unfeeling behavior of my cousin and my uncle, who undoubtedly was behind his niece's action, we now faced the practical problem of finding feed for the horses and cows. How could we feed them if the mill was sealed?

The mill had been closed early in preparation for the Sabbath, so many of the peasants who came into town with sacks of buckwheat had to wait until sundown on Saturday before the buckwheat could be processed. Father was afraid he would be unable to return the sacks of grain to the peasants because of the seal and that this might lead to trouble. My own few sacks of grain had also been listed and sealed.

My mother had three brothers, two of whom had emigrated to America more than twenty years before. The third brother lived in the Poltava region where he taught Talmud in a Jewish school. Mother also had a sister who lived some thirteen versts distant (almost 9 miles) from our town. She was a wealthy woman, owner of a very successful dry goods store. Her husband was a lawyer who was permitted to practice only in the lower courts. He was a fascinating person. Aside from being a lawyer, he was a gifted scholar with a profound knowledge of Hebrew. He considered himself a freethinker but politically was quite reactionary.

However, two of his older sons, students at St. Petersberg, played an active role in the 1905 revolution. Uncle was on good terms with a number of government officials, including the Governor himself. However, he lived in another province and so could not help us with our problem. He did advise us not to touch the seal but to cut a hole in the wall and to carry out as many sacks of grain as we wanted. In their place we were to return an equal number of sacks of straw and other worthless matter. Thus, we would have the grain and the law would have the requisite number of sacks.

That helped. We were able to return to the peasants the grain that was rightfully their's and we had food for ourselves and our animals. But still we could not use the mill. We ran from one government official to another but the seal remained unbroken and the mill remained closed. In the meantime it was agreed by my father and my uncle to submit the matter to arbitration. My father, my uncle and my aunt signed a document agreeing to abide by the decision of the rabbinical court. Although my father's sister also signed the agreement, she made no claim at all. She did not want even a single kopeck.

As it turned out, my uncle had also brought grandfather's old promissory note into court, the one he had grandfather sign years before, before giving him the 1,000 rubles. He had obtained a judgment on the note, which he renewed every five years, and now he was determined to get the money back, plus 18 years' interest. He had assured my father years before that he had torn up the promissory note.

When grandfather lay paralyzed in his bed my uncle came to visit him only once. He watched as my mother nursed him, washed and fed him and said:

"You are a saintly person. I will never forget this."

The arbitrators ruled that my uncle and aunt were entitled to nothing. But, since my other aunt was in urgent need of money, father should give her 100 rubles. As soon as the verdict was announced my uncle snatched up the papers he had signed and stormed out of the rabbi's house.

My other uncle, the lawyer, instructed us to break the seal and reopen the mill. Since I was not yet an adult and therefore not legally responsible, I was given the task.

By then, however, we had eaten most of the grain and the season was over. By Passover the situation was very bad. We couldn't even buy new clothes for the holiday.

Uncle went back on his word. He repudiated his agreement to abide by the rabbinical court and took the matter to the Russian courts where it dragged on for several years. Eventually the Russian Revolution settled the whole matter. Little more was left of Grandfather's inheritance than the ill feeling between my father and his younger brother.

SELF EDUCATION

THAT WINTER I BECAME FRIENDLY WITH Reuben Berls. He was several years older than I, tall, with a big black mustache and a large nose. He had three commendable qualities: He realized he was not clever, he was honest, and he loved to read. Despite a rather superficial intelligence he had a great influence on me. It was through him that I began to read books in Russian and Yiddish.

The first Russian book I read was called, *Under the Power of Light and Darkness.* I can't recall the author. We often read together and afterwards discussed what we had read. Reuben was well informed on Russian and Jewish politics. Together we subscribed to the Russian daily, *St. Petersberg Newsletter.* We read of events that had occurred some time before but to two young boys in the small town of Pobolov everything that happened in the outside world was new.

We also subscribed to the Yiddish dailies, *Friend* and *Moment.* We read the newspapers from the first line on the first page down to the last line on the last page. Reuben even read the advertisements. I disliked the advertisements and even to this day rarely look at them.

The blood accusation against Mendel Beillis—based on the slander that the Jews were using Christian blood in the preparation of Passover matzoh and other food—made no impression on me. I was certain it was a hoax and that it would soon be exposed. However, when the chief witness, Vera Scherback, a Ukrainian, and her accomplices were exposed and sentenced, I read every word.

During that winter also I became much friendlier with my older sister Rachel. In a way we came together through books. She read many Russian books but none in Yiddish. She felt they were not important. She also taught me some Russian grammar.

We had a mutual respect for each other. Rachel taught me to know myself, pointing out my strengths and my shortcomings. It was she who gave me the inspiration to control my temper and I succeeded. She also tried to teach me to be more tolerant and diplomatic in discussions with my elders. Alas, in this she was not so successful. She tried to teach me good manners and in this she was equally unsuccessful.

During that winter I began to feel my physical power. I was shaking myself out from under the milk-fed cloak of childhood and was beginning to emerge as a man.

My father was himself a powerful man, of medium height but broad of shoulder and laced through with muscles of steel. I began to do exercises and soon could lift to my shoulder a sack weighing eight pood, almost 300 pounds. My mother screamed out in fright but I laughed. I did it for the sheer joy and with the exuberance of newly-unfettered youth. Even years later I was still able to tuck two sacks of flour under my arms, each sack weighing five poods, and walk off with them.

I could lift an iron weight weighing 80 pounds, throw it into the air and catch it as it came down. Later I was able to take an iron weight in each hand, throw them into the air and catch them as a juggler would catch two rubber balls. At the age of sixteen I would engage in a contest with the peasants. We would sit on the ground facing each other, with our feet touching. We would then take hold of a stick and each would try to pull the other off the ground. The one who succeeded was the winner. I invariably won.

Yes, I was a strong young buck and enjoyed my new-found strength very much.

A BOYHOOD TRAGEDY

IN THE SPRING OF THAT YEAR I SUFFERED another painful personal experience. Another fellow, H., had become attached to Reuben. He was five years older than I. H. was small, skinny, and more cunning than clever, although he considered himself very intelligent. He came from a poor family. He would always come up with ideas for a good time but never had a kopeck to contribute to the expenses.

I was at an age when a boy needs a confidant, one to whom he could relate his dreams and discuss his plans and hopes for the future. I held nothing back. I told him everything, the most intimate details of our family life. Once my mother asked me, "Why do you tell H. everything that happens at our house? There are some things we keep to ourselves."

Mother was annoyed. She gave me a long lecture. And as it turned out she was justified, H. blabbed all that I had told him to others and, to make matters worse, ridiculed me into the bargain.

I was terribly hurt. I felt betrayed. I ran out of the house without uttering a word and went into the forest where I sought solace from the constant trees. They would never betray me! When I calmed down I realized that it had been my own fault. If I could not keep my secrets to myself why should I expect H. to do so? I swore that never would I reveal to others that which I did not wish strangers to know.

Many decades have passed since that painful experience. I have been very friendly with many people and many have confided their innermost secrets to me. But never have I violated my oath to keep my confidences to myself. I have never forgotten, nor forgiven, my so-called friend H. for his treachery.

AN ORCHARD

FATHER LEASED AN ORCHARD FOR THE summer, a large orchard with many trees, too many, because it was an off year.

The work started right after Shavuoth in June. I went into the orchard as soon as the trees started to bloom to keep the peasant boys from picking the blossoms. There was a cabin in the orchard where we stayed all summer, until after the fruit was picked. That was until shortly before Rosh Hashonah, the Jewish New Year, which fell in September.

We lived virtually in our clothes throughout the season. Meals were prepared over an open fire outside the cabin. When it rained we got soaked to the skin. The thatched roof offered little protection from the rain. Meals consisted mainly of bread, millet cooked with oil, and potatoes. And after the fruit was ripe it had to be guarded night and day to prevent it from being stolen.

Many families in our town depended on the orchards for their livelihood for the entire year. Mostly they were small, from a handful to some twenty trees. I was considered a full partner in the venture. Father even owed me some money. I was pleased that my decision not to open a store had turned out to be a wise move.

Father sold the apples to one of our relatives. I insisted that a contract be drawn up and that he agree to take all the apples. Father scolded me angrily for doubting our relative's honesty. I argued that it had nothing to do with honesty but with a written understanding. So it was that when it came time to pack and ship the apples, the relative took the good apples only and shoved to a side the cheaper ones, those that were smaller and those that were slightly bruised.

I protested, insisting that he take the cheaper apples first.

When my protests went unheeded I walked to the gate and with a wooden stave in my hand physically prevented his wagons from leaving. The peasants hired by our relative were afraid to force their way past me. My relative ran and brought my father who demanded that I let the wagons through. The relative said he would come the following week to take the cheaper apples. Of course, he never returned.

The other merchants did not want to buy the cheap apples without the good ones and so we were left with a harvest of cheap apples after having sold the good ones at an average price for both grades.

I threw the remaining apples into a wagon bedded with straw and left for the fairs in the smaller towns to sell at whatever price I could get. But the fairs were flooded with fruit. My venture was a failure. I had to do business mainly with women. God bless the women with all manner of good things but may He keep them away from me in business matters! They would climb into the wagon and pick and pick five kopecks worth of apples. When they got through, the straw and the apples were mixed up like a giant compote. The bruised apples dampened the good ones and all in all my wagon looked like a garbage heap.

I traveled to the fairs with my aunt, father's sister, several times. She knew how to handle the women and after she had sold her own wagon load of fruit she took over the sale of mine. For the entire summer's work we profited not a single kopeck. All we gained was some 20 poods of apples for our own use during the winter months.

After Succoth I was once again confronted by the question, what next?

My brother Sholem was drafted into the army. Although he was eligible for deferment he was still drafted; a vindictive anti-Semitic official named Burakov saw to that. My father spent large sums in an attempt to get him deferred, as was coming to him by law but it did no good. My brother left home for the dubious honor of serving in the Czar's army.

That winter was a bad one. The harvests were poor. The peasants brought very little buckwheat to the mill. We had no money to buy buckwheat for ourselves and my savings were rapidly disappearing. I had about 150 rubles and I used that as capital to lend out at six per cent interest. This I kept secret from my parents.

My father grew more introspective and more pious. Eagerly he sought some sign from the Almighty for an easing of the distress that faced his family. Once I overheard him say to himself, "God must be punishing me."

I offered father money to buy buckwheat so that at least we could feed the animals. But he refused. "You had better keep your money," he said. "If you put it into the mill you'll never get it back."

Since Sholem was in the army I remained at home and helped father in the mill. I also did some tutoring during the evening hours and was at least able to earn money for my own expenses.

My brother Chaim, three years younger than I, became Bar Mitzvah. He was a handsome boy, tall and slim, and not overly studious. He was a good boy. We got along very well. He too came to work in the mill. I also got along very well with my older sister. We liked each other and were very close. My younger sister was only a few years old. She was big for her age and suffered from rickets.

I read a lot that winter. I had a burning desire for learning and couldn't soak up enough knowledge. I read anything that had pages and printed matter. I began to yearn for the big city where I would be able to work during the day and study at night.

The Beillis case to which I paid scant attention before now occupied much of my thoughts. I realized that not just Beillis but all the Jewish people were involved. For the first time I became deeply concerned about the fate of my people.

And so the winter passed. Spring came, and with it a guest, a young girl, to visit Reuben's parents for the Passover holiday. I was completely captivated by her and struck up a friendship quickly. At that time there were no girls in our town near my age and my relations with the opposite sex were limited. My mother was afraid, Heaven forbid, that I should become involved with someone below our station in life, a seamstress, perhaps, or a servant girl!

That was of little interest to me. I fell in love with the visitor without asking her background or references. A new world opened up for me. Feelings I had never experienced before surged through my body. The male animal in me had come to life. It was a tame animal, though, one content merely to walk and chat with her.

AT MY UNCLE'S MILL

THERE WAS HARDLY ANY WORK IN THE mill after Passover. Father and my younger brother were easily able to handle what little work there was. So, I went to Bobruisk to look for work, perhaps as a salesman, or a clerk in a store. At about this time my father's younger brother came to visit us. He was not in very good health and was still mourning the tragic death of his son a few weeks before in the mill lake. He needed someone to help him in his mill and thought I might be just the one.

My father was not at all anxious for me to work for his brother. Nevertheless, after considerable discussion and consideration, it was agreed that I would do so. The pay was good, thirty rubles a month, with bed and board. On Lag Be'Omer, just before Shavuoth, I left home once again; this time to work in my uncle's mill.

He had a busy mill. It was much larger than father's mill and it operated seven days a week. Uncle had a partner but the business itself was in his name. He was anxious to get rid of his partner but that was not easily done. The partner had a "holding privilege." That is, after a certain time his position could not be taken from him without his consent. In addition, he came from a family of distinguished rabbis. Uncle didn't dare throw him out!

The partner was tall, well over six feet, and was physically very powerful. But still he was a very gentle perosn, a simple man and very kind. He recited his prayers with difficulty; he was as naive as a child. His wife was as clever as he was simple and she was also beautiful. There were many children in their home, I can't recall the exact number. The noise was unbearable.

The partner, H. B., always came home with a twig in his hand and if the children failed to quiet down he would make as if to give them the feel of it on their backs. He did it without anger, rather with a smile on his face. The children would scream and scamper out the door and windows. Never once did I hear one of them cry out in pain.

Uncle informed me that my chief task was to watch the partner, to see that he did not steal anything. It didn't take long for me to discover that it was my uncle who had to be watched.

The partner suspected that I had been brought to the mill to watch over him but if he resented it he never showed it. In fact, I believe he liked me. We became good friends. He even let me hold the money that came in and take care of the bookkeeping.

The work was long and hard. It was a heavy load for me. We began work in the evening after the Sabbath and did not return to the house until just before sundown the following Friday. I stayed at the partner's home but we came only to eat. We slept at the mill. We never changed our clothing during the week. When I finally took off my boots on Friday they were full of rye, some of which, due to the heat and dampness had even begun to sprout.

HARD WORK

WORK IN UNCLE'S MILL WAS WHAT I IMagine prison labor is like especially in the punishment batallion. It often happened that the peasant workers drank too much and failed to show up. So we had to do the work ourselves—pour grain into the mill buckets, pour the flour into the sacks, and then beat the sacks with a heavy stick to shape them properly, and weigh them. And if the sacks tore, we had to mend them also.

Once I worked straight through from Saturday night to Tuesday morning, managing to grab a bite of food from time to time as I stood at the flour box. I had no time even for a nap. On Tuesday morning when the miller finally came to relieve me I sank down to the floor and slept through the entire day and well into the following night.

There were two sets of millstones to grind the flour. A third set was mounted on rollers; that was for the sifted flour. There were other sets for barley and buckwheat. Water was plentiful. It came from a swiftly flowing lake that was constantly refilled from another lake, which was called, appropriately enough, "the upper lake."

As for the millstones set on rollers, a carload of rye could be thrown onto it at one time and be ground into flour quickly and automatically. One had to watch carefully that the wheels had rye to grind. If they didn't they would simply grind against each other and wear themselves out. To be sharpened they had to be sent to Germany.

We used to sleep in the big basket full of rye. There was an opening on the bottom from which the rye spilled onto the millstones. In that way, as the rye emptied out of the basket, like the sand out of an hour glass, we sank lower and lower until we found ourselves with our heads down and feet up. Thus we were awakened in time to refill the basket with more rye.

One hot night my uncle's partner and I went to sleep in the basket, both of us very tired. As we slept one of the belts broke and if the partner had not awakened in time, and awakened me, I would have been dragged down into the rollers. All the belts had come loose, the place was a mess. We rushed to put everything in order. Since it was a hot, humid night, we worked without clothes. The flour on our bodies, mixing with the perspiration, turned into dough. When finally we finished we jumped right out of the mill into the lake to cool off and wash the dough off our bodies.

Under the water I spotted rats as large as dogs. Terrified, I panicked and would have drowned if my uncle's partner had not come to my rescue. He dragged me out of the water. To this day I cannot get myself to jump into the water.

I had little opportunity to read that summer but I did

manage to study some Torah orally. There was a melamed in the house where I stayed, the children's teacher. He was a very pious Hassid and prayed incessantly but I never saw him studying the traditional volumes. It took him forever to recite the "Shmoneh Esreh." He spoke very little but loved to tell stories of wondrous deeds accomplished by the Hassidic masters.

SOME THOUGHTS ON THE BEILLIS TRIAL

THE BEILLIS TRIAL IN 1913 WEIGHED HEAVILY on me, especially the reactionary slogan, "Kromeh Yevreyev." ("Kromeh Yevreyev" was a clause inserted by the Russians into their legislation to legalize discrimination against the Jews. Literally, it meant "except the Jews." Thus, a law might provide some benefit for the Russian peasant but it contained the added phrase, "but not for the Jews.")

It occurred to me that the Czar might be planning to expel the Jews from Russia just as Spain had done in 1492. I became more and more strongly convinced that one of us must leave for another country, settle there and be prepared to bring the rest of the family over should an expulsion actually take place.

Just before Succoth, the Feast of Tabernacles, I had another run-in with my uncle. For the thousandth time he warned me to keep an eye on his partner. It was to be the last time. I lost my temper and shouted angrily that it was he who needed watching and not his partner. Without waiting for the storm to break I fled from the office, seized my clothes and left for home.

Uncle's partner and his wife, both unaware of my outburst, tried to restrain me but I had had enough of my uncle's pettiness and would not change my mind.

As I drove into our town a funeral cortege was passing by. The old rabbi had died. Everyone was saddened.

The autumn rains came early turning the roads in our town into a sea of mud. They were almost impassable. Walking was agonizing. My own feelings were as gloomy as the weather and as heavy as the mud.

SOLDIERING

THAT YEAR MY FRIEND REUVEN WAS drafted into the army, leaving me without friends. The newspapers carried stories about the size of the German and Austrian armies and of the might of the Russian army. It all seemed to be building up to a war but the others in my town laughed when I voiced my fears.

I had saved some money and began again to deal in grain. Thanks to the experience I had gained in my uncle's mill, I was a better judge of grain products and I soon began to accumulate sizable profits. I bought myself some new clothes and struck up some superficial friendships with some of the older girls—of what we considered the upper class—and also with some of the young men, most of whom were a bit older than I.

The peasants in the surrounding villages had become restless; it was dangerous to travel alone at night. Twice I was stopped while on the way home from Bobruisk. One time I jumped off the empty wagon and fled in the darkness to the home of a peasant I knew. On the second occasion I was accosted by two peasants, one of whom punched me in the face. Blood spurted from my nose.

Fortunately I had with me a "nagaikeh," a whip with a piece of lead at the end of it. I struck the peasant with it and knocked him to the ground. The other peasant, the one who had stopped me, jumped off his horse and ran toward me. At that point I whipped my own horse into a furious gallop and made my escape.

I was naturally afraid to pass through that village again and so I began to use the railroad instead of my wagon. It turned out to be a fortunate move for it opened a whole new world for me.

I was well dressed during my trips and always stopped at a hotel. Even more important, my travels now took me to cities where I was able to see films and go to the theater. It was during one of those early trips that I saw my first Yiddish play. I met other Jewish merchants and reveled in my new experiences as fully as a child with new and wonderful toys.

My brother Sholem came home on leave dispirited and unhappy. Soldiering in the Czar's army was not at all to his liking. He was accustomed to life at home where he was able to do pretty much what he liked and when he liked. Now he had to accept the bitter lot of a Jewish soldier in a hostile army subject to the insults and indignities of every anti-Semitic Russian within reach.

Sholem wrote long letters home full of complaints. Mother cried with the arrival of every new letter. I determined that no matter how much I suffered I would never write complaining letters home. There was nothing my parents could do but weep but, alas, their tears did not make my brother's lot any easier. It was a decision I honored all my life.

I suggested to my brother that he desert and flee to America. I offered to give him the money for it. I even contacted a man and made tentative arrangements for a false passport that would get him safely over the border. My brother refused. For whatever the reason, he chose to return to his company to serve out his remaining two years of service.

The town had become too narrow for me. With the exception of my older sister I had no real friends. I enjoyed her companionship but at the age of seventeen one needed other friends.

The Russian slogan, "Except the Jews," still bothered me. Added to that spiritually deadening feeling was the certainty that war must soon break out. I tried to convince the townspeople that the Czar was planning to expel the Jews and that the war that was surely coming would bring harsh suffering to the Jews. I told them finally that I had decided to leave for America.

My parents refused to hear of it.

"What do you lack here at home?" they asked. "You are wealthy and you won't be called for the draft for another four years."

I didn't like to go against the wishes of my parents. I was torn by uncertainty. My sister encouraged me. "Go to America," she said. "There you will have every opportunity to study and learn."

I dreamt of becoming a student, of working during the day and studying at night—first in high school and later, perhaps in the university.

It was a sweet thought in those otherwise bitter days.

NEW HOPES

ONE SATURDAY NIGHT WE SAT AROUND the table chatting, my family and I. I contrasted for them the grim picture of a young Jew in a small town in Russia with the glowing possibilities of life for that same young man in free America, a land where truly a Jew could become President.

Perhaps it was that final argument, perhaps they were convinced all along but were reluctant to part with their son. In any event, it was on that night that my parents finally and reluctantly agreed.

"Perhaps you are right, my son," said my mother. "Go to America."

The very next day I made my way to Bobruisk where I contacted the man who would help me get across the border and on my way to America. I knew that the Police Commissioner would never give me the documents I would need for a government passport. A week later, on Sunday, just before Purim, I began my long-dreamed of, long-awaited journey to the United States.

During the week before I left, a rabbi came to our town. Father wanted me to consult the rabbi, to ask him if I was wise to go to America. I was afraid the rabbi would counsel against it but I was determined to go nevertheless.

As I entered the room where the old Hassid sat I burst out "Rabbi, I am going to America."

He looked at me for a moment and said, "Noo, for gesunter heit." ("Go in good health.")

Father took me to the train. I will never forget that scene. Father ran after the train as it began to roll down the tracks trying to keep abreast of the car in which I sat, my face glued to the window. I could see him biting his lips, tears welled up in his eyes. My own vision was blurred by the tears that filled mine. It was a moment that wrenched my heart.

I had been under the impression that stealing across the border would be child's play. My agent had taken my money and was supposed to supply me with everything I would need, including passage on the ship. He instructed me to go to Lublin, go to a certain hotel and give them a password. The hotel was an evil looking, ill-smelling inn. A man came to me and told me we would make the crossing that night. One look at the man was enough to freeze the blood in my body. He had the face of a highwayman and when he asked me to buy him a drink my fears multiplied.

WE STEAL ACROSS THE BORDER

WE TRAVELED BY TRAIN ALL NIGHT. WE dismounted at a small railroad station and there the man turned me over to a peasant with whom I had no means of communication. He was a Pole and did not speak Russian. I was stopped by a policeman who examined my resident's passport. He regarded me and the passport with suspicion and was on the verge of arresting me when a bribe allayed his doubts and I was again free. The peasant led me to a barn where I found some 70 men, women and children, both Jewish and non-Jewish. All were waiting to steal across the border.

Not one of them knew where we were or how far we were from the border. At night two other peasants appeared and motioned for us to follow them. We filed out of the barn, each carrying his bundle or basket, and made our way along the back roads. Some of the women carried babies in their arms as well as packs on their backs. A few fell; their burdens were too heavy. They did not trust the men to carry their children, and their few meager belongings were also too valuable to trust to anyone else—even to a fellow Jew.

We walked most of the night, stopping at intervals to rest. In the morning we were divided into smaller groups and led to some stables where we let ourselves sink wearily to the ground. We were warned not to make a sound. Came the night and we continued our journey. By then we numbered some 300 souls. We had no idea where we were nor who the men were. We were completely at their mercy. It was dark and we had to keep moving. If anyone halted the peasant would prod him on with a stick.

The ground under our feet suddenly became softer. We were passing through a forest. Soon we were led into a swamp with the water reaching up to our knees. A Jewish woman with two children, a girl of about twelve and a child of three had become attached to me and clung to me as we made our way. The poor woman kept crying for fear that I would leave her stranded. I tied her child on my back. I held my basket in one hand and with the other hand held onto the woman. The girl held on to her mother's skirt.

The weather, bad to begin with, became worse. The rain combined with gusts of wind, slashed at our faces. Suddenly several shots rang out. The mother halted in the water, petrified. She gripped my hand in a clutch of iron. Some began to cry and the peasants ran among them hitting them with their sticks to quiet them.

After a while we were led off in another direction. We walked for about an hour and came to the edge of a lake. The peasants drove us into the water with their sticks. We waded in until the water reached up to our waists. And then, suddenly, we were on the other side. We had crossed the border!

IN GALICIA AND GERMANY

WE WERE TAKEN ON PEASANTS' WAGONS to Rozvodov, a Galician town in Austria. It was Saturday morning. The Jews were on their way to the synagogues. I was famished. I had sent my baggage ahead to Sosnowitz and had only the basket I carried. Originally there had been some food in it but I had eaten it all during the week.

The owner of the house where we were lodged was a tall young man of about 30. He wore a long coat and on his head he had a "shtraimel," the fur trimmed headgear that Hassidic Jews wore on Saturdays and holidays. A pious man, he did not wish to desecrate the Sabbath by selling us food. A cautious man, neither would he sell to us on credit. To buy non-kosher food was out of the question. So we sat there in sadness and in hunger and watched the very pious man sit at the table with his family leisurely enjoying their meal.

When the man finished eating he began to pace around the room—his entire home. He kept his hands in his trouser pockets and as he walked he jingled what sounded like coins. Suddenly he turned to us and asked which of us wished to exchange our rubles for marks. What audacity! He wouldn't desecrate the Sabbath by selling us food but here he was ready to do so to exchange money.

Turning to the others I said, "Fellows, let's eat." With that we all ran to the corner of the room that served as the kitchen and grabbed all the food in sight.

The Hassid tried to stop us but we were impelled by equal portions of outrage and hunger. Soon everything that was edible disappeared from the table. The Hassid became abusive so we gave him a bit of a beating in the bargain.

Suddenly the chief officer of the town appeared and the

melee subsided. The old table and several stools had been thrown over. A single white unbitten roll lay on the floor in the corner.

We were all put under arrest—some twenty men and two women, all Jews. We agreed to pay 20 kopecks per person for the food we had taken and saw right then and there how the official and the Hassid divided the money between them. We were then set free.

I took a walk around the town in the afternoon. A swarthy man sidled up to me and whispered that he would take care of my passage and that I should trust no one else. I said no quietly and moved away. He remained at my side. He invited me to play cards with him, or at least to have a drink with him. I may have been a small town boy but that stupid I wasn't. I tried to get rid of him but he persisted, like a fly around the tail of a cow. He refused to leave my side until I warned him that I would punch him in the nose if he didn't stop bothering me. At this point he decided that I wasn't worthy of his beneficence and walked away.

We left by train the following morning. After a short ride we transferred to another train that was filled with emigrants. This was the famous World War I car that bore the inscription "40 men or eight horses." There were forty people in each car. The cars had no benches and were so crowded that soon the air was stifling. The doors were locked from the outside. We were given one ticket for all forty miserable passengers. For some reason the conductor picked me to be the ticket holder.

At the next station I descended to the platform, walked around a bit and purposely missed the train as it moved off. I went into the station master's office, showed him the ticket and explained in a combination of Yiddish and German that I had missed the train. He put me on the next regular passenger train to catch up to the emigrant train and so, for a while at least, I traveled more like a person than an animal. It was a good trick. I used it four times before reaching Berlin.

We changed trains in Berlin. We were led through fenced-in alleys to prevent us from desecrating the sacred soil of the German capital with our Jewish boots. From Berlin we made our way to Bremen. There we were led to barracks, the men and women separate. There were no tables and no chairs, just one bench along the wall of the long room which served for sleeping. In the middle of the dormitory was an oven that was supposed to warm that tremendous hall. We ourselves had to go and bring the coal. We also had to keep the barracks and the yard clean.

We ate in a separate room and, surprisingly, the food was not bad. The yard was surrounded by barbed wire to prevent anyone from entering or leaving.

I was called into the office the following morning for a medical examination. While I was there a clerk asked me if I wanted a second or third class steamship ticket. I told him that I already had an agent who would attend to the matter. At this he muttered, "Damned Jew!" Without a second thought I let fly with my fist to his mouth. I was arrested. Several hours later I was freed. I learned that the Hebrew Immigrant Aid Society, more popularly known as HIAS, had intervened to obtain my release.

A man later came to the barracks to lecture us on how to behave. I could hardly understand his German-Yiddish, or Yiddish-German. I was told that he was a HIAS representative.

I spent several weeks in Bremen. I was tired and bored waiting for the agent to send me my steamship ticket. Our youth, boredom and general curiosity got the better of our caution and a number of us made our way over the barbed fence one day. We toured the city, visiting the museum and the library, we walked through the city park and hungrily drank everything in with our eyes. We couldn't get our fill of the wonderful sights of the big city.

We enjoyed it so we went over the following day and several days thereafter. One day we were stopped by a policeman. We admitted we were transmigrants. He escorted us back to the barracks and warned us not to show ourselves in the city again. We remained in the barracks the following day, bored to death.

The superintendent, an old, sickly German, pestered us incessantly. No matter how much we cleaned the barracks and the yard, it was never good enough for him. Once he burst in on us in the middle of the night and began abusing us with vile insults and curses. Why? Someone had urinated in the yard instead of the toilet, which was a considerable distance from our part of the barracks.

The superintendent stood in the open door berating us and threatening to freeze us out. Several of us younger men became quite angry. One stole up behind him, threw an overcoat over his head and began to beat him. The wiser ones among us ran up to him and stopped him lest we all get into deeper trouble.

An investigation was held the following morning. Since the superintendent was unable to identify his assailant, the police could do nothing. They finally gave up in disgust. Just to play safe, however, they broke up our group and divided us among the other barracks.

ON THE SHIP TO AMERICA

ON THE 13TH OF MARCH IN THE YEAR 1914 (according to the old Russian calendar) I embarked on the *S.S. Kassel* and thirteen days later, on the 26th of March, I arrived in the city of Baltimore in the State of Maryland. Those thirteen days were a period of great spiritual stress. I had had difficulties even before I boarded the ship. I suffered many discomforts but managed to survive. Even more, some of the experiences brought forth from me strengths I never suspected I had.

On the ship, however, I was confronted by a force I could not cope with. As we boarded the ship, we Jews were directed to a special section deep in the hold and told to stay there. Several hours later we were ordered to bring our baggage to the deck. There we learned that while we were stowed below the officers had rented their cabins to other passengers and took for themselves the area that had been assigned to us. We were forced to remain on deck.

It was not long before I began to feel seasick. That didn't help my disposition. I organized a committee of ten to place our grievance before the captain. I was in the lead, the others followed behind. The nearer we got to the captain the farther behind the others fell. By the time we—I—reached the officers I was standing alone. The officer in charge of between decks tried to stop me and grabbed at my jacket, tearing the lapels. I gave him a sharp kick in the shins and he backed off. I reached the bridge and found myself face to face with the captain. After hearing my charges he ordered the officers to find quarters for us.

From out of nowhere a number of seamen appeared and carried our baggage down to the belly of the ship where they divided the eighty or so Jewish passengers among some 600 non-Jews, most of them from Balkan countries.

Down in the hold the seamen led us to sections where double bunk beds were arranged in dormitory style. Whenever they came to an empty bunk they assigned one of the Jews to it. When the seamen left the Balkan emigrants threw the Jews out of their beds.

By then I was terribly seasick. I was unable to fight back when my European countrymen threw me out of my bunk. I had no strength to move. I remained on the floor where they dropped me. One Jew, who had been to America before, fought back but was hopelessly outnumbered. He received several knife wounds for his efforts. I admired his courage. Eventually he was to have a share in my destiny.

In the morning we complained to the officers and two seamen were assigned to each section as guards. After that we weren't bothered any more. Physically, that is. While we weren't molested, neither could we sleep in the midst of such a multitude of people, smells and noises. We Jews tried to make the best of it. We gathered in a corner. Some had bunks, the others bedded down on the floor. The air in the room—if it could be dignified by the term—was stale to the point of suffocation. Everything was damp.

Each of the passengers was given a tin can, a spoon and a tin cup for tea. We were not given any knives. For our meals we had to climb up to the main deck, and wait in line to be served. We were not permitted to take the food into the hold and had to find a place to eat on the deck. There was no place to sit, we had to eat standing.

All things taken together, I was ill almost the entire voyage and ate hardly a morsel. Finally, after thirteen days the agony ended. We had arrived in America.

Part Two

**In America;
Years of Struggle**

IN AMERICA—A GREENHORN

IT WAS EVENING ON THE 26TH OF MARCH when we reached the port of Baltimore. It was a Saturday night and also the first night of Passover. Since there was no matzoh on the ship and I would not eat "chometz" (leavened bread) I went without food. I stood at the ship's rail, wondering about the city lights in the distance. "What," I asked myself, "What kind of life will I find in the new world?"

Some days before the ship reached port I had telegraphed a cousin that I was coming and asked him to meet me at the dock. When the ship finally moored, I was among the first to descend the gangplank. Immigration formalities were simple. An immigrant had to possess $25. I had only $18. I changed a couple of larger bills into singles and when I showed the "roll" of dollar bills, no one bothered to count.

I waited seven hours for my cousin to show up. It seemed an eternity. Finally, at 4:30 in the afternoon he appeared. After a brief greeting he led me to a trolley for the ride to his house. I had to carry my bundles by myself. My cousin told me he was ashamed to be seen carrying "European" bundles. We finally reached his house and I was offered a seat. I thanked them with a Russian "spasibah." To my surprise, this infuriated my cousin's wife.

"You greenhorn of an animal, here one says 'thank you,' not 'spasibah,' " she shouted at me.

I felt as if she had thrown a bucket of cold water in my face. After all I had been through, with all my learning I was now a greenhorn of an animal.

(All immigrants and most first generation American Jews will surely remember the denigrating "grineh chaya" that plagued so many of the Jewish newcomers. Unfortunately this insulting epithet loses some of its sting in the literal translation, "green animal." It's not the color but the "greenhorn" part that is supposed to hurt. Perhaps I can impart some of it by translating it as "greenhorn of an animal." In any event, I am sure most of my readers will not miss the contempt in which Jewish newcomers were held by so many of their own kind—even by those who preceeded them by only a few months.)

My cousin, A., who had come to America at the time of the Russo-Japanese War, had married a woman who considered herself a "Yankee." To her Yiddish was an abomination so she ended up being unable to read either Yiddish or English. Newspapers and books were only for "greenhorns," according to her. She quickly absorbed all that was cheap and coarse in the new world. The main thing was to have a good time! It was she who wore the pants in that family.

My cousin was a kindhearted man, tall and handsome. He could neither read nor write. The best he could do was to sign his name, but with great difficulty. He was a saloon keeper and also owned the house he lived in. By the standards of those days he was thus a wealthy man.

In addition to my cousin's family, the house sheltered my cousin's sister and a brother, both from a village near my own. They had arrived a year before. The brother, J., was my age. In Russia I was considered an intellectual. He was just a village lad, with not too much learning—or promise. His sister, B., much older than I, had been a seamstress in the old country.

How did America welcome me? What has she given me? Up to this point it has been easy to relate my reminiscences. Before my life had been narrow, the horizons limited. In America, the horizons were broadened. My experiences were more numerous and more profound.

It is not possible to describe either the feelings or the experiences in detail. I must pick and choose. However, there is the danger that I will dwell mostly on the more dramatic, those experiences that left a deeper mark on me. That might be more interesting reading but it would not be a true picture of the life of an immigrant in Amerca at that time. I will write about the every-day occurrences. It may not be as interesting but it will be true.

My cousin, and especially his wife, took me in hand to "Americanize" me, to wash the greenness out of the greenhorn in me. First they changed my name from Beryl to Benny. Then they decided that I must have my mustache shaved off. After supper, my cousin J. took me to the barber, but being ashamed to be seen walking with me, he had me walk on one side of the street while he walked on the other.

On Sunday my cousin J. took me out to see the sights. We took a trolley, changing four times to be able to get a long ride for one nickel. We finally arrived at a park. There I asked him about life in America.

"Here one has to work all week long and on Sundays he has a good time," he answered.

"What is a good time?" I asked.

"Ach, you're a greenhorn," he said. "A good time is a good time!"

It's no use, I thought, I'll have to find out for myself.

I saw young couples getting into carts which took them on a swift ride on tracks up and down steep curves. I learned later it was called a roller coaster. As I watched I suddenly heard a crash and cries of distress, I saw several of the carts turn over. There was a great commotion. People crowded around the scene of the accident. Two couples were taken to the hospital. If this was a good time in America, somehow it did not find favor in my eyes.

On the way back my cousin informed me that they would not charge me for board for that day but beginning the following day I would have to pay $5 a week for room and board. I wasn't sure of what he meant by board but I had a fairly good idea.

The following day, Monday, my third day in America, my cousin's wife took me shopping for clothes. She spoke to the salesmen in English but I was able to make out some of the words. She asked one of them to give me a smaller size shoe. The ones I was wearing, she said, made me look too much like a greenhorn! I protested but it was no use. I left the store with my feet painfully squeezed into shoes that were much too small. I told my cousin's wife that it was difficult to walk in those shoes but she said that she knew better what was good for me.

It didn't take me long to realize that I ought to get a job as quickly as possible and get out of there.

A MILL AND A SHOP

I HAD NO DESIRE TO BECOME A SHOP worker. Even though I had never seen the inside of a shop I knew I would hate it. However, I had no choice.

An acquaintance of my cousin took me to a very large clothing factory where many of the newly arrived immigrants, "greenhorns" they called us, found work. The din in the shop was unbearable. It was impossible to hear someone talk. Hundreds of machines, lined up in even rows, screeched wildly while parallel rows of human beings sat facing them, quivering and squirming as they fed cloth into the roaring machines.

I could not get myself to become part of this insanity, even though I had a good share of experience in mills where a variety of machines made their own noises. But in the mill each machine had its own special sound, its own rhythm. I could tell by the knocking and the humming whether the machine was working properly. If anything went wrong, if a belt came off or the grain basket emptied out, I would know immediately by the change in the rhythm, the sound was different.

Just as a conductor of a symphony orchestra can hear the false note of a single instrument so we millers could detect the slightest variation in the smooth operation of the mill.

So, when the foreman of the tailor shop told me he had no place for an apprentice at the moment, I was relieved and secretly very happy about it.

My cousin lived so far from the Jewish area that I was unable to get a Yiddish paper. I missed the newspaper very much. I was eager to learn what was going on. My $18 had already been spent on clothing so I took a long walk to the Jewish part of town and bought a newspaper, *Varhait*, (Truth). I also made the acquaintance of a young fellow. He lent me Tolstoy's *Resurrection* in the original Russian.

I returned home happy. In the twilight, after supper, I sat outside on the steps and lost myself in the book. Unfortunately my cousin's wife spied me reading the book and when she saw it was in Russian she grabbed it out of my hand.

"You greenhorn of an animal," she shouted. "You are no longer in the country of Fonye the Thief. Here one does not read books in that pig tongue."

In a moment of fury I almost lashed back at her. I had to fight to restrain myself. After all, I was eating at her table, a guest in her house, even though a paying guest.

Everyone was on the lookout for a job for me. I had dreams of becoming an automobile mechanic, but that would require an extended period of training. I soon realized that I had to take whatever job came along so that I could leave my cousin's house as soon as possible.

RAGS

ON FRIDAY, JUST BEFORE SUNDOWN, MY cousin came home with a broad smile on his face and announced that he had gotten me a job in a junk shop owned by a man who came from a town near mine in Russia. My salary was to be $5 a week and for that munificent sum I was to work six days a week from 7 o'clock in the morning until 6 o'clock in the evening. I was allowed an hour for lunch.

I already had an idea what a junk shop was like. My cousin had previously been a junk dealer and there were a number of people from towns near mine who were still in the business.

I went to work on Saturday morning. The boss led me to three Negro women who were seated before a mound of material. They were picking rags. He said something to them and left. The three women were very friendly. They quickly taught me the "art" of rag picking. I observed how they sorted the rags by color and did the same. Later a Negro man showed me how to compress the rags into a bale. He put the rags into a machine. He stood at one side and I at the other and when the rags had been pressed we moved the bale onto a pile alongside and took another bundle to feed into the machine.

The work was hard. The day was long and hot. Suddenly I realized that I was working on the Sabbath. I thought to myself, my father and the other Jews back home are in the Synagogue now. It was time for the reading of the weekly Torah portion. A deep sadness came over me. My heart was heavy with guilt and shame. Was it for this that I had come to America? To become a rag picker and desecrate the Sabbath? The agony loosed a flood of tears that I could not control. My Negro co-worker didn't understand what was happening but his sympathy was quick and genuine. He tried to console me. He patted my shoulder and spoke softly to me. Later he brought me a pitcher of beer and made me drink some of it. "It'll make you feel better," he said.

Before coming to America I had never seen a black man. When I did see my first colored person, I must confess I was surprised, and also a bit frightened. Somehow that act of friendship, of humanity, that drink of beer helped to break down the wall I myself had put between us.

The boss come over to us. He too spoke gently and calmed me down. Still, I could not shake off the feeling that I was facing a terrible battle for survival in this golden land.

My lodging—bed and board—came to $5. My salary was $5. That left me at the end of the week exactly where I started, without an extra cent for my soul. Some weeks later I asked for a raise. To this the boss replied: "This is what you get for doing a greenhorn a favor! If it weren't for me you would have died of hunger." Nevertheless, at the end of the week he raised my pay to $6. I now had a dollar a week to feed my soul!

HATRED OF YIDDISH

EVERY NIGHT I RETURNED FROM WORK tired, hungry and dirty. There was no bathtub in the house. Twice a week I went to the municipal shower paying three cents admission. From the shower I went to the library and sat there for several hours reading. Since I was still living at my cousin's house, I did not bring any books home lest we get into a quarrel.

Somewhere I heard that there was a place that some rich Jews had established, whose purpose was to help "green out" newly arrived immigrants. The name I soon learned was the Jewish Educational Alliance and I found out where it was located.

Entering the building gave me the same feeling I got when I once entered the church in our home town, cold and strange. One was not permitted to speak Yiddish in the Alliance building! I left the building without waiting to hear what the other rules were. Several days later I was chased off the steps of the building for speaking Yiddish. I stopped going there. I looked upon the leaders of the Jewish Educational Alliance as missionaries trying to convert the Jewish immigrants to another faith.

I had become accustomed to my job, resigned to it would be a better word. But I couldn't get used to the coarse, almost anti-intellectual atmosphere in my cousin's house. I made more frequent visits to the library returning late at night to my room. The others were already asleep so I took off my shoes and walked quietly to my cot to avoid waking them.

IN PHILADELPHIA

I BEGAN TO PLAN A WAY OUT OF MY predicament. My mother's oldest brother lived in Philadelphia. I knew that his sons, my cousins, were all well educated and I felt that I would be happier in their company. So I wrote to my uncle, I.M., informing him that I was in America. He replied telling me he was delighted that I had come and that if the opportunity arose, perhaps I could come and visit him.

To me this meant: "I'm glad you're here but stay where you are." My first impulse was to forget about him and his family and find my own way. But the insult rankled, it stuck in my craw choking me.

I wrote my uncle a second letter telling him that I had brought regards from his mother whom he had not seen for at least 30 years. I also wrote in the same letter that I did not know if in America people still had some feelings for their mothers but that in Europe they did. This my uncle could not ignore. He invited me to come for Shevuoth.

I found my uncle to be a tall man, with a long gray beard. Stately, he gave the appearance of one of the Biblical patriarchs. His eyes were sharp and clear. His mind was equally clear. He was indeed a clever man. His wife, my aunt, was short, heavy set and walked with a limp. She was not a very friendly person and did not go out of her way to make me welcome.

Uncle was courteous, I thought a little too much so. He notified his three sons and daughter of my arrival and all of them came to see me the following day at noontime. My uncle's daughter in particular made a special effort to befriend me. She invited me to visit her and I gladly accepted.

My cousin lived in a beautiful spacious home with a

servant girl to tend to the housework. She had four children: M., a young man two years older than I; F., a girl about my age; B., a girl a year younger; and H., a boy of twelve.

My cousin's husband was short, very agile and lively. He had studied in a yeshivah in his youth and knew the Talmud well. Despite the 30 years he had spent in America he still spoke English as if he had just come off the boat.

The atmosphere was pleasant, like a noble family with genteel manners, where everyone showed affection and consideration for the others. The children spoke to the parents as if they were addressing friends. It was the first time I had ever witnessed such close parent-child relations.

I was given my own room, for myself, alone, with no one else! I felt as if I were in the Garden of Eden. They did not want me to return to Baltimore and tried to persuade me to remain in Philadelphia, with them. They would try to find work for me. It sounded delightful. I felt it was all a dream. Many young people came to visit my cousin's children. They were high school and college students. Perhaps I could make friends with some of them.

But, again I was to suffer disappointment. Some weeks later the children had a party at the house and invited many young people. I was not invited. To make matters worse I overheard my cousin, the children's mother, suggest to her son that he invite me to the party, otherwise I would be offended. But the son replied, "I don't care!"

After that when friends came to visit I left the house.

I BECOME A PEDDLER

MY UNCLE'S THREE SONS, MY COUSINS, never invited me to their homes. Apparently I held no interest for them. As far as they were concerned I did not exist.

My cousin's husband was a wholesaler of household goods, especially kitchenware. I was anxious to work for him. Instead he advised me to become a peddler. It was his belief that in America one should go into business for himself and not work for others. To stir up my interest he listed the great merchants who began their careers as peddlers. He himself had been a peddler for a number of years.

One day he pushed a basket of fly paper into my hands and sent me off by subway to another part of the city. He also thrust into my unwilling hands a piece of paper on which he had written what I should say when a housewife opened the door to me. All day long I knocked on doors—my earnings for the day, five cents, one nickel! And that five cents I felt was more charity than a purchase.

The following day he gave me a basketfull of stockings and lingerie. This time he sent me into a poor neighborhood. Again I went from door to door trying to peddle my merchandise to unwilling customers. Unfortunately I knew only a few phrases in English and when a housewife asked me something that wasn't on the paper I was lost. Rather than a self-employed business man I felt like a beggar going from door to door for alms.

I felt I was intruding on the women. Often a housewife had to walk down from the second floor to open the door. Some were justifiably angry and let me know it with a string of unfriendly words, most of which, fortunately, I did not understand.

Once I knocked three times before I heard footsteps. A

woman opened the door and I began to recite the phrases I had learned by heart. She didn't even wait until I had finished but spat in my face and slammed the door shut. That was the last door I assaulted. When I returned to my cousin's store I begged him to give me a job. One of the workers had left and I pleaded for his job. He told me to take off my jacket and go to work. I was overjoyed.

I had to unpack large cases of merchandise, sort it and put it on the shelves. When the need arose I went off on errands, and delivered packages. I was satisfied for the time being. I was hoping that when I learned to speak more fluently I could become a salesman. My salary was the same five dollars a week I had gotten when I started as a rag picker! However, I paid my cousin $3.50 a week for my food, at my own insistence, so I actually fared better than before.

My first major problem was to learn the English language. My cousin read *De Yiddish Velt* (The Jewish World), a local Yiddish daily. There were also some books in the house in both Yiddish and English. This was not of too much use. I enrolled in the Baron de Hirsch Night School to speed up the learning process.

In addition to English they gave courses in arithmetic and other general subjects. I progressed satisfactorily with the English but the other subjects were sheer torture, they were so elementary. I felt I needed a private teacher. One of my cousin's daughters, F., took upon herself the task of instructing me. She gave me several lessons but after a while began to find excuses to put off the lessons. "Later," she would say, or, "Not now."

After a while I stopped asking her and obtained the services of a young man who was a distant relative. He gave me two lessons a week in English. I was able to learn to read and write well enough but I had trouble speaking the language. My tongue was heavy and clumsy with English. Even to this day I speak with a heavy accent.

After supper on my free evenings, I would take the Yiddish newspaper and head for the Yiddish theater. At the entrance I bought a ticket for 10 cents, which entitled me to a seat in the gallery. By the time I finished my paper it was time for the performance to begin. I went two or three times a week.

In time I also found a friend, Miss B., a cousin of my cousin's husband. She was about my age, not very good looking but intelligent and well read. She took me to concerts and lectures and on Sundays we rode to the park. She insisted on paying for me and made it appear as if it were the most natural thing in the world. She had money and I had very little. So, what could be more natural than for her to pay for me?

God bless her wherever she may be at this moment. I have always had a warm feeling for her. She was a true friend when I needed one. She was like an older sister to me.

WAR AND THE TROUBLES OF A GREENHORN

THUS IT WAS THAT MY LIFE IN THE NEW world began to take shape. The war I had prophesied broke out. Even though I predicted it a good two years back I was nevertheless deeply distressed when it finally did erupt.

My brother Sholem was serving with the Russians at the Russo-German border, right in the thick of the fighting. Somehow the war turned me into a Russian patriot. I espoused the Russian cause and tried to convince everyone that Russia would defeat the Germans.

The work in the store was difficult, not only because of the volume but also because I had no time to learn how the business was run. It was not my intention to remain a clerk for the rest of my life.

There were two other young men in the store, both older than I. Sam, short and skinny, weighing less than 100 pounds, was a native-born American. He spoke Yiddish, enjoyed prize fights, and often shadow-boxed around me flicking short jabs into my body at will. He usually did this when I was carrying packages and so could not defend myself even if I wanted to. No matter, his blows hardly made an impression on me and they were not delivered in anger.

Sam liked to play practical jokes. The store handled over a thousand different articles and for each article there were several sizes or styles. Naturally I had not had sufficient time to learn the stock. So, when my cousin would ask me for a dozen pieces of a particular item, I would ask Sam. He would give me the wrong information and make a big joke out of it. My cousin, though annoyed, said nothing and would go himself and fetch the items. However, when this happened when a salesman asked me for something he would snarl at me, "greenhorn of an animal!" Sam would stand off in the background bursting with laughter.

Sam found this so entertaining that he played the trick on me almost every day. I pleaded with him to stop. He would promise to do so and then, at the next opportunity, he was back again with his cruel joke. In desperation I told my cousin about Sam's practical joke and asked him to persuade Sam to stop. My cousin did nothing about it.

It was inevitable that one day I would lose my temper and so it happened. Sam had played his usual trick on me. In a rage I walked towards him, my hands full of boxes of colored paper. Sam jumped around me like a boxer dancing around the ring, jabbing me and slapping my face. I hurled the boxes on the floor and continued towards him. Disregarding his jabs, I seized him by the belt on his trousers, lifted him high over my head and threw him over the table into the shelves beyond. He fell to the floor half screaming and half whining. The pots and pans on the shelves above rained down on his head. Needless to say, Sam never bothered me after that. Nor did I ask him for help with the stock.

Since this form of amusement was at an end he tried a different tack. We used to change our street clothes for work clothes when we came to the store. Sam would hide my clothes, each day in a different place, making me look for my clothes and wasting precious time at night when I was anxious to get out of the store to get to night school. Once he put dirt into one of my pockets. In retaliation I took his yellow-colored shoes, his hat and his suit, put them in the basin and wet them down thoroughly. Then I left the store.

The following day I learned that Sam was beside himself with rage when he found his clothes soaked. He was especially distressed over the damage to his yellow shoes. I freely admitted that I had done it and asked Sam what he intended to do about it. The other employees, long aware of Sam's tricks, upheld me completely. Apparently Sam was convinced of the errors of his ways. He promised not to play any more tricks on me and said from that time on he would really help me with the stock. I didn't believe him and didn't ask his help but he no longer gave me any trouble.

A NEW NAME,
A REVOLT, AND I LOSE MY JOB

A NEW MAN APPEARED IN THE STORE, A man with the title of "General Manager." I didn't like him right from the start. He was short and fat. He limped and his round face was frozen in a perpetual smile of self-satisfaction. He had the beady eyes of a blackguard.

There were strange activities going on in the store. Strange people came and went and everything seemed cloaked in secrecy. The workers told me that the new man was a scavenger who always seemed to turn up when someone was about to go into bankruptcy. He would call me "greenhorn" or "John," a cynical joke he explained away by saying that he wanted to distinguish me from another employee named Ben.

I asked the manager to call me by my right name but he persisted in using the two degrading names. I ignored him when he would do so and he would almost burst from shouting. I remained deaf until he used my right name.

He ordered me around and tried to make an errand boy out of me—for personal reasons, not for business. I was always ready to do anything for the store but to run out and get him a bottle of soda or a pack of cigarettes, that I could not tolerate. He would make me work overtime, for which I was not paid. All in all the job became much too unbearable.

One day the manager sent me out to buy half a dozen rolls for him. When I returned he looked into the bag and shouted, "Hey, you greenhorn, these are stale. Go back and exchange them."

There were several people in the store. All heard the man, some were embarrassed by his boorishness. I took six cents out of my pocket, put them on the table, opened the door and threw the rolls out into the street.

"You are fired," bellowed the manager.

"Are you the owner of the store?" I asked.

"Yes," he replied.

At that moment my cousin appeared. The manager told him of my impudence. My cousin turned to me and from the look on his face I knew that I had better leave. That evening I told my cousin, "We are finished. You as boss and I as worker. But as a cousin, tell me what to do now."

To this my cousin answered. "Do what you want. You can bang your head against the wall."

This I did not expect from my cousin. My total wealth at that moment consisted of two dollars and ten cents. What to do? First thing was to find a job. I went to stores similar to the one I worked in so that I could say I had experience. Wherever I went I was asked if I was the cousin of J.S. When I admitted it I was told that they did not need any help. I began to look for any kind of job but could find nothing. In the meantime my friend, Miss B., advised me to move out of my cousin's house. From what she said I gathered that he had asked her to do so. Miss B. had already rented a room for me in her neighborhood.

Without even seeing the room I packed my things and left my cousin's house. My cousin's wife, relieved at my leaving or guilt stricken by her husband's shabby treatment of me, asked me to visit them often. I said nothing.

A NEW HOME—A NEW JOB

I MOVED INTO MY NEW ROOM, A SMALL room on the third floor of a large house. The rent was $2 a month. The only window in the room looked out on a dark wall which I could almost touch with my hand. There was an iron cot at the window. A small table and a chair stood beside it. There was no room to pass. When I entered I had to remove the chair, enter the room and then bring the chair back in. The washroom was on the second floor. There was no heat at all.

I gave the landlady $2 for my first month's rent and was left with exactly three cents in my pocket. That night I went to sleep without supper. The next morning I was out looking for work but again without results. I returned to my room and lay back on my bed, tired and hungry. I tried to console myself that it was not too bad. It was quiet there, the sounds of the street couldn't penetrate that brick wall opposite my small window. Nevertheless, I couldn't console away my hunger.

As I lay there brooding someone called from below, "There's someone here to see you!"

My friend, Miss B. had come to take me to a concert. Apparently one look at my face was enough to make her realize that I was hungry. When we reached the street she turned to me and said, "I forgot something. Come to my place for a moment."

When we reached her room she busied herself at the little gas oven and within minutes had made an omelet which she set before me with bread and butter and a glass of milk. Not wanting to embarrass me she said she had suddenly gotten hungry and asked if I would join her. I started to laugh.

With a little persuasion from her I told her about the sad state of my finances. She offered to lend me some money. Much as I was reluctant to accept money from a girl, I borrowed a dollar from her. Several days later she came to me with news of a job. She gave me the address and told me to be there the following morning ready for work.

It was a wholesale glassware store. The pay was great, $9 a week. I had hardly completed congratulating myself when I learned that the store was about to go into bankruptcy and the same monster, F., who had plagued me in my cousin's store, was here to do the job. I learned also that he had asked for me. I couldn't understand why. I soon learned.

It seemed that for such a bankruptcy it was necessary to have an honest employee in the place. This bankruptcy was to be on a grand scale. Wagonsfull of merchandise came into the store. We were ordered to erase the names and markings on the crates and substitute different ones. Then we shipped the newly re-marked crates out. Some merchandise was repacked into different crates.

Among the items that arrived were silver platters and even gold watches.

The owner had his two brothers working for him. They were paid miserably low wages and now they realized that they would be left with nothing in their old age while their brother stuffed his pockets with money robbed from others. So, they reasoned in their desperation, why shouldn't they too steal? The two unhappy brothers grabbed whatever they could, even by the wagon load. The owner saw it all but had to remain quiet.

One day as I was preparing to leave he asked me to return later to repack a very valuable shipment he was expecting. Each time this happened I got an extra dollar for my work. The whole thing was offensive to me. I felt as though I were an accomplice to the thievery. But when I remembered the gnawing hunger pangs of a few weeks before I remained silent and stifled my sense of outrage.

A MISFORTUNE

IT WAS THE EVE OF ROSH HASHONAH, THE Jewish New Year. I was loading crates into the elevator and somehow got my leg caught between the elevator and the floor of the building. I couldn't pull it loose and began to panic. I screamed, more out of fear than pain. Everyone came running but no one knew what to do.

I suddenly asked myself, why do I scream? Failing to find a suitable answer I became silent. My co-workers became more frightened. They thought that I had fallen unconscious, perhaps even worse. I gathered my wits about me and began to tell them what to do. First I instructed them to cut off my boot so I could straighten my leg and ease the pain. I then told them to wedge some heavy iron bars under the elevator and try to raise it, or push it back far enough to free my foot.

My new-found calm soothed the others. But I was annoyed with their clumsiness. They were unable to move the car the slightest. I took a deep breath and with a great heave pulled my leg free. In the process I cut my foot badly, especially around the heel where I scraped the flesh away right down to the bone.

I walked down the staircase and when I got to the bottom I fell to the floor unconscious from the loss of blood. I was taken to a hospital where a cousin of mine, H., was the chief physician. He told me to clamp my jaws shut and clench my fists. Then he poured iodine over the open wound. A little later he bandaged it. He asked where I lived and promised to come see me. Neither of us believed that he would. He didn't.

For three days I lay in my bed. No one knew what had happened to me. In addition I developed a fever. The landlady, failing to see me come and go, became alarmed. She came to my room and found me half conscious. It was three weeks before I returned to work. My leg was still bandaged and I was barely able to walk even with the help of a stick cut down from a broom.

My boss was not very sympathetic.

"You greenhorn," he yelled at me. "Why aren't you more careful; getting hurt and staying away just when I needed you!"

He did not pay me for the time I was disabled. Unfortunately I knew nothing about workmen's compensation at that time.

Some days later I made a package of some clothing that I had left in the store when I was injured and when I went home at the end of the day I tucked the bundle under my arm. I had walked a few blocks when I heard a voice calling me. It was the bookkeeper. The boss had seen me leave with a package and was certain I had stolen something. He sent the bookkeeper chasing after me so he could see what was in the package. As he came up to me, the bookkeeper whispered, "If you took something from the store, throw it away immediately."

I was shocked. I felt as if someone had thrust a hot knife into my flesh. To be accused of being a common thief! I walked into the office, my face clouded over in anger and humiliation. The boss tried to grab the bundle but I pulled it out of his reach. "Let me see what's in it," he shouted. I tore the package open, lifted my jacket and shouted at him: "You bastard, you are the thief, not I."

I walked out of his office, trembling but happy. Stunned at my impudence, the boss shouted through the open doorway, "You're fired!"

I had been walking around too much, not giving my leg

a chance to heal. It bothered me still. My finances were down to $7.50. My situation was not very bright. But at least I did not know that worse was still to come.

SICK, HUNGRY AND OUT OF WORK

I REALIZED SOON THAT IT MIGHT BE SOME time before I was able to find work again. I stopped taking my dinners at the landlady's house and instead I bought some stale bread and fruit and that was my supper. I searched everywhere for work. However, my leg had still not healed so I couldn't take very heavy work, work that would require me to be on my feet all day.

Since the most important thing was to get my leg better I decided to take care of that first. I took to my bed as much as possible to speed the healing. Unfortunately it was not much. My day began at 4 o'clock in the morning. While it was still dark I rose, dressed, walked to the offices of the *Philadelphia Enquirer* and bought the morning paper. I looked over the want ads, noted those that seemed promising and then walked from one address to the other in search for work.

I hoped I would be the first to arrive but always there was one, sometimes two or three early birds ahead of me, apparently even more eager for work. I returned to my room late in the afternoon very tired and very hungry. All I had eaten was some of the stale bread I had brought with me. Supper consisted of an apple and a slice of bread. I had marked the exact size of the slice before I cut it so I should have some left for the next day. When I bought a bread I marked it into portions and never permitted myself to go over the line.

Conditions at the end of 1914 were bad. I was alone. The future looked bleak.

I began to look inward, to analyze myself, study my relations with other people. I had made a strenuous effort to control my temper and to moderate my language. Even during that winter when I suffered so from pain and hunger, I had made a conscious effort to better myself. And self-control was at the head of the list.

Looking back I believe that this exercise in self discipline was a kind of armor, protection against the difficulties I was facing. But it could have ruined me as well. I exercised self-control to the point of total denial and as a result developed deep feelings of inferiority.

I came to believe that I was not as good as others, that I was homely and a bit of a fool. I couldn't understand why a girl would want to be seen walking down the street with me. And I was so anxious for the company of women, especially B., the young lady who had befriended me before. I saw her rarely. I remained away not wishing to arouse her pity.

I came more often to my cousin, A. E., but never during meal time. I was afraid that I would not be able to resist the invitation to sit down at the table to eat with them. And what would have been so terrible if I had? But pride can be a terrible thing at times and so I said not a word about my situation.

DIFFICULT DAYS

THE WEATHER TURNED COOLER. IT WAS October, and then November, and still no job. I had no warm clothing. Whatever winter clothing I had brought from home I threw away at my cousin's behest. They were not "in style" and besides, they smelled too much of the ship's hold. If I had only known that a dry cleaning would get rid of the smell—style or no style, they would have kept me warm at least.

So, I had no choice but to continue wearing my summer clothes and freezing. Occasionally I found odd jobs for a day, sometimes for several days. One such job was hauling bricks up to the third floor of a new building—not up any steps, up a ladder with a hod of bricks on my back. The foreman who hired me was terrified that I would fall off the ladder, bricks and all. I often wondered whether it was my life he worried about or spoiling his bricks!

Once I got some work in a fish market. My job was to unload barrels which were covered with burlap. When I pulled the nails off and peeled off the burlap I was amazed to see turtles crawling over the top. My stomach turned when I saw how the black workers chopped the heads off the turtles, and then cracked their shells off. Much as I forced myself, I couldn't take it and had to quit.

Twice I turned to my uncle, I. M., for help and also to my cousin, A. E. Not far from my lodging house was a candy store run by a young fellow. The store was closed during the day because the young man went to school. When he returned late in the afternoon he opened it and remained open until late at night. The store also had a bed in the back.

The young man had finished his courses and was prepared to start practice as a dentist. All that remained was to sell the store and open his office. I saw a great opportunity for myself. I too would study by day and run the store at night. And by sleeping in the store would even save myself rent money. I spoke to him and we agreed upon a sale price of

$250. Of this he was to receive $150 immediately and the balance in installments. I dared to dream again. I could see myself going through law school. Nothing appealed to me as much as law.

But where was I to get the first $150? My friend B. offered to lend me the money but I didn't want to borrow a large sum from her. I went to my uncle. I knew that he was not poor. Besides, he had a very wealthy son. Surely $150 would not be such a princely sum for him to invest, or lend, for he would surely get it all back, with interest! After all, it was for a career.

My uncle heard me out. He did not refuse me. Neither did he say he would lend me the money. Instead he said nothing. Thus we sat in silence. When the silence became unbearable I left without a word.

I went to my cousin. She thought my plan was very practical—but did not offer to lend me the money. I did not ask her. My dream ended.

I came a second time for assistance. I had found a job as a cutter. Then, even now, the cutter was considered the aristocrat of needle trade workers. It was a well paying job, work was steady and a man could hold his head up. The only trouble was that I would have to work for two months without pay—until I "learned" the trade. It was a matter of less than $50. But alas, even this small sum I couldn't get from my relatives.

I took a job as a paper hanger. Again I had to work for a month without pay in order to learn the trade. After two days of climbing ladders with heavy pails on an empty stomach, I gave it up. My boss wouldn't even give me the five cents I needed to ride home from work every day. I had to walk from 63rd street where I worked to 9th street where I lived.

And so I was without a cent. I had paid my rent to the first of December. My room was freezing; there was no heat at all. I had no quilt or blankets, only a pillow and some bed sheets to cover myself. The bed sheets were mine—at least these I hadn't thrown out with my European clothes. It was so cold at night I had trouble falling asleep.

I BECOME A VEGETARIAN

TO GET IN OUT OF THE COLD I ATTENDED all kinds of meetings and lectures. One of them was given by a vegetarian, Dr. B. Lieber. Listening to him I became convinced that to be a vegetarian was not only noble but also healthy. I was proud that I did not eat meat. I explained to myself that it was good not only for my body but also for my soul.

Of course, if I could have gotten a morsel of meat or a sliver of herring, I believe I would not only have eaten it but my soul also would have celebrated the event. One day Dr. Lieber said that cold showers were good—also for both the body and the spirit. Since both of mine were in such low spirits, I felt that anything would be an improvement.

There was no shower but there was a bathtub on the second floor of the house where I rented my room. The water was going all the time to prevent the pipes from freezing. Having nothing to lose I tested Dr. Lieber's theory. I filled the tub with water, took a deep breath and stepped into the freezing water. I barely got myself wet, then jumped out and wrapped myself in a bed sheet. My towel was big enough to wipe my face only.

Thus, mostly wet, I lay down on my bed and soon felt

a warm glow spread through my body. I fell asleep and slept soundly until about 2:30 in the morning. By then the cold had penetrated through and through and I could sleep no more. I lay there huddled in my sheet with my teeth chattering and my shoulders shaking with cold. Finally I got up and dressed. If shivering and shaking were not enough, hunger began to add to my torment.

My misery deepened. I had lost my confidence. I considered myself next to nothing, a nobody, a misfit. I tried to console myself that this was only temporary but it did no good, my depression wouldn't pass. I argued with myself that certainly I was not a worse person than I was at home and there I was respected. Somehow, respect has more meaning on a full stomach.

I began to avoid people. I spoke little. When I would see people come toward me on the sidewalk I would step into the gutter to allow them to pass unhindered.

What right did I have to walk where people walked?

THOUGHTS ABOUT DEATH

THE FIRST OF DECEMBER HAD COME. MY rent was due. I did not have the $2. Why should I occupy a room if I couldn't pay the rent? The landlord, himself a poor worker, could surely rent the room to someone else and get some badly needed money for it.

I packed my few belongings into my valise and left it with a family I knew. I told them I had to go away for a while. They were kind enough to keep it for me.

I began to walk the streets in search of work. By evening I realized fully what it meant to be homeless. The air was dry but very cold. I walked and walked seeking some kind of refuge. My stomach was crying out for food. I had not eaten all day.

Cold, hungry, miserable, I was full of self pity. I began to think why not put an end to all this suffering? The Delaware River was not far away. I turned in that direction. As I walked my life passed before me. I had not had much of a childhood and enjoyed little more as a youth. My luck had been more bad than good.

As the gloom deepened over my shoulders I suddenly remembered the look in my father's eyes as he ran after the train taking me on the first part of my journey to the new world. I recalled the tragic face of my mother as she stood at the cemetery wringing her hands while her dead infants were lowered into their graves. The sadness in her face made me forget my own sadness for a moment. In her last letter she had written me: "Your brother Sholem is in the front lines. God knows what will happen to him. Our only hope is with you because you are in the golden land." The golden land, indeed!

How could I destroy myself when others suffered so much more? Surely I could have a bit more courage, at least as much as they! My parents, my brother, and others had more to cry about than I.

I spied a wagon parked on an empty lot and crept into it. There was straw in it. I covered myself as best I could with the straw and cried myself to sleep.

In the morning I awoke much calmer and with a determination to fight. I reasoned that my situation was bad but far from hopeless. After all, what did I need? Three dollars a week! As soon as I would find work I would actually be rich. I walked off in search of the elusive job. After a full day of fruitless looking I returned to where the wagon had been parked only to find it gone. So, I went to Fairmont Park and went to sleep on a bench.

I shook myself awake in the morning and tried to thaw out my frozen bones. To find a job I had to have a paper but I had no money for a newspaper. I walked around until I spied a stranger with a paper folded under his arm. I approached and asked him if he would let me see his paper. By this time it was late in the morning so whenever I got to the job that was advertised I always found many others there before me.

AIMLESS

BY THE FOURTH DAY OF MY FAST HUNGER overcame me. I went into the Broad Street station to warm myself. I felt faint. I went out and dragged my weary feet aimlessly along the street. Every few minutes I would stop and lean against a fence or the side of a house to rest.

Finally I found myself at 7th Street and Randolph. There was a farmers' market there. My eyes moved to several crates of garbage. I walked over to one and began to poke around in it. I found partly rotten apples and bananas. I tore away the bad parts and wolfed down the good parts. I looked over my shoulder to see if anyone was watching, although by then I doubt that it would have made any difference.

People scurried to and fro, making purchases, making deals. No one paid any attention to me. Gaining courage I approached a second crate of garbage. The market place became a veritable Garden of Eden for me. Whenever hunger pains reminded me it was time to eat I betook me to the market place for a feast.

I had made another discovery. Some of the farmers bought stale bread as feed for their poultry. I couldn't get myself to ask a farmer for a loaf of the stale bread. To steal was out of the question. But hunger forces compromises. I decided to take the loaf of bread without asking and if the farmer saw, I would start eating immediately. At least I would get a few mouthsful of bread. Several times the farmers caught me in the act and began to scream at me but when they saw me begin to eat the stale bread they became embarrassed and fell silent.

And thus I survived in December 1914. I made my bed mainly in Fairmont Park. When it rained or snowed I would find a freight car and creep into it, warming myself as best I could. The weather grew colder. I still had no job and I was in a constant state of semi-hunger.

I was afraid of two things: being arrested and looking like a tramp. I managed to avoid the first. The police seldom chased me from the park. My appearance, however, was another matter. My clothing became more and more worn and wrinkled. The soles of my shoes were almost gone and what was left was wet through and through. I put pieces of cardboard into my shoes to keep from walking on my bare feet. I managed to shave two or three times a week but my face had a constant stubble and my hair grew long and thick. I'm afraid I had begun to look like a wild man.

I kept my shaving paraphenalia in the small office of a livery stable. The watchman was a Russian peasant and I could converse with him. He was afraid to allow me to stay longer, the boss might find me there and fire him for allowing a tramp to stay there. He might think I would start a fire.

I FIND FRIENDS IN CAMDEN

IT WAS TOWARDS THE END OF DECEMBER when I accidentally bumped into a man I had known before. After the usual small talk I told him I was looking for work.

"Meet me tomorrow morning at the Camden ferry," he told me. "I'll help you find a job."

I slept little that night. I got up long before I had to, shaved and tried to smooth out the wrinkles in my suit. I met my benefactor and at 5:30 a.m. we arrived at the Victor Talking Machine Company, across the river in Camden. My friend went in to report for work after indicating to me at which door I was to wait. There were eight people there ahead of me. I got in line behind them. Soon more people came—and more. People began to stream in from all sides. The police came to keep traffic lanes open.

At 10 o'clock two young men came out of the door and walked towards the densely packed line. Instead of starting with the head of the line they went to the rear and began to pick men. Someone said they had chosen thirty men. I didn't notice. They disappeared inside the door. The others, not realizing that the job hunt was over, remained there, milling around. Suddenly, as if they had received a signal, the police moved in and began to chase the job seekers. In their haste to get away the people began to shove one another. Someone started a fight. More police were called. Several patrol cars appeared. The police used their clubs freely, hitting everyone within reach. Hemmed in as we were there was nowhere we could run. I got a nasty crack on my shoulder.

I edged away from the crowd and managed to climb over a fence to another street. Later I learned that there were some five hundred men gathered there for the thirty jobs.

I was free of the police clubs but not of my problems. How was I to get across the river back to Philadelphia? The ferry cost three cents and three cents I did not have. I stood at the entrance a long time watching the ferries come and go. Several times I wanted to beg the three cents but my tongue would not make the words come out. Nor would my hand reach out for the pennies.

As I stood wondering what to do next it occurred to me that Camden was also a city. Did it matter where I was unemployed? I might just as well look for work in Camden as in Philadelphia. I walked through the streets stopping into the stores asking for work. I deliberately kept to the stores because I knew that a cousin of my mother's lived in Camden and there was always the hope that I might find her. I had never seen her but I had seen her husband back home in Russia. Besides, I knew the family name and thought I might recognize it. Also, I felt that if I saw her or her children I would recognize them and they would help me.

And so the day went by. I was hungry again, and very tired. I began to wonder where I would spend the night. In Philadelphia I knew several places where I could stop in and warm up, like the office of the stable. The watchman knew me and let me sit there, near the stove. But here in Camden there was no friendly watchman to let me come in out of the cold!

I found a small park a distance away from the center of the city and there I lay down on a bench. I couldn't sleep. The hunger and the cold were almost too much to bear. I curled myself into a ball to keep my hands and face warm. After a long time I managed to fall asleep.

I had a beautiful dream. I was flying through space somewhere. It was warm, I came out of my dream and was half awake when I felt rather than saw myself being dragged by the hands. Someone was pulling me into a saloon. I was propped up in a chair alongside a hot stove and another person poured some whiskey down my throat. I was opposed in principle to alcoholic drinks but made no effort to resist. The liquor warmed everything inside me on its way down to my stomach.

I was told what had happened. After I had fallen asleep I fell off the bench. As I lay on the ground it started to rain and the rain soon turned to ice. In a short time I was almost covered with ice. Two men, also homeless, found me and dragged me into the saloon.

The saloon keeper, a German, questioned me. I replied hesitantly. He gave me a bowl of hot soup. In those days the saloons provided a free lunch counter for those who bought beer. I ate so quickly I began to choke. I ate and ate. No one bothered me. After I had had my fill I dozed in my chair near the stove.

At about 1 o'clock in the afternoon I thought it time to be on my way. My clothes were dry—and so were my bones. The saloon keeper wanted me to stay longer but I thanked him for his kindness and left. I wanted to find the Jewish section and inquire about my cousin's family. After several hours I found someone who knew my cousin and gave me her address. When I reached it I found a small wooden house with a sign on it that read: "F. Cleaning and Repairing."

I hesitated, finding it difficult to believe that my cousin's husband, who had been a violin teacher, could have turned into a tailor in this golden land. I waited on the opposite side of the street. I thought perhaps I could recognize someone from the family. After a while a girl came out of the door. She was dark, yet the face had a familiar look. It must be someone from the family, I thought.

With my heart pounding, partly in fear and partly in hope, I knocked on the door and entered. I asked if indeed the lady was my mother's cousin and explained who I was and where I came from.

"Yes," she replied. "And you are Benny. Where have you been all this time? We have been looking for you."

As we stood talking, her husband came in. He no longer looked like a violinist. He now looked like a tailor. My clothes must have told them more than my words for he said to me:

"We'll chat later, let's eat now."

To his wife he said: "We have such an important guest. Go, prepare something to eat."

He led me into his workroom and asked me to take off my clothes. He mended them carefully and pressed them in no time at all. When I returned to the kitchen to eat not only did I look like a new person, I felt like one.

As we ate they told me that they had known I was in America and had been trying to find me. They told me they had received a letter from her brother who lived somewhere in New England telling them that he had prospered and inviting them to come and live with him. He had a good job, with a private office for himself and, they asked, why shouldn't I go up to see him? Perhaps he had a job for me?

I liked the idea very much, especially since I had known her brother from the old country. When I studied at the yeshiva in Boruisk I used to patronize his shop. He was the owner of a teahouse and would often sell me tea on credit. Surely he would remember me!

I sent off a letter to him and in the meantime stayed at my cousin's house, at least until the answer came. "Come immediately." He also told me in the letter that there were evening schools there and that I would be able to study at night. The only problem that remained was to get the money for the trip.

My cousin R., gave me $2. I spent five cents for a shave, ten cents for a hair cut and fifty cents for half soles on my shoes. I went to Philadelphia to the girl who had befriended me so many times before. I found her sick and in bed. She was angry with me for not coming to see her for so long—ever since I had given up my room. I did not tell her of the difficult period I had gone through. She felt hurt. She thought I had deliberately avoided her, that I had been a false friend.

From there I went to my uncle, I.M. I showed him the letter. He was delighted and offered to lend me $15 to cover my expenses even before I asked him. I wanted to thank him but the tears clouded my eyes and I was unable to speak.

I did not return to my lady friend. I felt suddenly awkward and decided to write her instead. We kept up a correspondence for many years. In time she married. Many years later I sought her out in Chicago. I then lost track of her again. I still think of her often and hope that fate was as kind to her as she was to me.

IN A NEW PLACE

I ARRIVED IN GARDNER, MASSACHUSETTS, on the 14th of January, 1915. There was snow everywhere. I had to take a sleigh to get to my cousin's house. The streets, the fields and the forests were white. The snow crunched under foot. It reminded me of my little town in the old country. If I closed my eyes I could easily imagine I was still there. The frost bit into my face. Fortunately I had used $2.50 of the money I had received for an overcoat. I needed it.

My cousin R. lived in a tiny four-room apartment over a store. If he had prospered his home didn't show it. One room was so small that it was impossible to get around the furniture and so it wasn't used. The kitchen led off to two bedrooms, one for my cousin and his wife and the other for a boarder.

Poverty whistled out from all four corners of the apartment, such poverty I had seen only back in the old country.

R. was tall, over six feet, and as thin as he was tall. He looked like a stick. His wife was morose, nervous, perpetually angry, and was always spewing invective. They had three chilrden, a girl of seven, a boy of four and a five-week old baby. The boarder, about my age, came from a town near mine. He was black as pitch with piercing black eyes. He was intelligent and likeable.

After a frugal supper I inquired about the possibilities of getting a job.

"Don't worry, you'll get work," said my cousin.

R. got a folding bed from God knows where and set it up for me in the kitchen. I didn't like the idea, sleeping there right in the center of the apartment. I looked for a more likely corner. From the unused room the door opened onto a closed-in porch where they kept several chickens. I decided if the chickens didn't mind I would bed down there. They tried to talk me out of it, warning that I would surely freeze. I thought to myself it would be better than a freight car. Besides, the thought of having a corner of my own appealed to me.

I would use my overcoat for a pillow but what about a cover? I looked around and saw a soft piece of carpet on the floor. Perfect! I picked it up and dusted it off and that was my blanket. Sleep was still a stranger to me. No matter how much I cleaned the room the smell of the chickens was overpowering. It choked me. Besides, the carpet wasn't very warm! The New England winter was much more severe than in Philadelphia. I turned on my bed so long that it collapsed.

It should not be surprising that by that time I no longer believed in a personal God. I could no longer address my complaints to Him. But I did to myself. Why did I deserve such misfortunes? Millions of people live like human beings. Rich or poor, they managed to fashion a decent life for themselves. Why couldn't I? Every dog finds his own corner, but not I. I came here to my cousin who wrote such a glowing letter and the whole scene fizzled out, as if some unseen hand had turned a switch!

I still had part of my expense money. I decided then and there to go to Baltimore. I might not find much culture but at least I would have food and a place to sleep. Culture would come later.

To begin with I needed a secure home, a corner of the world I could call my own. Still planning my life in Baltimore I drifted off to sleep. In the morning I was awakened by a woman's agonized crying. I jumped up. R. had gotten up at six o'clock to go to work. The baby didn't feel well. He gave her a spoonful of medicine—in the dark. Instead of medicine, he gave her carbolic acid and went off to work. Shortly after the baby began to retch and cry. When I came into the kitchen I found the mother pacing to and fro hysterically with the baby in her arms.

I sent the older girl to the factory to fetch her father and I ran for a doctor. The doctor examined the child and said there was no danger. The baby had spat out the carbolic acid. She had just burned her mouth slightly. He gave me a prescription which I took to the drug store. I paid for the drug out of my precious expense money. As the doctor was getting ready to leave R. called me aside and asked me to give him the $2 to pay the doctor. He said he would withdraw the amount from the bank later and repay me.

R. did not return to work. Instead he took me for a walk around the town, and also to see if there was work for me. On the way back he took another dollar from me, also with a promise to repay. With it he bought some food for supper: two herrings, a small sack of potatoes, some bread and a bottle of beer. When his wife saw the beer she began to seethe, rising in volume as her anger increased. She finally ended by cursing him long and loudly.

Although it was my money that had paid for the supper I choked on every mouthful. I left the house and walked the streets for a long time. I was debating with myself whether to stay or leave. The trouble was that I no longer had enough money to get me back to Baltimore. I did have enough to get me to New York and there I still had another cousin. He was working in a tie factory. We had grown up together and I wouldn't have to be ashamed to tell him about my adversities. He would help me get a job.

Or, perhaps I should stay here in New England. If fate had brought me here perhaps it was meant to be. I could stay here and help R. climb out of his poverty.

I decided to remain, at least for a while. R. took half days off to take me around to various factories to find a job.

He himself worked as an oiler in a large furniture factory. He was very tall and the long oil can made him even taller. So, like a giraffe, he could reach all the machines without having to use a ladder.

The barrels of oil were stored in the cellar. R. placed empty boxes around the barrels and this was the private office he had described in his letter.

There were many factories in the town. He took me from one to the other and could still get to his factory in time to punch his time card. He worked from 7 o'clock in the morning until 6 at night, six days a week. For this he received all of six dollars a week.

(Now, in December, 1970, I learned what had happened to Miss B. Her husband died years ago. She herself had been paralyzed for some years. A nephew took care of her. Not knowing his name I was unable to contact him. Fate was not very kind to her.)

IN AN IRON FOUNDRY

WHEN R. COULDN'T GO WITH ME I WENT around by myself to look for work. Luck was with me and I found a job as a helper in an iron foundry. If there is such a thing as hell on earth, this was it!

The iron was poured into molds of earth. The earthen forms were shaped in the morning. At about three o'clock in the afternoon, when the forms were ready, the molten iron was also ready. Instead of using machines to pour the iron as is done nowadays, it was poured out of huge kettles which had to be carried by hand. When it came time to pour the molten metal we shed all our clothes but our trousers and shoes. The fiery metal had to be poured quickly. Holes would appear in the iron blocks if the metal cooled too soon.

The dust swirled around as we poured the melted iron into the wet sand. By five o'clock we were all black, covered with a layer of mud. I worked there only for a few days. I wasn't employed by the boss but by one of the workers as his helper. I was to be there only until his regular helper returned. The pay was quite good, nine dollars a week for a 55-hour week.

A whole month passed until I was able to land another job, this time in the junk shop of R's brother-in-law. I worked sixty hours a week for a wage of five dollars with the understanding that after 30 days my wages would be increased to nine dollars a week. The thirty days came and went but I did not get my promised increase. A second thirty days passed and still no increase. Finally, after four months my employer got around to fulfilling his promise. I was now getting nine dollars a week.

My tasks were simple. I had to do everything that had to be done in a junk shop: sort rags, squeeze them into bales, chop iron into manageable pieces, load freight cars, receive, pack and ship and, if time permitted, try to keep the warehouse reasonably clean.

Since I was still paying off debts accumulated during the period I was out of work, I couldn't afford to buy the necessary clothes and equipment, such as work gloves. As a result I had to work with the iron with my bare hands. Ordinarily that wouldn't be so bad but at feezing temperatures the iron would sometimes stick to my skin and rub my **hands raw.** And if working outside in the cold with iron was bad, working indoors sorting the rags was even worse. There was a broken stove in the middle of the room and it smoked constantly, filling the room with sickening fumes. I would have shut it off but there was an old man, a fellow Jew, also working there and he needed the warmth.

My employer, Y. was a giant of a man and as powerful as he was tall. He fled the Czar's army during the Russo-Japanese war and made his way to America. He settled in Gardner and became a junk man, buying and selling old rags, old clothes, anything that could be reclaimed or re-used.

When I came to know him he was already well off. He had become a wholesaler and his profits went even higher. He was a crude man, could neither read nor write. He lost an eye in an accident and that gave his face a wild, distorted look. His wife was stricken with tuberculosis and spent most of her time seated in her chair. Her father lived in the same house wth them. There was also a daughter, several years younger than I.

The father-in-law was short and heavy and was well along in years. Nevertheless he helped out in the warehouse. For this, his son-in-law, my employer, paid the old man three dollars a week and room and board. He gave him his salary in checks. Several years later, when the old man died, they discovered all the old salary checks hidden away under his mattress.

The house and the business were located about two miles outside of town. I had to walk those two miles to work in the morning and back from work at night. And if that weren't enough, I made the trip again at lunch time. If it happened that I was a few minutes late returning from lunch, the boss would shriek like a madman—this despite the fact that I was forced to work overtime, without pay, almost every day!

The town of Gardner had a population of about 9,000. It was noted mainly for its factories that produced cheap furniture. Most of the workers were of Slavic origin, peasants who had immigrated to America. Wages ranged from six to ten dollars a week for six ten-hour days. There were seventeen Jewish families in the town; eight of them were in the junk business. There were two wealthy families, real estate dealers. There were also a tailor and a shoemaker. The rest were small storekeepers.

The town had a small synagogue which I attended on Rosh Hashonah and Yom Kippur. Kosher meat came by special delivery from Worcester, the nearest big city. The town also had a lodge of the Order of Brith Sholem, although exactly what it did I still don't know.

How did the work affect my personal life? Although it was quite hard, I found it generally satisfying. I still had plenty of energy left after work but unfortunately there was little opportunity to make use of it. So I engaged in all kinds of gymnastics, developing my body physically. During the four years of my stay in Gardner I became a bit of a "strong man." I was able to lift a rag bale weighing some seven hundred pounds and carry it on my back from one part of the room to wherever it was needed.

Socially I didn't fare too well. My friend, G., who lodged in the same house, although younger than I, already had a sweetheart and spent most of his spare time with her. There were two girls with whom I was also friendly. They were both simple girls, from the old country, nice to talk to but not very stimulating. There were other young people in the town but they were considered upper class while I was of the working class.

It was a topsy turvy situation. In my home town I was considered to be of the upper class and here it was quite the opposite.

Culturally, R.'s estimation of Gardner was correct. There

were evening schools in the town. I enrolled in one of the evening schools but had to drop out. Most of the students were former Slavic peasants who were still trying to learn the alphabet and to add two and two. The only alternative was self education. I was a regular visitor to the library, taking out English translations of books I had already read in the original in Russian. Thus, reading in English what was already famliar to me, I was able to perfect my knowledge of English.

My room, which was very cold, was ideally suited for study. No one came near it and my evenings were undisturbed. Immediately after supper I would go to my room, put on my overcoat, cover my feet with rags to keep them from freezing and sitting thus, bundled up, I was able to read until two o'clock in the morning. That was my schedule every night for several years. I read hundreds of books and became quite proficient in English in the process.

I kept in contact with Jewish life by reading the Philadelphia Yiddish daily, the *Jewish World,* and later the New York daily *Der Tag.* The local library did not have any Yiddish books so I scrounged around for Yiddish books in every Jewish home in town. I doubt that there was a single book I missed. After a while I was able to save enough money to begin buying Yiddish books for myself.

I corresponded regularly with my parents. From them I learned that my brother was a prisoner of the Germans. I sent him packages through the Red Cross in Switzerland. The five dollars were quite a drain so I managed to get along without the less important necessities. What was worse was that I had no way of knowing whether or not my brother ever received the parcels. Nevertheless I mailed out the packages regularly. In later years my brother told me that the food I sent him had reached him and had kept him from starving.

The food in my lodging house was monotonous and poorly prepared. I rose each morning at 5:30. At six o'clock we had a glass of tea with a slice of dry bread. For lunch we had something fried in crisco and some bread. Meat we got on Saturday—one and a half pounds for the entire family! The lady of the house, in addition to being poor was also a bad housekeeper. She whined constantly about her lot, but the sad fact is that she was fit for nothing else.

She had a mania for scrimping and hiding away savings from the frugal allowance she got. From the household expenses she managed to accumulate a nest egg, a little "bundle." She managed it by giving everyone, her own family included, just barely enough to sustain the souls in their bodies but not enough for the body itself. I was in a constant state of hunger until I finally reached the stage where I was able to buy some additional food on the outside.

Just to mention a small incident: I used to come home from work later than her husband and found my supper on the table, the husband and wife having left to see a movie. And so it was each night for the next six days. Only on Sunday was the movie theater closed. When I came home that day my supper was cold and sour.

Since I worked in the junk shop I naturally came home with dirty hands. Facilities for cleaning them at the shop were not very good. At the house there was only one sink. Always when I washed my hands in the sink I saw a bowl with pieces of bread in it. I never knew why until a brother-in-law on a visit one day unraveled the mystery.

He was a great eater but couldn't stand her cooking. Understandable! She would often make puddings so the brother-in-law would often ask me, "What kind of Japanese pudding is she making today?"

Seeing the saucer in the sink with the pieces of bread, he suggested she probably used those leftovers for her puddings. I scoffed at the idea telling him that for ever so long I had been washing my hands in the sink right over that bowl of bread. Even as I protested it occurred to me that perhaps he was right. I emptied the bowl. The next day she apologized for not having any pudding for supper. I laughed so hard I had to leave the table.

The spoons and forks were made of tin and were never clean. I called this to her attention several times but it did no good. In order to cure her, I contrived to drop the tableware in such a manner that they landed under the stove. Since she never cleaned under the stove she complained that spoons and forks were missing. One fine day, however, she "discovered" several dozen spoons and forks under the stove. She surmised that it had all been my doing but after that she took care to see that the spoons and forks were properly washed.

In the meantime, my employer had formed a partnership with another junk dealer and with two non-Jews, wealthy factory owners. I was also permitted to purchase shares in the new corporation. If I had had more money at that time I would have been able to buy a full partnership. Since my finances were still on the meager side I was only able to buy a 14th share of the business.

They obtained a large tract of land from the railroad and made it into one of the largest and best junk shops in New England. They began to do business on a grand scale. The railroad gave them the land for nothing on the basis that it would profit from the hauling of the freight. The two non-Jews got credit at the bank without difficulty and so they had both the money and the opportunity to engage in all kinds of commercial transactions. They were not active in the business, only we three. My employer was the treasurer of the company and also the manager. The other partner was the buyer and I was the plant superintendent. The buyer covered all of New England, visiting factories that had been destroyed by fire, buying up salvageable metal. My job was to go there and make sure that the metal had been cut down to manageable size for shipment to the foundry.

We began to specialize in buying up large boilers. We broke them up with heavy hammers and chisels. Each boiler had from five hundred to a thousand rivets, and each rivet had to be broken off. The trick was to break the rivet off with a single blow from the hammer. If not, the rivet would simply bend and then at least twenty-five additional strokes were necessary before the hammer sheared off the rivet.

The biggest sledge hammer weighed some 18 pounds. We ordered a special hammer weighing 26 pounds. Not one of the workers succeeded in breaking off more than three rivets in succession. After that he would have to rest. I was able to knock off ten rivets in a row without a breather. With this kind of work my muscles bulged and I was no longer able to buy ready made clothes.

On this job I also began to drink a lot. I used to put away at least a quart of whiskey a day. The working day started early and everyone would greet the new day by drinking a tea glass full of whiskey. As we worked we all helped ourselves from a gallon jug that stood nearby. Each could take as much as he wanted.

The work eased up a bit when we were able to use the acetylene torch to cut the metal apart. I became quite an expert with the torch.

Whenever I had to go to a distant town to arrange for cutting down and shipping the boilers I would bring along some books to read on my lunch hours. Once as I sat in my dirty overalls, a book in my hand, a man came by. He was dressed like a farmer and carried a pitchfork in his hand.

"Excuse me," he said, "What are you reading?"

"*Prometheus,* by Aeschylus," I replied. I had no wish to engage in unneccessary conversation and I confess my reply was rather brusque. The farmer touched the book and said:

"Young man, I would consider it a favor if you would come to my house for supper."

I was reluctant to accept since I had no other clothes but the work clothes I was wearing. But the man was so gracious I felt that I could not refuse without offending him.

When I entered his house I was surprised to find a large room full of books. The man I had taken to be a New England farmer, I learned, was actually a professor at Harvard University.

The family received me in a most friendly manner and made me feel at home. However, I was very uncomfortable because of my dirty clothes. My English was very poor and I spoke more poorly than usual because of my self-consciousness. As I prepared to take my leave my host said to me: "Young man, as a junk dealer you are too much of a philosopher, and as a philosopher you are too much of a junk dealer."

At this point I would like to set down my reactions when I read in the press that the Czar had abdicated and that the Russian revolutionists had won out. As I read the news on a trolley car, tears of joy streamed down my face. I felt as if the chains had been lifted from my own back as well as from the Russian people.

Although I was living here in America, without the thought of ever leaving it, I still loved Russia. I never faltered in my opposition to those who felt that Russia had to be defeated in the war. I even went so far as to call for a Russian victory even with the Czar still on the throne. My hatred for Germany, inborn to begin with, grew even more intense when I first put foot on German soil and heard the insult, "Damned Jew!"

This took place in the beginning of 1917. Industry was thriving and our own business was doing very well. True, I was working hard but I enjoyed it. I saw a great future for myself. I had acquired a wide acquaintanceship in the business world. In my lodging things became much better as everyone's finances improved. In order to keep my expenses down when I traveled I slept in the ruins where we dismantled the metal. When some important or risky work had to be done I did it myself rather than trust it to the less experienced workers. Because I wanted the profits to accrue within the company I was satisfied with a modest wage of $25 a week. But my workers, whom I supervised, and often protected, were getting as much as $40 a week.

BETWEEN LIFE AND DEATH

DURING ALL THE YEARS THAT I WAS ENgaged in dangerous work I managed to survive without accidents. I was proud of my record. However, that record was broken, with almost tragic results, one day. It was either late in May or early in June, 1917. I had just finished a long and difficult job and I was tired.

I was loading an iron roller weighing 4,400 pounds of metal. The chain suddenly snapped throwing me to the ground and the roller up against my chest. I was rushed to the hospital but the doctors weren't too optimistic about my chances of surviving. The bones in my chest had been bent, my heart was squeezed out of position and the arteries were pinched together. My circulation was slow and painful.

For a week I hovered between life and death. In my lucid moments I reflected on my predicament and found it difficult to understand how I could die at the age of 20—without even having lived. What made it even worse was that it had to happen at this time, when I was finally beginning to climb out of my poverty. I was prospering and my future looked bright as the partner of a thriving business. I was determined to live.

And live I did! I don't know what helped me, whether it was my determination or the grass that my landlady brought from her mother's grave and placed under my pillow. Whatever it was I had begun to recover.

I was bedridden for several months. I felt well enough, strong and capable. But I couldn't stand on my feet. The doctors were at a loss to explain it. Even considering all my adversities, it is hard for me to recall a more desperate time, especially when I feared that I would become an invalid, without legs! That was the worst part.

My doctor advised me to eat chicken soup but not the meat. The landlady used to buy the chicken but she was embarrassed to take it to the ritual slaughter so I would ask one of the children to do it. All this kept me in a constant state of nervousness and didn't speed my recovery.

One day my non-Jewish partner took me to a specialist in Boston who treated me and helped me regain the use of my legs.

THE END OF A PARTNERSHIP

WHEN MY LEGS WERE STRONG ENOUGH I returned to work. The doctor warned me not to exert myself too much and not to do any heavy work. However, the job was naturally difficult and some weeks later I suffered a heart attack and was again confined to bed for several weeks. When I returned once again to my job I learned that a meeting of the corporation had been scheduled. At the meeting one of my Jewish partners proposed that I be fired. The motion hit my ears with the force of a thunderclap.

"But," I protested, "You promised me an increase in salary and also that I would become an equal partner in the business."

My partner said the promise had been made before the accident. Now that I could no longer work, there was no further need of my services.

I turned to another partner, my former employer. I asked if that was his feeling too. He said he agreed with his partner.

I turned to the non-Jewish partner.

"What do you expect of me if your own brothers want to throw you out?" he asked.

Sick at heart and overcome with humiliation and anger I shouted at my partners and finally threw a chair at them. Unfortunately I missed. My partner refused even to buy me out. And since they did not pay me during the time I was out after the accident, all the money I had saved went to pay the hospital and doctor bills. I didn't have enough left to start another business.

All this affected me very deeply. My heart cried out for vengeance. I could think of nothing else. Two years later the firm went bankrupt, but there was little consolation in

The author at the age of 20, when he worked in a junk-shop, Gardner, Massachusetts.

it for me for the shabby way they had treated me.

Years later I met J. in a mid-western city. He had lost all his money. I gave him $300 worth of merchandise on credit to help him get started. He never repaid the loan although he had made good and was well able to do so.

However, the moment I advanced the $300 in credit to him I became inwardly calm again. I was no longer filled with a desire for vengeance. So, perhaps it was I who got the better of the deal after all.

I stayed on in Gardner after I was fired and did some business on a modest scale. Even so I was successful. I had many acquaintances and enjoyed a good reputation at the bank. I had no trouble getting credit. If I had remained in Gardner there is no doubt that I would have become quite successful. As it was, within the space of some six months I managed to accumulate about $2,000.

However, a man I knew, a small business man, wanted to move to a big city and asked me to join him in a partnership. He wanted to open a business in Springfield. He said he had enough money and was willing to put us as much as necessary. I agreed to go along with him.

I went ahead to open a junk shop while he remained behind to wind up his own business. To open the junk shop cost more money than we had figured and he became very uneasy about the undertaking. I put my own $2,000 into the venture and worked very hard, from seven in the morning until midnight. I tried to do everything myself to avoid hiring additional help, even the bookkeeping. My partner came every Sunday to see how the business was progressing. He began to suspect that I was stealing some of the money. He didn't accuse me directly but I could tell from his actions that he was suspicious. That hurt me very much. Since he did not make any accusations I could not defend myself.

In the meantime he had moved to Springfield. I demanded that we engage an accountant to check over the books. This was done and when everything was found to be in order I proposed to him that since it was I who actually established the business and since it was on a going basis and he himself in town, that he repay me my $2,000 and take over the business by himself. He finally agreed and the partnership was dissolved. This was in the year 1918.

LABOR ZIONISM AND FREEDOM

I ENJOYED A VERY ACTIVE SOCIAL LIFE IN Springfield. It was there that I became acquainted with the ideology of the Poale Zion, the Labor Zionist movement. There were many lively debates between the Labor Zionists and the general Jewish Socialists, both at open meetings and at private gatherings.

I was caught up in the excitement of the political ferment and in order to discuss the conflicting ideologies intelligently I had to read up on them. I even bought a copy of Karl Marx's *Das Kapital*. I struggled through that ponderous volume but to tell the truth I didn't get too much out of it. At least I was able to say I had read *Das Kapital,* which was more than many of my friends could say.

It was in Springfield that I regained some of my self confidence, especially as a result of frequent chats with a young friend named Mirsky or, as he called himself, "Murphy." He had a great influence on me and helped me to regain my self respect.

The revolution in Russia and the civil war which followed made regular correspondence impossible. I had not received any mail from my parents for a long time.

Despite my worry over my parents I felt a great sense of freedom, due in great measure to having given up my unfortunate partnership. It was a happy-go-lucky feeling and I didn't much care where I was going or what I was going to do next.

From Springfield I came to New York. I didn't even bother to look for a job or try to open a business. The city just didn't appeal to me. Besides, I still had the feeling of having thrown off all worry and thoughts of the future.

I BECOME A COAL MINER

WHEN I TIRED OF LAZYING AROUND IN New York I made my way back to Philadelphia. From there I returned to New York, spending money as freely as if I had never had to earn it and as if there was no end to my treasure. Then, one morning I suddenly felt the emptiness of this sort of existence and decided to become productive once again.

I must say that I was influenced in my decision partly by the teachings of the Jewish radical writer and theoretician, Dr. Chaim Zhitlowsky. As a result I left for the mining region of Pennsylvania determined to become a coal miner. I wanted desperately to become part of the laboring masses, the Jewish proletariat.

I boarded in the home of a Lithuanian woman whose husband and son both worked in the coal mine. There were four other boarders. In those days the workers were paid by the ton and not by the number of hours they worked.

The atmosphere in the house was stultifying and suffocating. Most of the people were half drunk most of the time. They drank more whiskey than they ate food. Apparently it made it a bit easier to face the new day of toil. First thing in the morning everyone took a tea glass full of bootleg whiskey. Then they reached for their dinner pail and left for the mine.

My job in the mine was to load the coal onto a cart. When we got back to the house everyone reached once again for the glass of whiskey and then sat down to a meal of stew containing large pieces of meat. At first I couldn't stomach the food but in time I became used to it. After dinner they continued to drink until one after another they staggered off to bed. Two persons shared each bed.

In the morning when the day shift workers left for the mine, the night shift workers came home and occupied the same beds. The bedding always looked black, even when it was newly changed. They would often get into fights and I was drawn into some of them against my will.

Once there was a discussion on religion between an Irishman and a Syrian Mohammedan. As luck would have it they decided to ask my opinion. Having no desire to adjudicate a difference of opinion in a religious matter, I replied that all religions were good—for nothing! Suddenly everyone in the saloon pounced on me. I was one against more than a dozen. Chairs and bottles flew at me from all sides. I was bleeding all over, but several of my adversaries were also bloodied up and lying on the floor.

This incident cured me of my desire to become one of the masses. I left town and took it easy for a while—until I came to Atlantic City. In that ocean-front city lived another of my cousins. A.E. She was happy to see me and made me welcome. She was a calming influence on me and under tender, almost motherly care I began to think of doing something constructive with my life. I decided to return to Baltimore. During my absence from that city my father's sister

In America; Years of Struggle

and her husband immigrated to the United States and settled there. I was anxious to see them again and that was where I headed.

IN BALTIMORE

RETURNING TO BALTIMORE I FOUND MY uncle with his nose high in the air. He was no longer a "batlan," an impractical man. His beard had broadened and was well combed. The people called him "Rabbi." In the synagogue he sat in the upper pew and was accorded all the honors of a distinguished religious leader.

My aunt was even more of a surprise. When she arrived in the United States several years before she couldn't even recite the prayers, let alone read or write. Now she had learned to recite the prayers from the prayer-book and how to read and write in Yiddish. Such an accomplishment for a woman over 65 was truly a marvel.

Both my uncle and my aunt had begun a new life here in Baltimore. Their children, all working, provided for their basic needs. True they were not very well off but then, they were never accustomed to better. They had enough to enjoy an active social life and were held in high esteem by their neighbors. What more could an elderly couple ask?

My aunt was active in community affairs. She was especially active in the burial society and was often busy arranging funerals and consoling the bereaved. I boarded with my aunt. The apartment was over a junk shop and consequently was usually infested with insects. Nevertheless she kept the house clean as she could and was an excellent cook. She would be offended if I failed to finish the generous portions she served me.

I invested in a small junk shop and soon I began to accumulate a modest profit. However, I had to work for it—from five o'clock in the morning until ten o'clock at night. The fact that I was making a profit impelled me to work even harder. In less than two years time I had netted a profit of $30,000.

YIDDISH SCHOOLS

I BECAME INTERESTED IN YIDDISH SECUlar schools which used Yiddish as the language of instruction. Since Baltimore had no Jewish school with the exception of a Talmud Torah, I began to urge the Poale Zion, the Labor Zionists, to open a Yiddish school. Years before, long before I arrived there, they had a Sunday school but by 1919 it was no longer in existence. Although the Poale Zion was very active it was not quite strong enough to support such an undertaking.

So I joined the Arbeiter Ring, a labor order which was known in English as the Workmen's Circle. There I found two other members who shared my wish to establish a Yiddish school. We began to send notices around to the fourteen branches of the order trying to rally additional support.

The old guard, led by the local manager of the Jewish *Daily Forward*, was against us. The *Daily Forward* was also against us and used all kinds of propaganda to kill off the idea. We wanted to finance the program by a $1 tax per member per year and although it was really a very small sum, it held us back.

Whenever we would persuade a branch to adopt the school tax the opposition got to work undermining us. They pushed through a special meeting and managed to mobilize enough votes to rescind the school tax. The discussions frequently led to violence and sometimes chairs flew across the room.

But luck and determination won the day and we finally opened a school. J. B. Beilin, Educational Director of the Workmen's Circle was a great help to us in our campaign. The first teacher was a well known Yiddish Writer. I hope he will forgive my harsh judgment of him. But the fact is that while he was a good writer he was poor as a teacher. He did us much harm. He finally left in the middle of the semester and we had to scramble around for a replacement. We were fortunate and secured the services of a capable man who remained with us for the next year. He got along well with the children. The school became a source of great pride with us.

At just that time the *Jewish Daily Forward* issued several editorials calling for the anglicization of Yiddish. This set off the fight around our school program once again but with increased intensity. Fortunately we had managed to win over many of the non-active members to our side and with their help managed to stave off the renewed attack. To safeguard our program we agreed that each of us would be present at each meeting of every branch and if the school program came up for discussion the member present would immediately notify the activists. They, in turn, would mobilize all our forces and thus we were able to turn aside every attempt to destroy our school.

I started reading again, concentrating this time on Yiddish literature. Every new Yiddish book or magazine that came out was a welcome and joyous experience. I had to get each volume, each magazine and read it from cover to cover. The home of our teacher became our cultural center. A group of us would meet there regularly staying until late at night, or rather until early in the morning, talking, talking, talking.

The teacher's wife, pleasant and lively, helped make the gatherings interesting. As for me, I had no material worries at the moment and for several years enjoyed a pleasant and culturally stimulating existence.

CRISIS

AND SO THE YEARS 1919 AND 1920 PASSED. Toward the end of 1920 a financial crisis struck the country. Prices began to fall. Actually there were warning signs at the beginning of the year but my business didn't begin to feel the pinch until the end of 1920. Prices tumbled so rapidly that we were unable to plan ahead. Not having experienced such an upheaval before and not having parents or older experienced associates to advise me, I failed to appreciate the seriousness of the situation.

If prices declined, I reasoned, then they would also rise. I continued to buy goods at the market prices. I had my own money and did not seek any bank credits. I paid for everything in cash, especially since I held contracts to supply goods at higher prices. Unfortunately it was a very cold winter and because of unusually heavy snowfalls the railroad was unable to transport the goods. I did not know that an embargo, such as the one the railroad declared, nullifies a contract. I was certain I would be able to complete my transactions as soon as the embargo was lifted.

In the meantime I continued to buy at the going prices. When the embargo was finally lifted in 1921, I sent out letters notifying my customers that their shipments would be arriving shortly. I was stunned to learn that two of my customers had gone bankrupt and that the other firms refused to reinstate the orders saying that the embargo had invalidated them and they no longer wanted the merchandise.

On my part I had a tremendous inventory, all purchased at high prices. If I sold the goods, even at a loss, it would not have been too bad. If I had known my economics better I might have saved myself several thousand dollars. But at least I was solvent.

Wanting to familiarize myself more with the way things were done in the United States I put a lock on my door and took off for a six-month tour of the country.

I returned to find that prices were still falling. My lease had expired and the landlord was asking for an increase in rent. I refused and he rented the store over my head. I sold the goods for less than $1,000.

Discouraged, I decided to get out of the junk business entirely. Many of my friends looked down their noses at my work.

"Why should a young man as intelligent as you waste his life in the junk business?" they asked.

Perhaps they were right, I thought. I sold my business at a time when prices were at their lowest point since the days of the Civil War.

I GET MARRIED AT A BAD TIME

UNTIL THAT TIME I THOUGHT LITTLE about marriage. Women had played a minor role in my personal life. Why this was so I find it difficult to explain. Perhaps it was because of my changing moods. I had been through great trials and had a rather poor image of myself.

I felt that women would not find me at all interesting or attractive.

Then there were times when I felt myself much superior to the girls of my acquaintance. The girls were just not up to my standards. Between the two it is impossible to determine what were the real reasons. Nevertheless, it was a fact that I had few female friends and they had little influence on my life.

It was in 1919 or perhaps 1920 that I began to think about getting married. I felt I didn't have enough money. I wanted a home and servants and a car. I reasoned that if in the two years of my stay in Baltimore, to which I had come with $300 in my pocket, I was able to save some $30,000, I could in a few years time save $50,000 or $75,000 and that was a tidy sum to bring to a marriage.

But fate determined otherwise. In 1921, with business poor and my losses mounting, I fell in love and in a couple of years I was married. My financial situation at the time was very bad. I decided to get out of the junk business. For $2,400 I bought a half interest in a grocery and meat store. Since I did not have that much money I borrowed $1,000 from relatives and the balance on my insurance policy.

My partner was gifted in social activities but in business he had two left feet. I realized this the day after we became partners. I tried to cancel the partnership and asked for my money back. He refused. Things went from bad to worse. Every day there was money missing from the till. I asked him how it happened.

"We are two partners," he replied, "It is either you or I."

I understood what he was implying. If I accused him, then he could very well accuse me. Some would believe me and some would believe him. So, rather than be thought a thief even by a few I remained silent.

The partnership lasted for two and a half years. They were years of torment, insult and humiliation. Never had I thought that one person could cause another so much anguish. Many times I pleaded with him to pay off the debts and take over the business by himself. I would leave without a cent. I offered to let him out and I would assume responsibility for all the debts. I would even give him $500. Still he refused.

The business continued to deteriorate. We took food from the store to feed ourselves and each of us received $20 a week as wages. Unfortunately the store's income was not enough to cover expenses.

And that was the moment I picked to get married.

What made me fall in love with Chana Leah Golomb instead of the other girls in our group? There were other beautiful girls but Chana was not merely beautiful, she was stately, almost majestic. She dressed magnificently. She fashioned her own clothes according to her own styles and not those decreed by the stores. She sewed all her own clothes. Frequently the stores would be showing the clothes that Chana had designed for herself a year or two before.

But this was the outer Chana. It was what first drew me to her. When I became better acquainted with her I became aware of her inner qualities. Chana loved music, especially Jewish folks songs. She knew many of them by heart and would love to sing them. She read books in both English and Yiddish. Above all she loved the truth. She couldn't stand hypocrisy. She detested those who spoke of idealism and behaved selfishly.

Our crowd those days, in the years 1918 to 1922, was mainly idealistic. We loved the freedom we enjoyed in America and the opportunities that were open to all. But we wanted more. We wanted an end to poverty. We felt that everyone was entitled to a free education, including college. We wanted to make America better.

We all worked hard but we did not mind it. Most of us were Zionists and many of us went from door to door collecting coins to send to the settlers in Palestine. It would make Chana furious when one who spoke avidly of the need to help the settlers would refuse to make a personal contribution. She used to call such people "mouth idealists." All these things endeared her to me and the more I came to know her the more I loved her.

The fact that she came from a poor family was no handicap. As far as I was concerned it was in her favor. I was determined never to marry a girl who came from a rich family, even if it were to mean great financial advantage to me.

What made her choose me I don't know. I do know that there were boys who were wealthier and better looking than I who proposed to her. The only answer that comes to mind is the old Jewish saying, "It is written in the book of old, that 40 days before a child is born a voice in Heaven calls out whom he or she is destined to marry."

I had to forget my dreams about servants and automobiles. We had to live on the $20 a week which the store was barely able to provide. At the end of the two and a half years we were able to sell the store, pay off our debts and divide between us $84 that was left over. That left me with $42 in cash. I also had about $2,000 in personal debts to pay off. There was the original $1,000 I had borrowed to buy into my partnership and the other $1,000 I had to borrow to sustain myself and my wife during the period of the partnership.

Nevertheless, when I came home and placed the $42 on the table in front of my wife, I danced for joy. I had gotten rid of the grocery store. I felt as if I had gotten rid of a plague. I told my wife I had no idea what I would do or how I would make a living but at least I was rid of that monstrous yoke around my neck.

MY FAMILY GOES HUNGRY

ALTHOUGH I HAD NO MONEY I NEVERtheless tried to get back in the junk business. One of the many problems confronting me was getting a license to open such a business in parts of the city where I could find a loft suitable for such a venture.

As I struggled to get back on my feet my wife gave birth to the first of our children, a beautiful baby girl. And now in the midst of my financial difficulties and my family happiness I was unable to provide for my wife and child. There were times when we had no food in the house, not even milk for the baby. I can never forget those terrible days.

My wife had been brought up in poverty. Her mother was widowed early in life, with six little ones to care for. My wife, the oldest of the children, had to go to work in a shop to help support the family. My mother-in-law worked very hard herself and managed to give each of her children a good education; one son even became a lawyer.

By the time I met my wife-to-be she had advanced quite a bit and was earning $40 per week, a tremendous wage in those days. She dressed elegantly. After our marriage and my financial reverses, I couldn't even give her $3 for a pair of shoes. At least she was able to revamp some of her old dresses so she had something decent to wear. It grieved me that I was unable to give her even the bare necessities of life. I began to berate myself again, to blame myself. I was terribly depressed and again that feeling of worthlessness came over me.

In later years my wife and I both recalled a specific incident that happened during those dark days. We had been invited to a wedding. My wife had no decent shoes. In desperation we finally got her a pair with $3 borrowed from an acquaintance. And so we went to the wedding and mingled with former friends of my wife, all of them dressed expensively and in the latest fashions.

At this point I would like to relate an incident having to do with money. When I had money I donated generously to a number of institutions—and I enjoyed doing so. One of the institutions I contributed to each year was the Jewish Teachers' Seminary in New York. That year the representative called at a time when we literally had no bread in the house. He was a writer, well known in Jewish cultural and literary circles. When I told him I would not be able to contribute anything that year he drew himself up arrogantly and said:

"I consider this extremely rude, a swinish act!"

Stunned, but unwilling to create a scene, I took $5 from the money I kept for our weekly rent and gave it to him. I paid rent by the week because I couldn't accumulate the large sum necessary for the entire month's rent. I found it easier to pay by the week. At least we were assured a roof over our heads.

I gave him our rent money and was relieved that my wife was spared the embarrassment of hearing the abuse I had taken.

AN ENTHUSIAST OF LITERATURE

DURING THE YEARS 1919 TO 1923 I DEVOTED as much time as I could to promoting Yiddish literature. I I greeted each new poem with joy. Every new story in the newspaper and between hard covers was an event and they often led to lengthy discussions and analyses.

When a book salesman arrived I considered it a pleasure and an honor to accompany him on his rounds and help him sell his books. This was not without its problems, however. Once a writer, gifted but not very ethical, came on a selling tour. I invited him to my home and even provided a bed for him. He took money for his books but then failed to send the books to the purchasers. The people came to me complaining and since I felt a certain sense of responsibility, I made a trip to New York, found the writer and threatened to thrash him unless he honored his sales. He finally sent the books out.

In 1923 I was most surprised by a very pleasant discovery. I had read in *Di Zukunft,* a Yiddish monthly literary magazine the opening stanzas of a lengthy narrative poem, "Kentucky," by Israel Jacob Schwartz. It was a revelation. I felt as I imagined a man wild with thirst would feel on finding a well of sweet water in the middle of a desert.

I had grown tired of reading Yiddish works of life in the old country, in the shtetl. Most of the Yiddish writers, even those who had lived in the United States for several years, showed a remarkable ignorance of this country. They continually wrote nostalgically of their home towns, forgetting the misery and the persecution. Even those who wrote about the American scene seemed to concentrate mainly on life in New York as if nothing existed outside of New York City and the Lower East Side.

And when they wrote of life in New York the authors saw life not as it really was but as they saw it from their coffee houses and their clubs. I was drawn to one writer, Isaac Raboy. I particularly enjoyed his stories of the American prairies. His tone was fresh and lively although some of his characters were stilted. He showed great promise and I hoped that he would find his way as a writer.

Joseph Opatoshu captivated me with his stories, masterfully fashioned. He was the father of the actor David Opatoshu. Whenever I got my hands on one of his stories I devoured it greedily, regretting as I neared the end that it did not go on and on. His work was real fictional art.

Schwartz's narrative poem was deeply satisfying, spiritually and intellectually. It was as refreshing as a swim in a cool stream on a hot summer's day. His verses, his characters, his descriptions were all so natural, so captivating. I made inquiries about the author and later was able to establish contact with him. Eventually we became intimate friends.

HARD WORK

I ENJOYED MY ASSOCIATION WITH WRITers and books but I had to earn a living. I got a job as organizer for the Butcher's Association; it was the best I could do at the moment. I didn't like the job but the $35 a week salary provided me with an adequate living.

Some six months later I was offered a job in a rag company as shipping and receiving clerk. The salary was $40 a week. I accepted. With this job a new chapter was begun in my life.

The bosses were two brothers, Jewish. One of them, J., was my age. The other, B., was two years younger. J., one of the most competent men I have ever met, was honest, direct, fast thinking and a hard worker. B. was a suspicious person. He watched over every penny. Everything in the shop was his business. B. was also a hard worker but he was stubborn and had deep feelings of inferiority.

The two brothers did a big business despite the cramped quarters they were in. Hundreds of tons of merchandise went in and out of the loft each month. My first few weeks there were difficult. One of the foremen took a dislike to me and tried to get me fired by telling the boss I was taking graft. Several times my employers asked me questions that sounded strange—there seemed to be no logical reasons for such questions. They had known me from before, when I was in business myself. We often competed but never was there a hint of dishonesty in our dealings.

Once I said to them: "You realize that several years ago I would never have come to work for you. I took the job because I did not have bread in my house. I would rather starve than work under suspicion. I demand to know what you were told and who made the accusations against me!"

When I promised not to take any action against the informer they confessed that one of the men, a non-Jew, embittered and crippled, had made the false charges. Although they insisted that they knew the charges were false, years later I learned that they had hired a private detective to investigate me. It was the detective's report that had convinced them of my honesty.

I worked very hard. The years I had spent in the grocery store had sapped my strength and I did not have the energy I had in previous years. However, I forced myself, refusing to admit even to myself that I had slowed down.

Despite a fair salary my financial situation was not good. Of the $40 I received each week, I had to pay off debts and the balance was hardly enough for the barest necessities. What was worse I saw no future for myself in my work. I was at a dead end, not meeting people, not knowing prices or procedures. I would remain a shipping clerk for the rest of my life if I didn't get out of there. However, to quit the job at that time was out of the question. Being stuck in the warehouse I had no time or opportunity to look for another job.

Instead I decided to work so hard and become so valuable that my employers would be unable to get along without me. In two months time I took over the whole warehouse operation. At first the foremen tried to sabotage me but when they were convinced that I meant them no harm, that to the contrary I meant to befriend them and make the work easier, they came over to my side. Once when one of the foremen made a mistake, B. came charging into the warehouse shouting furiously. I took the blame on myself for the error. This proved my loyalty and the two foremen became good friends and loyal co-workers.

With their cooperation I was able to function at top efficiency and saved the company hundreds of dollars each month. As a result I was able to persuade the employers to raise the salaries of the two foremen. But the extra load began to affect my health. I suffered a breakdown and had to be taken home.

The summer of 1924 was a very difficult one. I came home exhausted from the day's work, with hardly enough strength to eat. Often I fell into bed without having eaten, without even removing my clothes. I was physically broken. Even talking became too much of a burden. Some of my wife's relatives began to pass remarks that I was lazy, that I was making believe I was sick so that I wouldn't have to work.

I was deeply offended by their insinuations but what could I do? What could I say? The fact was that I was consumed by ambition. I worked beyond my capacity. That they did not see. They could only infer what seemed to them to be obvious; that I was too lazy to work!

When I began to feel more secure in my firm I asked to go on the road. At first they resisted but when I informed them that I had no intention of remaining at that job, even at the $50 a week I was then getting, they finally agreed. The arrangement was that I was to visit nearby towns for two or three days a week and spend the remaining time in the warehouse on my old job.

As luck would have it I was successful on my very first trip. After all, I was experienced in this line of work and I had engaged in commerce from my earliest days, so it really wasn't too surprising that I should succeed at what I knew!

Two weeks later my employers called me into their office and told me:

"We are convinced that it would be better for all of us for you to spend more time on the road than in the warehouse. Find someone to take over in the warehouse and you can spend full time as a traveling salesman."

But getting someone to replace me was not going to be easy. The job required experience, ability, strength, common sense and a willingness to work. Again luck was on my side. A young man, a Jew, came by the very next day asking for a job. He said he had had experience; he left his job after a disagreement with his father. I told him that my job was available and since he was experienced in our line he might get it if he asked for $40 a week instead of the $50 I was getting. He agreed and I instructed him on how to conduct himself during the interview with our employers. He went in.

When he emerged he nodded that the job was his. "How much?" I asked. "Twenty-five dollars," he replied. I knew then that he wouldn't work out. He remained for exactly a month and during that time he almost ruined the warehouse. He was sent away.

That didn't affect my status. I remained an outside salesman, traveling all over the country, the very first in all of the United States in my line of work. True there were other salesmen, but they went on occasional business trips and for only short distances. I was on the road constantly. I had no office work. That was the responsibility of J. and B.

I would travel all week, returning home on Saturday morning. I would leave Sunday night or Monday morning on my next trip. The more my territory expanded, the longer I stayed away. First a week, then two weeks and later three or even four weeks.

My early trips were to towns near Baltimore where I would buy merchandise from small junk dealers. I gained their confidence immediately. I spoke to them in Yiddish and interlaced my speech with Jewish sayings and some quotations from the Bible. Many of the junk dealers were Jews who had studied in their youth, were still observant and never lost their love of Torah and learning. They were overjoyed to be able to talk in the old tongue and of things that were all but forgotten.

I was very scrupulous in my dealings with them. I did not try to beat down their prices and they soon respected me for my fairness and honesty. When I offered a certain price for merchandise they knew immediately that it was a fair price and that they would not do better elsewhere. I often bought goods for late delivery. And if in the meantime the price of that merchandise went up then I paid them the higher price even though I didn't have to.

Of course the sellers were delighted with me but not so my bosses. They argued, not without correctness and logic, that a deal was a deal. "And what if the price went down?" they asked. "Would your friends then agree to charge you less?"

I argued that the good will was worth it. Besides, I continued, if we did not give them the higher prices then the next time they would not sell me merchandise for future delivery and that would create serious problems for us. One day we had some sharp words. Here is how it happened.

I told them it was not they who paid my salary but the dealers from whom I bought the merchandise. If I did not bring merchandise for them to sell then surely they wouldn't pay me for my good looks. I impressed on them the fact that I was earning my way and a good part of their's as well. That put an end to the verbal wars.

Even better, I had a freer hand than ever before in my dealings. And why not? They earned good profits on the merchandise I was able to buy for them. For me it was another new world. I always liked to travel, to meet new people in new surroundings, to talk of business, books, the theater, the events of the day.

I began to travel greater and greater distances away from Baltimore. Also, instead of just buying merchandise I was also selling. I knew from the very moment I entered the firm that this would come to pass one day. I was not concerned only with the immediate profits of a two or three-week trip. I considered the ultimate good I could do for the firm over a long period. In short, I was laying the groundwork for a solid business that would profit and profit in later years from work I had done earlier.

I thought it was more important to find new markets in specific factories than to sell to other dealers. My plan was to create specific merchandise for every kind of job and sell it directly to the manufacturer. This often meant virtually creating something out of nothing.

The workers sorted the rags into hundreds of sizes and qualities. For each rag there was a different purpose. I had to be on the watch constantly for new outlets to move the merchandise. I studied the whole paper manufacturing process in order to learn the kinds of rags that would be most suitable for different kinds of paper. This meant getting to know the manufacturer and convincing him that the particular rags I was recommending were best suited for his purposes. When I proved to him that I knew what I was talking about the rest was easy. It was a long and difficult process but I was successful.

I put all my energy into my job. I liked it and I was desperately anxious to succeed. I had struggled for too long to fall back now. I felt I was on my way at last. I even neglected my wife and child. The business came first.

My employers were quite happy with my results and I, in turn, felt like a third partner. When I disagreed with their operating methods or business decisions I did not hesitate to tell them so. I recall saying during one such argument: "I disagree with you. I think you are wrong but I will do as you say because you are the boss. If I were the boss I would expect you to do as I say."

In the meantime I gained greater and greater experience. I was able to evaluate merchandise by just looking at it. I could even estimate the profit from each bale of mixed merchandise. I began to study the general economic structure of our country in order to anticipate future trends in our line.

I have no wish to credit my company's success to my personal wisdom but the fact is that during the four and a half years that I was with the company I never once made a wrong estimate on future prices. The merchants with whom I dealt were all under the opinion that I was a partner in the firm. Not only was this not so but my salary until 1928 was only $75 a week.

On my trips I met many traveling people, Jews and non-Jews. I often heard from Jewish salesmen but never from the non-Jewish salesmen—that they preferred to deal with gentiles rather than Jews. My own experiences were exactly the opposite. When a conflict arose over the quality of the merchandise (in this field controversies were very frequent), the discussion was sometimes quiet and orderly, sometimes stormy and not so orderly. But always an amicable agreement was reached—with the Jews, not the non-Jews.

The non-Jews invariably began the argument with: "Why are all you Jews swindlers?"

Arguments arose often because in our line the goods were not produced uniformly, not by machine. There were no set standards and so it was difficult to determine the quality.

With the non-Jew the quality of the merchandise was only secondary. First he had to know why all Jews were swindlers. True, not all gentiles were that way but far too many! And all too often I found that when a gentile started his argument with that libel that he was himself a liar and a swindler.

On such occasions I would let the gentile vent his spleen, to pour out all his hatreds, prejudices and hostilities. I would then try to cut the loss as low as possible and then have him sign a waiver of all further claims. After that I vented a little spleen of my own. I would tell him what I thought of him—good and loud so everyone could hear, not only those in the office.

I had started my job with a salary of $40 a week. But I had many debts to pay so the first years were difficult for us.

Toward the end of 1924 my wife took in four children who had been placed in an institution. For this she received $25 a week. It placed a heavy load on my wife, attending to four children when she had a little one of her own to look after. We kept the children for the entire year, until my debts were repaid. In the meantime my salary was increased and our financial situation eased considerably. We had enough for the necessities of life and a bit left over for charity.

During the years when I was unable to make my usual charity donations we became estranged from the social life of the community. The Labor Zionist movement in which I had been so active gradually forgot about us. Since we could not contribute to its various funds we had lost our importance. Now that we were once more on the contributors' lists, we became important people again. Once again our mail box was graced with engraved invitations to meetings and fund raising functions.

Now that I was well situated economically, I found many new "friends" who asked for business advice, and sometimes loans. It always galled me how these good-time friends always appeared when the weather was fine and disappeared when the skies clouded over. When I had business reverses and faced financial troubles these good friends would often say: "That Benny, he thought he was so smart. I knew he would break his back one day!"

And when the sun came out again for me financially, there they were, back again, shaking my hand, hanging on to my every word about business and again with the hand outstretched for a "business" loan. In those days it saddened me greatly. In later years I became more philosophical about it. There came a time when I was even able to smile at this human frailty. After all, we Jews are the chosen ones, but still we're not perfect!

I TRAVEL OVER THE COUNTRY

FOR BUSINESS THE YEARS FROM 1924 TO 1929 were very good years. For me personally they were excellent years. I was able to make lots of money for my firm and for myself as well. My territory, which extended throughout the United States, now included Canada as well. My travels took me to almost every state in the country and to many parts of Canada. Every trip began with a stop in Pittsburgh and from there I continued through the northern states and on to the west coast. From there the route turned south with stops in all the important cities.

While it was enjoyable, it was also arduous. It meant that I worked during the day and traveled at night. Each trip lasted about 36 days and not once during that period did I sleep in a hotel. The constant traveling began to affect my health. The end of each trip found me nervous and exhausted.

In 1926 a second daughter was born to us. I wanted to spend more time with my family. After all, it was for them that I was working, I should at least enjoy them!

My employers were a little afraid they were going to lose me. They weren't concerned about my health or my family, only their profits. They began to talk about incorporating the business and giving me some shares. My relations with my employers were correct and friendly. I knew the business perhaps as well as anyone else in the line and I liked the business. I was well known throughout the industry and had many friends and acquaintances. I was well thought of by them and was always given a warm welcome when I arrived. I knew even the intimate details of their business and often they would seek my advice knowing that I would not reveal confidential information to anyone.

Because my job kept me out of town so much I was not active in the community. Officially I was a member of the Workmen's Circle. My sympathies were with the Poale Zion, the Labor Zionists, and I contributed to all their funds. I continued to stuff my valises with books to read on the long journey.

Our social life I left to my wife. She invited whomever she thought I would most enjoy and we went out as guests to those whose invitations she accepted. To my wife's family I was the wealthy relative, the one to whom they all came with their bundle of troubles. And since I was the wealthy one it was my responsibility to help them. I helped each to the best of my ability.

And so passed the years to 1928. The firm grew bigger and bigger. When I started to work for the firm the total capital of the company amounted to $27,000. True the bosses did a bigger volume than their capital warranted. The business was smalltown in its thinking, purely a local operation and I helped to expand it. In the years I was there it took on a national and then an international character. We had business dealings with companies in Europe and Japan.

In 1928 a company on the west coast began to compete with us for business from Japan. They managed to make good connections and were getting better merchandise than we. Faced with this competition, we decided that one of us should make a trip to Japan and set up a complete operation. The merchandise would be gathered, sorted and packed ready for shipment to the American market without any further processing. I was picked to make the trip.

MY TRIP TO JAPAN

I LEFT FOR JAPAN IN MARCH OF 1928. Before going, however, I made an intensive tour of the United States and sold a large amount of goods hoping to fill the orders from Japan.

I will not dwell here on my impressions of the country or its people or customs. That is enough for a chapter by itself. I did see more of the country and its people than the tourists get to see since I had occasion to work closely with them and live with them, in their homes.

The trip lasted six months. When I returned I expressed the opinion that Japan was preparing for war and that it was only a matter of time before she would drag the world into a terrible carnage.

The trip itself was successful. I established excellent contacts both to buy merchandise and to ship merchandise to Japan, some of it for the first time. My trip also took care of our west coast competitor. We no longer had anything to fear.

But I found on my return also some threats to our future dealings with our European contacts. My employers were very nervous about it and urged me to make a trip to Europe immediately. My wife was expecting a third child and I didn't want to leave her until the child was born.

In June, 1928, my wife gave birth to a third girl. Although she was normal at birth she soon developed an ailment. When she was six weeks old she had to undergo surgery. By October the child was well again and I left for Europe.

I had with me half a dozen addresses of people with whom we were dealing. I had a double plan. First I would contact firms that would sort and pack the rags, bypassing the brokers entirely. Then I planned to study our line of business in Europe generally. My aim was to determine which merchandise could be imported from Europe with a fair profit and what sort of merchandise we could ship to Europe. This meant not only establishing contacts but also creating new markets where none existed before.

I also had in mind to explore the possibilities of opening a branch of our firm in Europe although my experiences in Japan caused me to have grave doubts about the success of such a venture.

MY TRIP TO EUROPE

MY TRIP TO EUROPE TOOK ME THROUGH fourteen countries. I visited almost every city and many towns of importance. I sought out dealers with whom there was the slightest possibility of conducting business, making copious notes of each individual and his mode of operation. I noted especially what he imported and what he exported, what kind of merchandise and the quality. Thus I was able to compile a register of our industry in Europe. I had more information than any of the directories in the United States or in Europe. Actually there was no directory of our business in Europe and gathering the information was tedious and painstaking.

Adding to my difficulties was my deficiency in languages. I spoke only English and Yiddish. I had great difficulty making myself understood, especially in the Latin countries. In the German speaking countries I was able to get by with my Yiddish. Because of my poor German some people thought that I was speaking Dutch. In Holland, on the other hand, they thought that I was speaking German. But somehow we managed. I took advantage of the opportunity to visit Russia and see my parents. I will refrain from writing my impressions of Russia. It is for another place and another time. I did see my parents. They saw me, they touched me but they couldn't really believe it was I, their own son, their Beryl.

A BITTER DISAPPOINTMENT

IT WAS THE END OF MAY IN 1929 WHEN I returned to the United States. I had been away for several months, including the end of 1928, when I was supposed to have received my year-end bonus. Each year my employers showed their appreciation for my efforts and since 1928 was an exceptionally profitable year, I expected a larger bonus. I was terribly disappointed, more for the lack of recognition than the money.

"Why?" I asked them. "You yourselves have been telling me that I made the firm what it is today; that your capital has grown from $27,000 in 1924 to over $700,000 by the end of 1928. Am I not entitled to some benefit from those profits, especially when you admit that it was largely from my efforts?"

"True," my employers agreed. "We had a good year in 1928 but we do not wish to give you a bigger bonus because if 1929 is bad, or not as good, and we would have to cut your bonus, or not give you one at all, you would resent it even more."

With such reasoning who needs logic? By the same token he should stop paying my salary because if he should go bankrupt in the next month then think how bad I would feel! I felt they were making a fool of me.

I then asked when they were planning to incorporate the business as they had promised. Finally flushed out, B. answered that they would never give an outsider a part of the business. I thanked him for his frank answer. B. was surprised. Why should I thank him? He didn't understand what was happening and showed his uneasiness. Why did I thank him, he asked?

I asked what they thought I should do after they misled me for years with false promises of a share in the business? At least I knew that there was no more hope for me here. I was still young, I had gained invaluable experience. I could certainly make a go of it elsewhere. Why did I have to pile up more and more profit for these two exploiters who didn't have either the decency or the intelligence to reward the source of their increased wealth?

I informed them that I was resigning. I told them that I would stay on long enough to straighten out the business and then I would go.

J. who was a bit smarter, perhaps greedier than B. tried to pass the whole incident off as a silly joke.

"We didn't mean it," he said. "You're tired and nervous, just home from a long trip. Go take a month's vacation and rest up. Then you'll come back fresh and we'll talk."

"No," I replied. "You are mistaken. It's not that I'm tired and nervous. I am well aware of what you have done. I helped build the firm because I believed in you and praised you to our business associates throughout the world. Now that I see your promises are worthless, I cannot go on doing business with these same people as I did in the past. There is no use taking my salary when my heart is not in the business any longer. It won't do me any good and after a while it won't do you much good either."

I returned home terribly depressed. I told my wife what

In America; Years of Struggle

had happened. She stood by me, agreeing that I had done the right thing. It was time I stopped working to enrich others, neglecting my wife and children and not even be honestly repaid for my efforts, she said. She was most reassuring at a time when I needed reassurance.

My employers did their utmost to convince me to stay. They offered me the phenomenal salary of $10,000 a year, with all expenses paid on my trips. I was not even tempted. I tried to explain to them that it was not the money but my lack of faith in them.

Since I had not visited our customers during the months I was in Europe, I agreed to make one last trip, around the country.

I made the trip but it was not as successful as my previous trips. I found I could no longer speak about our merchandise so convincingly—since I was not convinced myself. To make sales one had to be forthright and sure of his firm and his product. I was sure of neither. I had doubts about the merchandise that would be shipped and I wondered if my employers would honor the commitments I was making. I did not want to be responsible for a dishonest transaction. I never expressed these doubts but apparently I was not as persuasive as I had been on past tours.

IN PARTNERSHIP

IN DETROIT ONE BUSINESS MAN PROPOSED a partnership, that I buy a half interest in his company. I had had business dealings with him for some years and knew him to be an honest man, refined and courteous. Although the offer was tempting I told him that I was in town on business and since my firm was paying my expenses I had no moral right to conduct my own personal business on company time.

I asked if he would give me a month to consider the proposition. I promised him an answer by then. He urged me to examine his books but I refused and continued my tour. But this time I did not reach the Pacific coast. My heart was no longer in my work and I just couldn't get myself to continue the trip. It became tedious and agonizing. I was afraid if I didn't stop I would suffer a breakdown.

I lasted for three weeks and then wrote to my employers that I could continue no longer. I could have gone through the motions but I wanted to be honest with my employers and with myself. They persuaded me to take a vacation instead.

I discussed the dilemma with my wife. We came to the conclusion that I would take the vacation and use it to go to Detroit and look into the offer I had received while on my trip.

Here was the situation. B. was an honest and noble person but was more familiar with literature than with business. He was a wealthy man at the turn of the century but lost everything in the panic of 1907. In 1911 he went into business washing dirty rags and selling the clean ones to factories to be used as wipe rags—for the workers to clean their hands, the machines or to wipe a smudge of dirt off the wall.

At that time his was one of only three such firms in all of the United States. During the period from 1911 to 1929 he acquired a good reputation but not much capital. He was on the verge of bankruptcy because his inventory plus his accounts receivable were less than his debts. However, he did have machines that were fully paid for—all his own.

I spent several days in the plant studying his methods and trying to visualize the possibilities. I liked what I saw. I knew almost instinctively that the business had a tremendous potential. I signed a contract then and there. I bought a half share of the business. However, the building still belonged to my partner. The total price to me was $17,500 of which $10,000 was to be in cash and the balance I was to pay out of the subsequent profits.

The firm needed cash badly. We arranged that I would give the $10,000 to him and that he would put it into the business as a loan. His two brothers-in-law, one of whom was a judge and the other the owner of a large business, promised to get us another $10,000 from the bank. I insisted on the additional loan for without it I was convinced that the business couldn't continue.

But, again I was cheated. The brothers-in-laws made no move toward the bank and my partner, instead of leaving the money in the business as we had agreed, withdrew the $10,000 to pay off some of his personal debts. He owed some $30,000 to a previous partner. That I did not know when I agreed to buy into the business.

The firm had been incorporated so the books did not show how much he owed personally. He owned the building and our corporation had to pay him $400 a month rent.

As it happened he had to obtain a new mortgage. He came to me with a suggestion that the corporation sign a lease agreeing to pay him $600 a month rent but actually to pay him $400. In that way he reasoned, he could show the people from whom he wanted to obtain the mortgage that the building was earning more than it actually did. Since I trusted the man's honesty I agreed.

As soon as I began work I confirmed my opinion that it was a good business. I was convinced that it could yield substantial profits. But the company needed capital. We had to buy goods from people who had done business with us previously and knew that our credit was good. But they overcharged us. We could not buy from new firms for fear that they would not extend the necessary credit. We couldn't continue on that basis.

It was at this point that I decided to make use of my wide acquaintance in our line. I started buying goods from new sources at much lower prices, lower even than the usual market price. And because I knew which firms produced higher quality merchandise I was able to buy the best merchandise at the most favorable price.

The profits started to rise the very first month. For the first six weeks our profits totalled $15,000. In January we had to furnish the credit agency a financial report. To my amazement I discovered that my partner had reported net worth of $40,000 more than the books showed.

I was in a quandary. I had read the credit reports on our firm before I became a partner and I knew later that they did not conform with the books. I realized that if he signed a false report and if the firm went into bankruptcy he could go to jail. On the other hand, if we submitted a true report, the credit agency would assign us a lower credit rating. So I had to go along with my partner.

My partner was not only a poor buyer, he was an equally inefficient manager. I saw that it was costing us forty per cent more to produce our merchandise than it cost our competitors. In this I must confess that I was as unsuccessful as my partner. I was never able to get a full day's work out of our employees although we paid higher wages than the rest of the industry.

Perhaps the reason for this was that my company had never fired a worker since it was established in 1911. And so the better workers left us over the years and the poorer ones remained. Aside from that I was too much involved with the commercial side and could not devote too much time to production problems. Even though I couldn't pay attention to production, I never thought it important enough to hire someone to supervise production. I realize now that it was a mistake.

The firm used to get its orders by mail. My partner didn't like salesmen and he himself never went out to see a customer. But he advertised well and that succeeded in building up a considerable mail order business. Even so I felt that the mail orders would drop off in time and the business would come to a standstill unless we adopted more advanced selling techniques.

In 1911 when my partner first opened his doors there were only three such firms in the entire country. By 1929 there were 26 such companies in existence and during my trips around the country I saw that sooner or later every small town would have a similar company doing business there. People order things by mail when they cannot buy them at home. If they can buy the same merchandise at home at the same price, or cheaper if they do not have to pay shipping costs, they certainly wouldn't go to the trouble of ordering by mail.

To avoid such an eventuality I began to expand the firm's operation. First I began to sell to jobbers. True, the profit was smaller but the increase in volume more than compensated for it.

I became a partner on the 16th of July, 1929, and by September I had already formulated plans to open branch offices in Buffalo, and Cincinnati. In Buffalo there was no competition at all. In Cincinnati there was one small firm. My plan was to keep the laundry working day and night, cleaning and sanitizing the goods. Then the material could be cut, the metal removed, the goods sorted by color and thickness and then condensed into huge bales ready for shipping.

I planned to ship from Detroit. The offices in Buffalo and Cincinnati would be for sales only.

Perhaps I should explain a little more about my business. I would buy up large amounts of a special kind of rag, wash them in large laundry vats and sterilize them. I would then sort and cut them to specific sizes a bit larger than a handkerchief. The large pieces were cut into smaller ones and the smaller ones were sewn into larger sizes. These we would sell to factories to be used as wiping cloths—for the workers to wipe their hands or to clean their machines.

People in general, and Jews in particular, tend to deprecate this line of work. Its volume runs into millions of dollars annually. Any mechanic who wipes his hands after coming up from a grease pit, or a pressman cleaning ink off his rollers, hundreds and thousands of workmen in almost any line of work, will testify to the value of the wiping cloth.

Its worth was never more appreciated than during World War II. Huge amounts, millions of pounds, were ordered by the U.S. Navy alone.

The industry was established by Jews and about 90 per cent of it is still in Jewish hands. Some day I hope to write a book on the rise and growth of the waste material industry in America of which the wiping cloth is a branch. Many industries would have had to create their own waste material departments if we had not done so, at a higher cost and, most likely, not nearly as good as the industry we created.

DIFFICULT DAYS

I HAD FOUND A SUITABLE PERSON FOR one of the branch offices and was in the middle of negotiations with a man for the second branch when the crash came. No one who lived through those turbulent days in 1929 will ever forget the stock market crash that wiped out so many fortunes almost over night.

Although our firm was financially secure I realized that there would be a depression soon. I prophesied that the depression would last for five years. My partner laughed at my pessimistic prognostication. Others to whom I expressed the same fears thought I was insane.

They couldn't sway me. I was convinced, just as I was convinced in 1914 that there would be a World War. In any event, as a result of the Wall Street crash I decided not to expand our company, not to speculate, not to buy too much and to watch expenditures very carefully. Although we were still able to show a profit, financing was tight and I was frequently driven to despair to raise capital.

We bought goods on promissory notes due in three to four months and we found ourselves paying about $12,000 to $15,000 worth of notes every month.

That meant that we had another note falling due almost every day. There was no one in town from whom to get a two or three day loan without interest, except perhaps B., an old friend of my "green years" in Massachusetts. I had found him in Detroit running a small business and he seemed financially stable. I often came to him for a loan and he gave them without hesitation. But they were small loans and did not help much.

Business in the 1930's was not yet bad. But as the months passed the orders became harder and harder to get.

With a combination of hard work and careful financing we managed the year quite well all things considered.

My chief concern was where to raise the necessary working capital. I wracked my head day and night trying to get out of the tight financial box we were in. Often I would get up out of bed in the middle of the night and pore over my notebook to see how big the next note was, when it fell due, and where I was going to raise the money to cover it.

These problems plagued me when I worked and when I rested, at home and at social gatherings and while sitting in the theater. Above all I was especially careful to see that the checks we issued did not bounce back for lack of funds. If that happened our credit would have been ruined.

I have been using the first person pronoun because as soon as I entered the business my partner turned the financial worries over to me—also the production problems. He devoted himself to public relations—advertising and in general promoting the company in the industry.

Our relations were like that of a father and a bright son. He thought the world of me and I looked up to him with reverence as I would to my own father. When it came to introducing new methods or new machinery into the plant, it required great tact on my part. I knew that when someone conducted a business in a certain way for eighteen years and was getting on in years he would not take too kindly to innovations. I soon found the formula that enabled me to do pretty much as I wanted. And far from protesting, he was delighted with my suggestions.

I would talk to him about a specific problem or a new approach that would enhance our business. I would describe in glowing terms how our company would benefit. I would then drop the subject, knowing fully well that in a few days he would raise it himself and ask why I had done nothing about it, especially since he had expressed himself in favor of it. And so I got what I wanted. My partner was pleased, especially since he was under the impression that the idea was originally his.

He was naive, almost childlike. His chief concern was not to go into bankruptcy, not so much for the money he would lose but for his reputation. He dreamed of selling his part of the business and moving to a small town that had a well-stocked library and there spend his days reading.

Socially I did not exactly mingle with the upper strata of Jewish society. My wife, who had come to Detroit from Baltimore, leaving a mother, sisters, brothers and many friends, was homesick. To make her more at home I decided to create a circle of friends who would involve my wife in their activities and thus ease her homesickness. The first thing I did was to join the local chapter of the Poale Zion. My wife became active in the organization's schools and also with the Pioneer Women, a Labor Zionist group, the ladies Auxiliary of the Poale Zion.

My wife plunged into the activity managing to keep herself busy seven nights a week. Since we did not have any servants in the house I stayed home with the children. I didn't even have a chance to go to the theater or the movies. However, I did use the winter nights of 1929-1930 to make the acquaintance of all the latest Yiddish books. When I had finished those, I got to work on those that appeared in recent years, the years of struggle, when keeping alive took up more time than I could allow for reading.

Thus passed the year 1930. Early in 1931 the business took a turn for the worse. Prices fell sharply. A carload of goods bought one day, could have been bought for half the price the following day. However, we continued to show a profit thanks to new orders from jobbers. The only trouble was that the jobbers, in financial difficulty themselves, couldn't pay their bills on time. I was nervous about their credit but I couldn't cut them off. I couldn't suddenly refuse to ship their orders because that would have meant the loss of money they owed us and also an end to future orders. I tried to get as much money as possible and keep their accounts within manageable limits.

DEATH TAKES A HAND

IN MARCH OF 1931 I ATTENDED A CONVENtion of our industry. I telephoned my partner the morning after I arrived and was surprised when he begged me to return immediately, the same day. He said he was lonely and troubled. He wasn't feeling well. I packed my bags and prepared to return home but had one stop to make on the way, to see a customer. I joked to myself that my partner would have to wait another day before I returned. I regarded the whole business as a bit of comedy.

When I returned I found my partner in the hospital where he had been taken with a ruptured appendix. That same evening he died.

His passing was a severe blow to me. I wept bitterly. He was truly like a father and added to my sorrow was the feeling of guilt that I had delayed my homecoming by another day—just for an extra order, an extra bit of business.

I was shocked the following morning when his son and brother-in-law came into the office, opened the safe and took away all his personal papers. Their behaviour seemed vulgar. It pained me very much. I was suddenly faced with a number of questions. What would happen with my share of the business? How would our creditors react to my partner's death? Would they continue to extend the same line of credit to me?

The situation took a drastic turn for the worse when a firm I had worked for and done business with on a large scale informed me that I could no longer expect to receive as much credit as before. I had bought huge quantities of goods from the company, owing it as much as $20,000 at a time. I became panicky. I didn't know whom to turn to.

As I sat in my office trying to sort out my problems a man with whom I had been doing business walked in. He was an Italian. I told him what had happened and described my fears. He laughed and said, "Don't worry so much. I'll give you all the goods you want and without notes. When I need money I'll let you know."

When I explained that I might not be able to meet too many notes at one time he shrugged it off saying we could worry about that later. If necessary, he continued, he would extend the notes. His attitude reassured me, I felt as if I had gotten a new lease on life. I was convinced that everything was not lost. He immediately sold me $30,000 worth of merchandise without asking for payment. I later honored each and every debt, without having to extend any of the notes.

In the meantime I was paying the widow $100 weekly for living expenses. I didn't know how the accounts would turn out later but I felt I owed it to my late partner.

I discovered shortly after his death that my partner had borrowed $25,000 some years before and had given the man the company's stock as collateral. I learned that he still owed $14,000 against the loan. The lender, in the meantime, had sold the notes to a bank and I realized that if the bank did not receive payments on time it would demand half control of the business.

I knew that the widow did not have the funds to keep

up the payments of $1,000 a month. I discussed the matter with my late partner's two brothers-in-law. We agreed that I would continue the payments and the amount would be deducted from the widow's share when the business accounts were straightened out.

Negotiations were begun on taking over the widow's share of the business. They went on and on. First they were conducted with the business-man brother-in-law. Before he could make a decision he had to consult with the brother-in-law who was a judge. Then the judge took over the negotiations and before he could move he had to get the approval of the business man.

Since both were very prominent in the city and highly respected I thought they would negotiate like gentlemen and honor their commitments. During the negotiations I paid the widow $100 a week in advance in addition to the $1,000 payments I was making to the bank. I was also paying $400 a month in rent.

And so the years 1931 and 1932 creaked by. I paid up the $14,000 loan to the bank but business got worse from one day to the next. It was difficult to get cash. The jobbers held back on their payments. I still managed to eke out a profit but because of the debts I had paid off I was short of funds myself.

I urged the widow to get on with the negotiations. I was prepared to pay her dollar for dollar on the value of her share and take over all the debts, realizing that many of the bills owed us would never be paid. Nevertheless the widow and her brothers continued to delay, to procrastinate. I finally warned them I would stop my $100 weekly payments—and did so. At that point they agreed to resume negotiations.

They demanded that I sign an agreement to pay $600 a month rent for the next ten years and also to pay the difference between the $400 rent we had been paying and the $600 rent that was stipulated in the corporation contract. I explained that this was done in order to get a bigger mortgage but that the firm had never actually paid the higher rent. They replied that it was immaterial whether they knew that or not, they were not acting out of morality, they said, but according to the law.

I felt trapped. I searched for a way out. I realized what a mistake it had been to sign such a contract. True, I hesitated but it was not for lack of faith in my partner. I was afraid of what would happen if he died. And here I was confronted with the situation and my worst fears were coming true.

I wanted to draw up an additional agreement at the time, one that would take effect in the event of my partner's death and correct the situation. But I knew that like all elderly people my partner did not like to talk about or consider the possibility of death. I didn't want to hurt him so I dropped the matter and signed the agreement without the safeguards. I was to pay dearly for this act of kindness.

I had no lawyer to advise me at this stage of the negotiations. I had no wish to cheat the widow. On the contrary I wanted to provide for her for the rest of her life. But when her brothers-in-law pulled their swindle I went to a lawyer. He advised me to go into bankruptcy and negotiate with our creditors, get them to extend our notes for a six-month period. I was to hold a public auction and purchase the machinery and reopen the business under a new name. In this way I would discharge all the debts and at the same time be free of the contract on the building.

I told the lawyer that he was right technically and legally but that I could never agree to a procedure that would rob the widow of her rights. I summoned the widow and her brothers-in-law to arbitration but they refused to agree. I summoned them to a rabbinical court—the judge was a very religious man—and they also refused.

In the meantime I mailed a check for $400 for the month's rent but they returned the check. On the 11th of the month they put a lien on my bank account. I felt as if I had been stabbed in the back. Surely throughout all the negotiations it was I who was trying to reach a settlement and it was they who were procrastinating.

That same day the credit association notified all my creditors that my bank account had been attached. I went to the courthouse where the brother-in-law sat and created a scandal right then and there, hoping to be arrested and then being able to bring the whole dispute out into the open.

But the judge didn't go for it. He summoned me into his private chamber so that the public should not hear my accusations which were not made quietly or gently. I called him some nasty names and warned him to release my funds or I would ruin the firm and the widow would not get a single penny. I left him with a quotation that was actually Samson's last words: "May I die together with the Phillistines." (Judges XVI; 30).

An hour later I received a phone call from the bank notifying me that my account had been released. Although my contract provided that I could remain in the building for another year I decided to move, the sooner the better. I was aware that such a step was very risky financially, could even ruin me. I estimated it would cost $10,000 to move the machinery and establish myself in new quarters. Nevertheless, I was so disgusted with my late partner's family that I felt I could not do business with them under any circumstances and so decided to move despite the financial hazards.

I was lucky. The very next day I found a building that

was better suited for my needs than the building I occupied. Not only that, the rent was lower. For the first year the rent was set at $75 per month. The second year it went up to $250 per month. The same rent held for the third year but on the fourth year it was increased again to $350. There was also a stipulation that if some time in the future I would buy the building, half the rent I paid would be deducted from the purchase price.

I started moving the machinery immediately.

ON MY OWN

AS SOON AS THE WIDOW HEARD I WAS moving she came running with all kinds of threats. I explained that I had tried to act decently but if they, on their part could act in such bad faith then I would repay them in the same coin. After several weeks of tedious negotiations they finally signed the papers but not before I had agreed to give them $7,000 more than the figure we set previously. I didn't give it to them in cash; it was to be paid in installments. They also tried to insert a number of tricky clauses into the agreement but this time I was on guard and evaded all attempts to trick me into additional commitments.

According to my estimates it should have taken about a month to install the mashinery in the new building. It actually took almost four months. The expenses were greater than I had figured and by the time the move was completed I found myself in bad shape financially. I had very few orders to fill and many debts to pay.

In March, 1933 all the banks in Detroit closed down and soon they closed all over the country. Unfortunately the bank closing came at a time when I had just deposited a considerable sum of money. The checks had not had time to clear. In my industry, payments came in usually between the 11th and the 15th of the month I would deposit the money and immediately write checks to cover my bills. So the banks closed holding my deposited checks but they had not made payment on the checks I had issued.

The jobbers owed me large sums of money and were behind in their payments. They took advantage of the bank closing to stop payments altogether. Several of them went into bankruptcy. I settled with others until I straightened out all outstanding accounts, losing some $23,000 in the process.

I was without capital and without capital I could not run my business. I was in a worse situation than when I first started the business. My lawyer and accountant both advised me to go into bankruptcy. They saw no other way out of my financial difficulty. The economic situation throughout the country continued to slide down and down. I hesitated to accept orders from jobbers for fear they would not pay. The factories worked only part time and I had to sell them goods at very low prices.

To get extra business I went after **Government contracts,** especially from the U.S. Navy which used millions of pounds of wipers a year. I landed several large contracts. Although the prices were lower than usual, by working day and night, occasionally around the clock, six days a week, my company began to show a modest profit. Most important, I had begun to accumulate some capital—my customers started paying their bills—and I was able to pay my debts. As long as the money comes in a business can remain alive no matter how large the debts.

The work was hard. There were many problems. But in those hard days I considered myself lucky that I was able to continue in business and make a living. I found myself becoming involved in social activites although I had very little time for them. Whatever spare time I could find I devoted to reading about Jewish problems, mainly books of Judaica. I also hired a tutor to help me resume my study of the Talmud. And thus passed the years 1930, 1931 and 1932, a bad time for our country and for me. Both managed to survive.

I began to concentrate on government orders, and to increase direct sales to the factories. Mail orders had fallen off —as I predicted they would years before. Everything seemed to be running smoothly and I figured that my struggle to survive was over and that I would begin to reap the harvest of my labors.

But fate had something else in store for me.

In 1933 I received government contracts for 2,000,000 pounds of merchandise to be shipped to various Navy yards throughout the United States and Hawaii. Shortly after shipping the first carload of goods to Norfolk, Virginia, I was called by the Detroit inspector and told that he had been notified by the Norfolk inspector that the shipment had been rejected and to discontinue further shipments.

I had already sent off a second carload so I rushed off to Norfolk to find out why the first shipment had been rejected. There I found a confused situation. It appeared that there were some inspectors who had accepted goods that were not up to specifications and new inspectors had been sent from Washington to correct the situation.

Since they could not verify immediately that the merchandise I had sent measured up to government specifications, to be on the safe side they rejected sixteen carloads, including the two which were mine. The second one was rejected even before it reached Norfolk. I could get no answer to my angry questions on how they could reject a shipment they had not yet inspected.

Unable to get any satisfaction from the inspectors I went to the Admiral who commanded the Navy yard. He explained that he was unable to help me; the people in Washington had conducted the investigation and everything was in their hands. I replied that I had never expected an Admiral in the United States Navy to hide behind a woman's skirts. Instead of throwing me out he laughed heartily. He gave me his word that in this instance it was impossible for him to intervene.

I left for Washington immediately. I could get no logical or satisfactory answer there either. No one could, or would explain how the inspectors could reject merchandise without having seen it, before it even arrived. I reasoned that since I had received orders totalling 2,000,000 pounds, it might not be wise to make an issue of one shipment of 30,000 pounds and endanger the rest of the orders. I was afraid that some of the inspectors might try to take it out on me if I pressed the first shipment too vigorously.

Instead I persuaded them to take the first two carloads, but at a reduced rate. Before I left the office the chief purchasing agent of the U.S. Navy informed me that the government needed huge quantities of rags and that I could continue to ship them according to the orders I had received. I reminded him that the inspector in Detroit had a telegram ordering him to cancel the balance of my orders. He waved the matter off saying, "Nonsense." The telegram had come from Norfolk, meaning to discontinue shipments to that city but not to the other nine destinations.

Also, he continued, the sender of the telegram was not authorized to do so. I was delighted to hear this, but still fearful of bureaucratic confusion, I asked him to send off a telegram informing the Detroit inspector that I was to resume shipments. He promised to do so. However, when I got back to Detroit and went to see the inspector, he told me that he would not accept any goods from me without instructions from Washington. I telephoned the chief purchasing agent in Washington who promised to send off a telegram immediately.

Ten days passed and the telegram still had not arrived. By then I had made several calls to the nation's capital to no avail. In the meantime I had begun to receive telegrams from various government installations asking about delivery. They warned that if I did not fulfill my contracts they would cancel them and purchase the goods on the open market charging me for any increase in cost.

My factory was working day and night. I had sixteen carloads ready for shipment but the Detroit inspector stubbornly refused to inspect them. Without his approval I could not make the shipments. I got into a tight financial situation and didn't know what to do next. One morning, about 2 a.m., I received a phone call notifying me that a cable had arrived from Pearl Harbor cancelling my contract. They were buying the rags on the open market and were going to bill me for any increase in costs. Within the next few days all other government depots voided their contracts with me and started buying on the open market. According to the prices then prevailing I stood to lose over $55,000.

My letters, telegrams and phone calls to government officials were of no avail. I could get nowhere. I had no alternative but to close my business. I owed my workers four weeks salary and did not have an extra penny to my name. The following Monday morning I left for Washington, proceeding directly to the Navy purchasing office. There I explained the situation to the chief purchasing agent. I asked him why he had not sent the telegram to the Detroit inspector as he had promised. Instead of an explanation, I was insulted and accused, along with everyone else in my line, of being a thief and a blackguard.

Angrily I accused him of lying. I told him that I had not come to compare pedigrees with him. He waved me away angrily saying he could do nothing for me. I took out my key and threw it on his desk.

"What is the meaning of this?" he asked.

I replied that they were the keys to my business and that since the government was demanding $55,000 in cost differentials and the security bonds I had deposited with the government totalled only $50,000 that the bonding company would be taking over my business anyway and that I was therefore turning it over to him. I added that he could take pride in the fact that he had used the might of the United States Navy to kill a fly.

So saying, I went to a corner of his office and sat myself down. There I remained from nine in the morning until four in the afternoon every day from Monday to Friday. I was determined not to leave until I had straightened the matter out once and for all. The officials asked me several times during my stay why I was there. I told them I had no reason to return home, my entire wealth was sitting there on the purchasing agent's desk.

Friday morning he called me to his desk and asked me what I wanted. I told him all I wanted was to be able to fulfill my government contracts. He said it was impossible because the various installations had already bought the rags they needed in the open market. I asked him if he was looking for a way out for himself or was really interested in reaching a fair settlement. I told him he could easily telephone the various Navy yards and instruct them to accept my shipments; it was no great problem that they had already bought rags on the open market because they were using much more than my contracts called for. Instead of making another purchase three months later, they would make their next purchase in six months. By then they would have used up all their surplus.

The purchasing agent agreed and began placing his phone calls immediately. He asked me to wait around for the replies. By 2 o'clock all the Navy yards had answered that they were still willing to accept my shipments. I asked the agent for a letter testifying that I could resume deliveries on my contract and a second letter to the inspector in Detroit instructing him to begin inspecting my shipments.

The agent assured me the letters would be mailed and urged me to return home. But I had been assured before without result and was not ready to rely on his promises again. I asked him to write the letters while I waited. He did so.

He could not give me the letter addressed to the Detroit inspector explaining that it had to go by mail. However, I insisted on seeing the letter deposited in the mail box. I had my way.

I returned to Detroit and got to work on my shipments. Production had to be expanded, everything had to be speeded up. In the meantime, the government owed me some $12,000 which had been held up when my contracts were cancelled. Before leaving Washington I went to the office where government bills were paid. I explained that my contracts had been reinstated and that I was entitled to be compensated for previous shipments. They were delighted that the controversy had been settled and promised that a check would be sent to me in a day or two.

I waited for two weeks. The checks still had not come.

I telephoned Washington several times but without results. I made another trip to our country's capital and was shifted from one official to another. Nothing came of it until one clerk, sorry for the runaround I was getting, explained that when my contracts were voided a red tag was attached to my page in the ledger. That red tag could be removed only by the person who put it there or by his superior.

Tired and frustrated, I headed straight to the top. I called on the head of the American Navy and explained the whole ridiculous situation. He received me most cordially and asked me to return the following day. When I arrived the next day his secretary asked me to go to a certain room and there I found the checks made out and ready for me.

I returned to Detroit in a much happier mood. I felt relieved, my luck had turned at last, my troubles were over.

THE NATIONAL RECOVERY ACT

PRESIDENT ROOSEVELT SIGNED THE NEWly-passed National Recovery Act, popularly known as the NRA. Prices were brought under control and all employers who were covered by the NRA agreed to pay a minimum wage of $15 a week. I suddenly found myself in a price-wage squeeze. After selling a carload of rags, instead of making a 2 per cent profit, I found myself facing an 18 to 20 per cent loss.

Again I went to Washington. I explained my situation to the chief purchasing agent of the Navy Department. He reassured me saying that the President had foreseen such situations and had arranged to compensate merchants for losses on government orders. When I asked him to approve an increase in the prices on my contracts he said he had no authority to do so. He urged me to continue my shipments and that later I would be able to submit a bill for the losses sustained as a result of the NRA.

If I wished, he said I could cancel my government contracts; the government would not object. However, he advised me to follow the first course, meet my contract obligations and make up for the losses later on. He assured me he would approve the supplementary bill himself.

I showed him that I was not able financially to continue under those terms, that I would be the loser in either case and that I would be forced out of business if I had to ship at the old prices. At this point he suggested that I negotiate new contracts with the government and ship some goods at the new price and some at the old price and in that way equalize my losses until I could make a settlement later on. The government would not insist on fulfillment of old contracts at the time specified but would be willing to wait, he added. I followed his advice.

I was never able to determine the exact extent of my losses under the old contracts but I think they were anywhere from $20,000 to $25,000. It was impossible to figure it exactly because I was selling to private firms at different prices at the same time that I was shipping my government contracts. It was difficult to specify how much of my expenses were due to the government contracts and how much to my private shipments.

To obtain an adjustment in rates I had to submit 128 different affidavits and ran up an accounting bill of several hundred dollars. After all my trouble the Treasury Department sent me a polite letter, exactly two lines long, informing me that my request for an upward revision in my government contracts had been rejected. There was no explanation.

Since I had to be in Washington for other reasons I took

advantage of the opportunity to visit the Treasury Department and ask why my request had been denied. Someone in the bureau explained that my affidavits and reports were not honored because the chief purchasing agent had instructed the Treasury Department not to pay the price differential since I did not ship the orders at the times specified in the contracts.

I was very angry. The agent had trapped me. I had no recourse. When I returned home I sent a letter to the head of the Treasury Department explaining the entire situation to him. I described how the chief purchasing agent for the Navy had urged me to ship the merchandise and that he promised that he himself would help me get an adjustment in the price to make up for losses I was sustaining as a result of the National Recovery Act. If the purchasing agent was now telling another story, I added, he was a downright liar.

A LETTER BEFORE THE SUPREME COURT

I NEVER DREAMT WHEN I WROTE MY letter to the Treasury Department that it would end up in the hands of the Supreme Court of the United States. Here is how it happened.

It turned out that the Treasury Department refused compensation to all contractors who suffered losses as a result of the National Recovery Act. In 1938 the matter came before Congress which passed a law providing for compensation for NRA losses. I received a letter from a Washington lawyer asking me to let him handle my case. He was certain he would be able to get a favorable decision and his fee was to be 25 per cent of the amount I would receive.

I hesitated at first. I had wasted enough time and I was reluctant to squander additional valuable time on a doubtful cause. But since I would not have to lay out any money, I had nothing to lose. Besides, something might come of it. I told the lawyer to go ahead.

The case went first to the Court of Equity. I had to submit a new set of charges; they had to be formulated according to another set of laws. This cost me another $200. In 1940 there was a hearing before a Federal judge. For two days I sat in the witness box answering questions on my contracts, technical questions about shipping, billing, etc., about contracts that had been running for about six years. By the end of 1940 the Federal judge issued a verdict giving me $1,300. It was so small it made me laugh. But I was surprised several months later when I received word that the government was appealing the decision to the U. S. Supreme Court, the highest court in the land.

Thus, the Supreme Court had in its possession all the correspondence, charges, reports and affidavits on my case. My grandchildren and my descendants might some day benefit from the legal process.

The experience cooled my readiness to accept governments contracts, particularly large ones where I had less control on prices and stood to lose large amounts.

In 1937 business generally in the United States was not good. It had been better in 1936. But my business was thriving. In 1936 and 1937 I managed to make up my losses on the government contracts and show a nice profit besides.

Throughout all the years of economic struggle I always found time to take part in the social and philanthropic life of the Jewish community. I contributed to various campaigns and institutions. I never sent individuals away wthout funds when they came to me for assistance. I felt that the forest was composed of trees and that one must not neglect the trees while favoring the forest. In the long run the forest would suffer if the trees were neglected.

Assistance to individuals amounted mainly to small sums from several tens of dollars to several hundreds. In most instances it was a matter of listening patiently to the individual's story and advising him on personal or business matters. On business matters, sometimes I would instruct him on what course to take.

My wife's family brought all its financial troubles to me. My own family, residing in Russia, received funds from me regularly. The sums were not large, perhaps even too small. And there were some periods when I was unable to send anything.

My father died in 1935. His small mill had been confiscated by the government. My mother went to live with my sister in Mogilev-on-the-Dnieper and then I lost all trace of them.

I BECOME A FARMER

I DID SOMEONE A FAVOR IN THE YEAR 1936 and it cost me lots of money and lots of trouble. My wife's cousin had a large and well-stocked farm. It had a vineyard of 100 acres, 60 acres of farmland, a forest of 40 acres and a beautiful home that cost, in those days, $20,000 to build.

We visited the farm several times for a few days rest and always enjoyed it. We were enthusiastic about the way the farm was thriving. However, in the depression years my cousin was unable to keep up his mortgage payments and in 1936 the bank foreclosed. The bank was angry at my cousin for agitating among the farmers to hold back on their mortgage payments. Congress had passed the Frazier-Lemke Law providing that farms could not be taken away for failure to pay their mortgages.

When the Supreme Court declared the law unconstitutional the banks immediately swooped down on my cousin and seized the farm. The banks refused even to negotiate terms with him. He came running to me to save him.

The first mortgage happened to be held by a Detroit bank. I went there and was told that they would have no dealings with my cousin. However, if I wished to take over the mortgage, in my name, they would come to an understanding with me.

I decided to take the mortgage in my own name and save my cousin's farm. It was a $25,000 mortgage. I took it for two reasons. First, I believed that the farm could be run profitably and take care of its debts; secondly, the Michigan law then prevailing provided that if I did not pay the mortgage the farm could be taken away but I could not be held accountable for "deficiency." This meant that if the farm did not bring in enough to cover the mortgage payments, I would not be responsible to provide the difference between the auction price and the debts. Only the farm would be taken from me, nothing else.

I considered it a reasonable risk to make the $3,000 payments expecting that with me watching the business end of the farm, my cousin could still save it.

But the matter ended quite differently. As soon as my cousin saw that he would not lose his farm, he began to ignore my advice. In the first year there was a rich grape harvest but he put the money into his own pocket instead of into the farm, thus leaving me holding the bag.

I didn't want to go to court over the matter, and to throw

him off the farm was out of the question. So I had to make the mortgage and tax payments out of my own pocket. For three years I suffered in frustration until I realized that it was a devilish and hopeless game. I went to the bank and agreed that I would give them $6,000 against the mortgage and they could take the farm. I considered myself lucky because the Michigan Supreme Court had issued a decision that if a real estate auction did not cover the full amount of the mortgage then the owner was still responsible for the balance.

The entire matter cost me $13,000 in cash and several years of heartache. I had hoped that I would be able to salvage several thousand dollars from the farm inventory. But it turned out that my cousin was smarter than I. He borrowed money against the inventory without me ever knowing about it. If I took away the inventory, which had been put up as collateral, it would have meant prison for my cousin. It would have served him right but I could not get myself to take such a drastic step.

Instead I spat on the whole experience, vowing not to let it bother me any more.

The years from 1936 to the end of 1942, the year I am putting this chapter down on paper, were financially the most profitable years of my life. True, I worked very hard, perhaps too hard, and my strength was beginning to weaken. Nevertheless, I felt that hard work does pay in the end.

UP TO THIS POINT

I BUILT A HOME FOR MYSELF AND FILLED it with beauty and riches. It was built to our taste, my wife's and mine, without a second look at the costs. My business was now on a firm foundation and I was prospering as never before. Our reputation was of the highest and credit was no problem.

Even so I lacked an inner peace. I found myself haunted by the thought that as the wheel spun in my favor, it could just as easily reverse itself. I tried to convince myself that my fears were groundless but it didn't help. My subconscious prevailed over logic.

I pictured several situations. What would happen if I were suddenly to become poor? I would have to lower my standard of living. It was obvious! I would have to cancel my contributions to many worthwhile causes and, even worse, I would have to explain why I had cut my contributions.

Thoughts like these made me sad. It is one of the reasons I contributed to anything and everything as long as I had the money to do so.

Being somewhat practical, I took steps to protect my future against sudden poverty. I had numerous opportunities to invest in projects, many of which seemed worthwhile and showed promise of a liberal return. Yet I held back lest one of these ventures go sour and take my investment with it.

This was a strange feeling for me to have developed suddenly since I had always been a speculator, buying and selling carloads of merchandise. The price could have fallen before I could sell and I stood to lose a lot of money. At times I did, but in the main, I came out a winner. Now, on reaching the age of 46, I had suddenly become cautious. I was afraid to speculate. I didn't want to lose what I had fought so hard to gain.

Another contribution played an important role in my new economic thinking. I had two business ventures going at the same time and I spent so much time on them that I had no energy left to look for new investments. After a day's work, I came home exhausted. I didn't want to add to the workload lest it undermine my health.

In past years, I would hardly give a thought to the physical requirements demanded by my work. In later years, however, I began to feel tired by the end of the day and I realized that my health needed looking after too. I thought of death frequently and was resigned not to reach a ripe old age. I argued with myself that it was foolish for a man at the age of 46, of reasonably good health, to think of dying, especially when I had so many wonderful opportunities to enjoy the good things of life, the fruits of my hard labors. It was all very logical. It made sense. But still I couldn't shake off the depressing thoughts of death.

These morbid thoughts intruded themselves even into my work. I was careful to record every transaction to the smallest detail so that if anything should happen, if I should suddenly die, everything would be on paper, my affairs would be in perfect order.

This does not mean that I was terrified and immobilized by the fear of death. Not at all. I thought about death dispassionately and rationally. It was a practical problem that had to be faced, not avoided. I just did not want to reach the ultimate end at that time, when my children were still very young, before I was able to help them go into the world fully able to stand on their own two feet. I wanted desperately to be a real and good father to them and this I could not do from the grave. That was the reason. For myself, I could easily have made peace with my Maker.

The eldest of my four daughters was nineteen. The youngest was eight. Another was sixteen and the fourth was fourteen. The oldest had attended an elementary school of the Farband Labor Zionist Order, and for three years studied in its high school. She was thoroughly familiar with Jewish life and customs, and also its problems. She attended college for a year and then transferred to an art school to study painting. She was also interested in music but I feared that neither talent would be sufficient to provide her a living if she had to be on her own. She was a dreamer and like all dreamers found it difficult to concentrate on specific projects. She went from one dream to another in search of a way of life for herself.

My second daughter was about to finish the Yiddish High School. She was also in her senior year in regular high school and was preparing to enter college. She was of a more practical bent and had no fear of work. She was more Jewishly inclined than her older sister and took a greater interest in Jewish affairs. She had not yet chosen her life's work. After all, she was only sixteen, changing from a child into a young woman. It was too early for such a momentous decision.

I had always wished that my daughters would prepare for careers. In that way they would always be independent and have a source of livelihood if they had to fend for themselves. For that reason, I did not shower them with luxuries and tried always to instill a basic sense of modesty and a respect for traditions.

My third daughter had completed the Farband Labor Zionist School and was in the second year of Farband High School. She was a Jewish nationalist. Although she spoke only English she read Yiddish very well and was able to manage a bit of Hebrew. She firmly believed in the perpetuation of Yiddish. She was active in "Habonim" (the Builders), the Labor Zionst youth organization. She was a clever girl and had a ready answer for anything. It was too early for her to consider a career.

The youngest, then eight, was in fragile health and did not receive a formal Jewish education. We planned to start her in Jewish school when she was nine. My wife and I differed on the kind of education to give our youngest. My wife, who was religious, at least more religious than I, wanted to send her to a Talmud Torah. I was reluctant to do so. I feared it would introduce a dissonant element among the children, three to the Farband schools, and the last to a Talmud Torah.

My wife was adamant. Two of my daughters, then 14 and 16, sided with me. I was very pleasantly surprised to hear the strong arguments they put forth. They did not want the family unity to become disrupted by the youngest sister injecting a different philosophy into the house. They also argued that their youngest sister would feel strange in a home where the prevailing liberal spirit was so different from the strict orthodox training she would get at a Talmud Torah.

We kept a kosher home. The holidays were celebrated according to tradition but not in a strict religious sense. I spoke to the children in Yiddish and they usually replied in English. We understood each other quite well and communicated easily. My wife spoke to them in English exclusively. The children did not read Yiddish books although my library contained hundreds of volumes in Yiddish. I also had books in English but they were mainly reference books.

The children were avid readers but they preferred to go to the library to borrow books in English. They rarely reached for a Yiddish book on the shelves right in their own home.

It was 28 years since I had come to America. With the exception of the first few years, when I went to synagogue during the high holidays, I did not enter a house of prayer.

However, on reachng middle age, I began to think about joining a congregation. True, I did not attend synagogue. Still I was not a goy! We kept kosher and observed the holidays at home. In effect, my home was my synagogue. And who was to say I was not as pious as the Jew who went regularly to shul and occupied the front pew?

Exactly why my thoughts turned in this direction, I still don't know. Perhaps it was approaching old age. Perhaps it was the unsettled times, or my wife's wishes, or my children who asked me several times why we did not join a synagogue.

To sum up my life at that time, at age 46, sometimes I felt I had made a success of my life and at other times I had spent my life on matters of little value, that I exchanged life for small change. What gave me the greatest satisfaction, however, was the knowledge that whatever little I did accomplish I did strictly on my own, without help from others. On the contrary, while I struggled, while I was still pushing the wagon uphill by myself, I paused to give help to others.

I was also proud that what I had gotten I had gotten honestly and by means of hard work. In all my years of business, I never cheated anyone nor did I take advantage of a person's weakness or lack of knowledge in business transactions.

Thus ends this section of my memoirs. I hope that in the coming years I will be able to resume my writing and describe the events of those years.

Part Three

**Communal Activity;
Frustration and Fulfillment**

IN THE STRUGGLE
FOR A JEWISH STATE

TEN YEARS HAVE ELAPSED SINCE I WROTE the first part of my reminiscences. Now I will record the events of the following ten years. They were years of great achievements and years of deep despair. They were busy years, particularly in service to the community.

Ever since I first settled in Detroit in 1929, I was active in the Poale Zion, the Labor Zionist movement. During the early years I was especially concerned with the welfare of the Yiddish schools and for Yiddish books. I helped many writers get their works published and later helped them sell their books.

The Poale Zion Farband school had 120 pupils and one teacher, a Mr. Levine. He was a devoted and hard-working teacher. In addition to his teaching chores, he was secretary of the school administrative committee. He met with and assisted the women's club of the school and kept the books on tuition fees.

The school was open six days a week. However, because of the many duties the teacher had, the level of instruction was not quite as high as we would have liked. I led a continuous struggle on this issue with our school activists. Since they were concerned mainly with enrolling a large number of students, they were quite satisfied with the way the school was going. "Our school has more pupils than the Workmen's Circle School and the Sholem Aleichem School," they said proudly.

In those years, there was no coordination between the three Yiddish schools of the Jewish nationalist-radical movement and very little cooperation. Each school conducted its own affairs as it saw fit. The Central Committee of the Labor Zionists, sitting in New York, paid little attention to the schools and had no means of evaluating the quality of education in them.

The Poale Zion Labor Zionist Party, which always boasted of the Yiddish schools it had established, took little interest in what was happening in the schools. When a split occurred in the Poale Zion group in Detroit over a teacher, I was sent to New York to ask the Central Committee to send us a qualified teacher, one who would raise the cultural and educational level of the school.

Unfortunately the leaders in New York didn't even have the patience to listen to me. One by one they left the meeting until I remained alone with the empty chairs. It then became clear to me that many of the leaders were against the schools and would not help us in any way. Others did not oppose the schools but considered them an empty blessing. Nevertheless both groups bragged loudly about their Yiddish schools when it suited their purposes.

The Yiddish schools made great progress in the previous 23 years, especially in their budgets. Where it had been under $10,000 annually in the beginning, it soared to $50,000 20 years later. In the same period the number of pupils had increased by 40 per cent. In the later years we had 14 teachers, each of them conducting two one and a half hour classes a day or one two-hour class. Classes were held four days a week. Each teacher received an annual salary of $5,000. An assistant teacher received between $3,000 and $4,000. There was also a principal who did not conduct any classes because, he argued, he was kept much too busy with other chores. There was also a secretary in the office.

The budget was a heavy burden. The Detroit Jewish Welfare Federation contributed $8,000 annually. At the same time, the Federation was covering the total annual budget of the United Hebrew Schools. The $8,000 to the Yiddish schools was not for our's alone but also for the Workmen's Circle and the Sholem Aleichem schools.

If I complained about the high budget or the performance of the teachers, I was sharply criticized. So, gradually I withdrew from activity but continued to contribute to the movement. When necessary, I would advance loans to the organization or to the schools. I also conducted negotiations with the Jewish Federation on the allocation for the following year.

Eventually, the Poale Zion and Sholem Aleichem schools were united but it wasn't a successful merger. Each side expected the other to take on the greater share of the work and bring in the greater amount of funds. The match was later dissolved. "No longer a bride, once again single," as the Yiddish adage goes.

I came to the conclusion that Yiddish education cannot be in the hands of small groups. It must become the responsibility of the entire community, the organized Jewish community. The Welfare Federation was willing to take over the responsibility but only on the condition that there be a unified Yiddish school system with a minimum program for all schools. The Federation was willing to include Yiddish for those who were interested but specified that all boys would have to wear scull caps when the Bible or prayer book was being taught.

For my part, I insisted that the Federation cover the total budget, exercise control over expenditures, and oversee the functioning of the schools but that it leave the content or curriculum to each school to decide for itself. The Federation would not agree.

I realized that something would have to be done for our schools. Our Yiddish speaking members were interested in them but their ranks became thinner and thinner every year; their numbers diminished visibly month by month.

THE YIDDISH BOOK— REPROACHES OF A DEVOTED READER

I WAS ALWAYS PROMOTING YIDDISH books and helping Yiddish authors get their works published and circulated. I derived much satisfaction from this work, but also considerable aggravation. Writers are also human beings—but human beings of a quite different breed. Most of them are self-centered and show little consideration for their fellow men. However, if one understands them he can discount the discourtesies and enjoy their company and their idiosyncrasies.

To cite some examples. I took one writer to a place where he would have an opportunity to sell his book. I said nothing to the man except introduce him to the writer. The writer said: "Here is my book. The price is $5, pay me."

The prospective purchaser, a bit nonplussed, replied, "But Mr. A., I do not understand your writings."

Mr. A., the writer, not a bit embarrassed, then said: "Who says you have to understand it? Just give me the five dollars."

The man stood silent, struck dumb by the arrogant author. He handed him the five dollars. As he left, the author turned to me and said: "He also wants to understand!"

The writer, L. arrived in Detroit. A literary gathering had been arranged in his honor. There were about forty people present. L. held forth as follows:

"The entire Bible is not worth the skin of an onion. My small book is worth more than all the books of the Bible."

Later one of the guests asked him, "How could you talk that way about the Bible?"

In reply he said, "You asses, what do you know about literature?"

Another writer sought our help to get his collected works published. We formed a committee in Detroit to help him. We raised $1,480 which, for a city the size of Detroit, was a very fair sum. When we handed him the check, he said:

"Well, I will have to be satisfied with this sum. After all, I'm not a consumptive." This was a reference to an ailing Yiddish writer for whom large sums of money were raised in Detroit.

Another very important writer paid us a visit. He wanted the Jewish community of Detroit to raise $5,000 to enable him to publish his complete works. I explained that for a community of our size to raise such a huge sum of money for one writer was a bit too much. I softened the blow by explaining we were at that very moment collecting funds for two other writers. I asked if he wouldn't be content to publish just five volumes and publish the remaining five at a later date.

"My God," he exclaimed, "How can you ask me to choose which of my books I should publish now and which I should hold until later. Every single word I wrote in those books is as important as every word in the Bible!"

Or take the following experience. A writer, L., with whom I was on very friendly terms, had sent me a telegram notifying me that he was arriving at my home that Saturday and that I should arrange a gathering there in his honor. "I need money to publish a book," he wrote.

The telegram reached me at a time when my wife was ill. I wired back that because of illness it was impossible to fulfill his request. I also wrote a lengthy letter containing a more detailed explanation. Because I had refused his request, our friendship came to an end. He did not even ask about my wife. A year before, he had been our house guest for two weeks and my wife went out of her way to make his stay as pleasant as possible.

I realize now that these committees formed to help writers are to a great extent responsible for ruining the Yiddish book market. We turned it from a business into a charity. But that is the subject for another chapter.

During the past several years, the task of selling Yiddish books became a painful process. Even books we could well do without were being published. But there are many, many kind-hearted people who lend their names to a number of worthy, and sometimes unworthy causes. Letters are mailed around the country, all in the same vein, "We are turning to you as a lover of Yiddish culture." There were additional stock phrases, words to entice the reader, and the inevitable ending: "You know how difficult it is for an author to get his book published, the expenses are so great, so won't you send your contribution." etc., etc.

How can a lover of Yiddish not reply? Until some years

ago, I would mail my contributions regularly. Often if I received a reply at all, it was a letter of abuse because of the small contribution. The writer felt I should have written a much larger check. I'm surprised that he didn't just submit a bill listing the amount he felt I should give and then threaten to sue me if I failed to pay.

More recently I hold back my checks and wait until the books are published, and mailed to me. Some of them are trash, I am sorry to say. I realize that in the general book market in America, there is much that is written in English that is of no value. But at least the English books have a market in the hundreds of thousands, the millions, so there are customers for all sorts of books. But the number of Yiddish readers in some American cities is not greater than several times ten and they must buy everything that is published.

To me, personally, it is not only a question of spending money but also of wasting time. I often devote several hours a night to reading. Occasionally I find myself reading nonsense, only because it had just arrived and I had no prior idea of what it contained. To return them to the authors was out of the question. It would be too much of an insult. At least he feels his work is of great importance.

We have several Yiddish writers who are quite prolific. Every few years they issue a new edition of the "Complete Works Of." So I accumulated quite a number of duplicates, although each "Complete Works" was in a different format. Thus I have on one shelf of my library several books by the same author, each a different size or shape, a lilliputian miniature next to a giant tome which cannot fit on the shelf standing up, all with identical contents.

Another pet peeve is that many Yiddish books published here in America have no connection at all with Jewish life in America. The same book could have been written in

Chile, or Mexico or even in Africa. More recently, since the "Third Destruction," during the Nazi era, one often hears that it is important to depict Jewish life in Europe before its destruction by the Nazis. Well, and what came before the era of catastrophy? How many Yiddish writers in this country depicted Jewish life in America? Most of them wrote about life in the old country or about New York's East Side of years ago.

When my children were small and attending the Farband School, we inaugurated the practice at home of reading aloud selections from Yiddish books on Friday nights. I started with Sholem Aleichem, whom the children loved. Naturally I had to provide a running commentary along with the stories. I also read to them from Mendele Mokher Seforim, I. L. Peretz, David Bergelson and others. But the subject matter was too strange for the children. They simply did not understand these writers.

The children began to demand: "Papa, you say that Yiddish literature is so rich! So, let's read about Jewish life in America." But except from I. J. Schwartz's narrative poem, "Kentucky," I was not able to find anything suitable to read to them about Jewish life in America—of the life of the Jewish immigrant, of the sweatshops, my children were too far removed from those early struggles. America in the 1940's was not America of the early 1900's.

Many of our Jewish writers became uprooted from Jewish folklife. Books appeared in plentiful numbers but most are on historic themes, pure invention, and others are reminiscences of an era not long past. But where is our life today? Where are reports on five million Jews who make up the Jewish community of America today?

If one should read in a New York daily a description of Jewish life in a distant American city, it is usually shallow

Communal Activity; Frustration and Fulfillment 219

and inaccurate. In 1952 I read in a Yiddish newspaper that the Jewish community of Detroit was 100 years old. If the writer had taken the trouble to come to Detroit and learn the true facts instead of writing fanciful tales from secondary sources while sitting in his New York apartment or cafe, he would have written more accurately and more interestingly.

This was the state of Yiddish literature at the time, more hope than substance.

THE DETROIT JEWISH COUNCIL

EARLY IN THE 1930'S THE AMERICAN JEWish Congress awoke from a long slumber. After the San Remo Conference when the partnership between the American Jewish Congress and the American Jewish Committee was dissolved, it was thought that the Congress was free to become active in American Jewish life. Instead it went into a long and deep sleep. The Poale Zion tried to awaken the Congress but to no avail.

Finally, when it did awaken, it tried to set up Jewish community councils in each of the larger cities. Representatives of the American Jewish Congress made the rounds of the cities calling meetings and trying to organize chapters. The response in Detroit was favorable. The time was ripe. However, the time dragged. I don't know if it was the lack of funds or it had not yet completely shaken off the stupor of its long sleep. Finally the Detroit Jewish Federation took the initiative to organize a local communty council based on individuals not on representations of local organzations.

The Federation called whomever it wished to meetings.

There was a committee of 21 in existence. It was established several years before to build a Jewish home for the aged. The plan was to revitalize the committee and co-opt additional members as needed and the enlarged committee would then become the Community Council.

I was at that time president of the Poale Zion Branch No. 3 so I was invited to join the committee. One of the questions for discussion on the agenda was how the Council was to be formed and what kind of constitution it would have.

I realized from the start that my idea of what the Council should be and the idea of Kurt Peiser, director of the Jewish Welfare Federation at the time, were as far apart as east from west. Three factions were formed. One was the Federation group, which asked for a Council consisting of individuals who would not be responsible to anyone, only to public opinion. This meant, of course, a Council which the Federation could control.

Another was the Congress faction, to which I belonged. It demanded that the Council be composed of organizational representatives with each delegate responsible to the organization which designated him. The organization would have control of its delegates and could replace them if it so desired.

The third faction was neutral, indecisive. Those belonging to this group didn't much care how the Council was constituted.

We held many meetings but were unable to resolve the question. Our group was relatively small. It consisted of ten persons but all of them were experienced organizational men and could easily orient themselves to new situations. They could certainly prepare a workable, democratic constitution for such a group. All were General Zionists, Labor Zionists and representatives of the Arbeiter Ring (Workmen's circle), accustomed to procedural battles at meetings and conventions. We succeeded in preventing the Federation from creating a Council without us.

On one occasion, during a meeting, Kurt Peiser got up and said, "I will wait no longer. I'm going to establish a Council of individual members." I felt as if I had been stabbed in the back. Without thinking, I rose to my feet and banged on the table so hard that the dishes flew off. I shouted at Mr. Peiser, "Who are you to let us or let us not do what we wish? You are a hired employee. Today you are here and tomorrow you will be in another city depending on which will give you a thousand dollars more."

Very much chastened, Kurt Peiser got up and said, "If this is what the Jews of Detroit want, you shall have it. We will set up a Council of organizations."

Several months later, he actually left Detroit for a job in Philadelphia.

The democratic forces had won the first round. Now came the time to prepare the constitution. A committee of three was appointed. It included a judge, James Ellman, a former president of the General Zionists; Joseph Chaggai, a Labor Zionist and a powerful speaker; and me. We all agreed that the constitution should be as broad and flexible as possible and as democratic as possible.

We held innumerable meetings. We soon realized that to prepare such a document, it was not enough merely to be in agreement on the aims of the group. It was necessary to be able to envision how people would interpret the provisions and by-laws. We realized that the Jewish Welfare Federation would like to gain control over the Council and failing that would try to limit its scope on the pretext that some actions would be contrary to the constitution.

Ellman, as an expert on the law, devoted himself to the legal aspects. Chaggai was concerned mainly that the preamble be a work of literary excellence, inspirational and lofty. My own interest was to make sure that neither the Federation nor any other group should be able to take over control of the Council. It was determined that the cultural activities of the group include Jewish education for the young, active support of Zionism, and other positive programs.

The Federation appointed an expert to the committee, a professor. It was inevitable that we should have trouble with him, and we did. He was an orthodox Jew and insisted that the cultural activities be limited to instruction in English or Hebrew but not in Yiddish. He also wanted us not to use the word "national" in our by-laws. The professor did not have his way. But on one point I lost out. I wanted the budget to be covered completely by the participating organizations or by a separate fund raising campaign specifically for the Council. I realized that if the Federation would fund the Council, it would inevitably control it. Eventually the others came to agree with me, but it was too late.

By 1952, the Jewish Community Council of Detroit had 307 affiliated organizations. Its annual budget amounted to $75,000. By that time, I had been a member of the Executive Committee of the Council for fourteen years. I cannot say that I was completely satisfied with the Council and its activities. It came around more and more to the way of work of the Anti-Defamation League. Instead of a positive program to promote Judaism and the Jewish community, it engaged mainly in countering anti-Semitism, which I considered negative work.

There are four major reasons why the Council took this path.

Communal Activity; Frustration and Fulfillment 223

1. With the exception of Simon Shetzer, the first president, we did not have any distinguished leaders on the Council, men of prominence who were at the same time men of character, strong Jews with a deep understanding of Jewish traditions and history. I considered this important because I feel very strongly that the more Jewish a person is, the less he fears anti-Semitism and conversely, the less one knows of Judaism the more he trembles in the face of anti-Semitism.

2. None of the directors we had, with the exception of Isaac Frank, knew anything about Judaism or Jewish life. To this day we have no suitable instruction in Judaism for social workers. Most social workers come out of college with courses in psychology, sociology, and so on, and they are, therefore, so to speak, specialists. They do not know Yiddish and they know little about the life of the Jews. How can a blind person be a leader? They feel no need to study Jewish problems because they can make their way very comfortably as social workers. They are well paid and have no difficulty finding employment.

3. The Federation throughout the years prevented the Council from carrying on cultural programs, simply by refusing to provide the funds for them. The budget had to be submitted to the Federation which went over it line by line. Each part of the program was carefully scrutinized. How much for salaries, how much for postage, etc., etc. In this way it was able to head off any aspect of the program with which it disagreed, lectures, Jewish education, concerts, in short, anything that came under the heading of education was prohibited.

Under the budgetary system it was impossible to save money on one program and apply it to another, more important, program. If any money was saved it had to be returned to the Federation. And if $50 was needed for something not in the budget a special appropriation had to be obtained from the Federation. After a while the Federation adopted a get tough policy with the Council. The budget committee would comb the Council budget very carefully eliminating those parts of it they disagreed with, and all under the pretext of economizing.

Of course their real aim was entirely different. They simply did not want to permit the Council to conduct its business freely and prove that its members could make intelligent decisions on their own. The real boss, they let us know, was the Federation. They picked on trifles, an expense item amounting to $50 or $100.

It sometimes seemed to us that the Federation people derived a sadistic pleasure in torturing the Council's executive board. Some of us wanted to cover the small expense item out of our own pockets. But the Federation said, "No, if you do, we will cut the amount you raise from your budget."

4. A large measure of guilt for this state of affairs had to be borne by the organization and their representatives. They did not take too much interest in the work, were generally negligent and perhaps were not really suited for such a program. They yielded up the Council to the Federation by default.

To summarize:

We had in Detroit a democratic institution that could have become a well-organized, well-run "Kehillah," a Jewish community organization. That it fell short was due to a number of intangibles. We tried, but it was not enough.

That is not to say that the Council did not make worthwhile gains in the community. It achieved status by its mere existence as the united voice of Detroit Jewry. It spoke on behalf of the community. No longer could any individual claim to speak for the Jewish community, as had been the case before the Council was organized.

The Jewish Court of Arbitration also achieved a great deal, especially in settling disputes between Jewish organizations. During World War II and the period of price controls the Council was careful to prevent black marketeering in areas or trades considered generally to be Jewish. I took part in one such problem. One man had already been sentenced to prison for black marketeering and several others were to be indicted. Through intercession of the Council and with some assistance from Federal officials, we were able to head off the indictments and settle the problem.

When a committee of the Council called on the Federal official, he told us that the situation was very bad. He said that the black marketeering was on a large scale and that he was determined to stamp it out once and for all. He added that he had enough evidence to send another five or six men to prison.

We told him that we had not come to plead for the guilty ones. On the contrary, we agreed that it was his duty to prosecute anyone who broke the law. But, we asked him, how it was that he prosecuted only the small businessmen, the retailers, and not the manufacturers who bought the merchandise with under-the-table payments. Why, we asked, didn't he prosecute the buyer as well as the seller? If the manufacturer had not been willing to pay more for the merchandise than the OPA (Office of Price Administration) allowed, then wasn't he equally guilty of violating the law?

The official replied that he could not prosecute the manufacturer because the transactions were conducted by the employees and not the manufacturer himself. Thus, the owner could not be held legally responsible. This sounded ludicrous to us. So much so that I was provoked into an undiplomatic question. Bluntly, I asked him, "Is all this perhaps due to the fact that the dealers are Jews and manufacturers are Christians, and not only Christians but also rich?"

The official maintained his poise. He assured us that it was not so. I replied that perhaps he was being honest but that it didn't matter. What was important, I continued, was that the public would interpret it that way. We, for our part, I said, would issue a statement to the press asking him openly to explain why he failed to prosecute the manufacturers along with the retailers since they were both equally guilty.

The Federal official began to squirm. He realized that he was in a tight spot. He changed his tune. He began to assure us that he was not interested in sending anyone to prison. All he wanted to do was to put a stop to the black marketeering. He begged us to help. We assured him that that was the very reason we had come to see him.

Following a number of stormy sessions with the dealers we managed to establish some order. The truth of the matter is that a large part of the blame for the black market should fall on some officials in Washington. I was at that time a member of the National O.P.A. Committee. I told them at one of the meetings that they were driving the people into the black market with their contradictory and discriminatory regulations.

The situation had deteriorated to such an extent that many of the dealers would have been forced out of business if they had remained strictly within the OPA regulations. One national Jewish organization interested itself in the problem since the trade was largely Jewish-owned. The organization asked me to make a study of the problem and give it my recommendations. I did so and the recommendations were eventually forwarded to Washington. One of them was accepted and the second rejected. At least the problem was eased.

The committee set up by the Detroit Jewish Community Council to handle the matter consisted of three members: a rabbi who delivered sermons to the Jewish dealers in the name of the Jewish people and warned against "Hillel Ha'-Shem," against desecrating God's name by their black marketeering; an attorney who argued the law with them and warned them of the consequences (the dealers did not listen since they knew the law even better than the lawyer); and I, a businessman. I was well acquainted with this line and was able to talk to them in their own language.

The rabbi was the first to leave the committee. The lawyer soon followed suit and I was the sole surviving member of the Council committee. Nothing was ever reported to the Executive Committee and so little is known of this incident. Other committees were active in other lines. The dealers in my line remained my close friends because we spoke the same language, trusted each other, and besides, they realized that I had saved them from the possibility of heavy fines, or worse.

THE AMERICAN JEWISH CONGRESS

A COMMITTEE CAME TO ME WITH A REquest that I accept the presidency of the local branch of the American Jewish Congress. I refused. I was angry with the Congress for not having done anything from 1922 to 1933. The Congress had been created in 1917 or 1918. When it was formed, many Jews had high hopes for it. They believed that here was a group that would succeed in uniting all the forces of the Jewish community into one mighty organization.

It was to take the place of the older and more conservative American Jewish Committee which had dissolved its partnership with the Congress. This gave the Congress a free hand to be active on the American Jewish scene but, despite that, it did very little in the intervening years. It took a bloody flood in Germany to awake the sleeping Congress. The Poale Zion had tried to awaken it but without success. The Poale Zion had done much for the Congress. It was the strongest propagandist for the Congress in the early days. It also resigned later from the Jewish Labor Committee in order to remain a constituent body of the American Jewish Congress.

Aside from all that, the main reason for my lack of warmth for the Congress was the occasion of a speech delivered in Detroit by its president, Rabbi Stephen S. Wise in the late 1930's. He declared in his speech that from that time forth, the American Jewish Congress was going to devote all its energy, time and means to fight against discrimination wherever and whenever it appeared and against whoever was guilty of it. As long as a single Negro suffered discrimination, he said, we Jews were not safe.

At the end of his speech, I asked Rabbi Wise if the American Jewish community had given him a mandate to turn the Congress into another civil rights organzation. The name alone, American Jewish Congress, I argued was indication enough that the organization should devote itself to Jewish interests and the fight against discrimination against the Jews was but one aspect of the total fight for Jewish rights. The AJC included other programs, perhaps of even greater importance because they were positive in character;

Jewish culture, Jewish education for children and the democratization of Jewish life in general.

The Jews did not create the Negro problem, I continued. The attitude of the Jews toward the Negroes was much better than that of his white fellow Christians. Of course we should help, as Jews along with other groups, but to take the lead? I felt that was wrong.

Rabbi Wise replied that he had become convinced that Jewish life free of discrimination would not exist as long as there was another group suffering from discrimination. Since the Negroes were the chief victims of discrimination, he said, the American Jewish Congress must be in the vanguard in the struggle to eliminate discrimination against the blacks.

Immediately after that speech, the doors of the Congress were opened to liberals of different hues including pink and red, and differing programs and policies. I did not relish becoming the leader of such a mixed multitude.

Several years later, the Congress recognized its mistake and had to cleanse its ranks. The charter of the Detroit chapter was revoked by the national office and two new local branches were organized to get rid of the unsatisfactory elements.

A BATTLE AGAINST THE COMMUNISTS AND THEIR FELLOW TRAVELERS

DURING THE PERIOD OF THE SO-CALLED "United Front," the left wing International Workers' Order, a fraternal society, tried to affiliate with the Detroit Jewish Community Council. I was at that time chairman of the

Membership Committee and when the application came to me, I rejected it.

The left wingers appealed my decision to the Executive Committee. A delegation representing the I.W.O. appeared and argued that the Order was engaged in Jewish cultural work, that it supported schools for children, published Yiddish books and was generally a fraternal rather than a political organization.

Politically, all members of the Order were left wingers. This was generally agreed. But the delegation pointed out that they also had in their ranks some Zionists and even some religious Jews. Besides, they added, the Order did not concern itself too much with political issues.

Something odd occurred at the meeting. The affluent representatives of the American Jewish Committee, those of the Reform temple, and even of the Order of B'nai B'rith, were in favor of accepting the International Workers Order —all in the interests of unity. I carried on a vigorous battle against such a move and with the support of the Zionist groups and the Workmen's Circle, managed to keep the International Workers Order out of the Jewish Community Council.

The I.W.O. appealed the decision to the quarterly meeting of the delegates, the highest governing body of the Council. I knew in advance that the left wingers would be coming to the meeting well prepared and well organized so I prepared my own line of attack against them.

Firstly, the I.W.O. had been created by the Communist Party. Secondly, the I.W.O. was very active politically, despite what the delegation members said. Thirdly, the I.W.O. took its orders from the Communist Party. I brought with me documents to prove my accusations, to show how the policies of the I.W.O. changed according to the Kremlin

Communal Activity; Frustration and Fulfillment

line on the Arab pogroms in Palestine and on the Stalin-Hitler pact of 1939.

I argued that the Jewish Community belonged only to those Jewish institutions that put the interests of the Jewish people above all organizational considerations. I maintained that they, just like others in the Communist movement, put the interests of the Soviet Union and the dictates of the Communist Party above everything else. If it should come to a choice between supporting a foreign power or the interests of the Jewish people then they, the left wingers would in the future, as they had in the past, support the foreign power, even if it would harm the Jewish people.

The I.W.O. people came to the meeting with all their ammunition ready. They had already seen to it that all leftist delegates—from Landsmanshaft societies and other organizations—were present and ready to vote for them.

I expected a strong fight but, to my surprise, after I presented my argument, not a single representative of their group asked for the floor to defend their point of view. When the chairman called for a show of hands, not a person voted in favor of admitting them.

FUND RAISING

DETROIT BECAME WELL KNOWN FOR ITS generosity and success in raising funds for various causes. Since I was deeply involved in Jewish affairs, it was only natural that I should participate in many of the campaigns.

For campaign purposes, the year was divided into four quarters.

At the time of Succoth, late September or early October, the Labor Zionists launched a federated campaign that included the Farband Schools, the Habonim Labor Zionist Youth Organization, the Poale Zion Party, the Jewish Teachers's Seminary, the weekly Yiddish Kempfer, the monthly Jewish Frontier, and the operating expenses for our own local Yiddish school. This campaign lasted through the end of the year.

During this period, there were usually several smaller campaigns such as raising funds for the publication of a book by a Yiddish writer and the annual appeal for YIVO, the Jewish historical and research institute. During this period also, the Histradrut began preparations for its campaign which was launched officially right after New Years's Day.

The Histadrut campaign ran through January and February. In March the Allied Jewish Appeal began its drive. This took in the United Jewish Appeal and all local Jewish institutions. And between the Histadrut and the Allied Jewish Appeal, the Israel Bond organization conducted a limited campaign. Also sometime between the Histadrut and the Allied Jewish Appeal campaigns, Ampal, the American Palestine Economic Corporation, managed to conduct a drive.

In the middle of June, the UJA campaign was winding up, the Israel Bond organization launched a large scale campaign, with the Jewish National Fund coming close behind. Before the State of Israel was created, the JNF bought large tracts of swampland from the Arabs and turned them over to Jewish settlers who reclaimed the land and made it productive once again. Now it is concentrating on reforestation in Israel.

This is not all. I mentioned campaigns in which I was directly involved. There were others in which I was not directly involved. Still hardly a day passed that I did not have in my pocket a bundle of cards for solicitation for one cause or another. Sometimes I carried cards for three or four campaigns at one time, having had no chance to "cover" the cards separately.

Many contributors made me visit them several times. Others were not at home when I called and so I had to go a second, and sometimes a third time. Some, very few I'm happy to report, actually hid from me when I came to their home for their contributions.

We established a Jewish National Fund Council in Detroit with which all Zionist groups affiliated. It was a coordinating Council designed to bring some sense of order into the multitude of campaigns that stumbled over each other.

The major load of the campaigns was carried by the Poale Zion and the Mizrachi (the religious Zionists) and the least by the general Zionists. We collected between $100,000 and $120,000 annually. Of that amount half, sometimes sixty per cent, was collected by the Ladies' Auxiliary, formed exclusively to work for the Jewish National Fund.

Funds were collected in the traditional manner: the familiar blue and white boxes in the homes, the planting of trees in the homeland, golden book honor certificates, inscriptions in the Children's Book of JNF, and semi-annual tag days on Tisha B' Av and Purim when appeals were made in the synagogues.

During 1950-1951 I served as president of the JNF Council and in 1952 I was elected executive chairman of the Council.

ZIONIST ACTIVITY

IN 1936, FOLLOWING A LENGTHY DISCUSsion, Lawrence Crohn, a general Zionist leader, and I concluded that a general Zionist council should be formed in

Detroit to coordinate the activities of all local Zionist groups. Such a council would bring more order into our activities without in any way limiting the freedom or autonomy of any of the individual groups.

When I espoused the plan at Poale Zion Branch No. 3, of which I was a member, I encountered a great deal of opposition. I argued my point stubbornly and was able to swing a majority over to my side. I had to go through the same experience at meetings of the other two branches, the five branches of the Farband Labor Zionist Order and the three branches of the Pioneer Women.

There was no doubt. The time was ripe for such a council. The Arab disorders in Palestine were growing in fierceness. Large sums of money had to be collected—and very quickly. The press was unfriendly, often hostile to Zionist activity and thinking. The three daily newspapers did not report news from Palestine objectively and we had to make strong efforts to get more honest reporting. These and other tasks could be realized more quickly and more effectively in partnership than by individual action.

We had to awaken the Jewish masses to the dangers of the situation in the Holy Land. Even staunch Zionists had to be encouraged lest they sink into dispair. But what was so logical and self-evident to us was, regretfully, not accepted or so apparent to many Zionists in all the organizations. Their immediate goals and their party loyalty were of greater importance to them than the common good. They were afraid their organizations would suffer if they united with other groups to work on a joint, unified program, even for a limited time and for limited purposes.

In the meantime, I wrote to the Central Committee of the Poale Zion Labor Zionist Party in New York informing them of our plans. The secretary of the Central Committee

Communal Activity; Frustration and Fulfillment 235

immediately forbade me to take a hand in the formation of such a council, claiming that it was against the best interests of the party. I tried to explain that the unity and the independence of the party would not be diminished in the least and that the council would be able to accomplish collectively what the Poale Zion could not do individually.

To this came the reply that if the Central Committee thought it advisable to form a council it would have done so on a national scale. Detroit had no right to do so on its own, I was told, not without the permission of the Central Committee. If I continued to work for the creation of a council, it would be a violation of party discipline and proper steps would be taken, I was warned.

I did not obey the Central Committee and helped to establish the General Zionist Council of Detroit. It consisted of a broad representation of all Zionist groups in the city. The constitution was flexible. It provided that each affiliated group join on a voluntary basis and when it did so it did not surrender any of its autonomy. Any group could withdraw from the Council at any time if it felt it necessary to do so. The majority could not coerce any individual organization into following a certain course if it violated the organization's program or beliefs. Any group could choose not to participate in any specific action.

I mailed a copy of the constitution to our Central Committee in New York to which they did not reply. Needless to say, there were no dire consequences.

Less than two years later a similar council was established on a nation-wide basis, the Zionist Emergency Council. By that time we had a well-functioning General Zionist Council and were destined to play an important role in the struggle of the Jewish community of Palestine and later of Israel.

There was no inter-party or inter-group strife in the council. There were some frictions, but they were mild and were confined mainly to individuals, not to organizational groups. The council functioned very well indeed, as we had hoped.

THE WORK OF ZIONIST COUNCIL

RIGHT FROM THE OUTSET, WE CONCENtrated our efforts on the three daily newspapers. As I reported earlier, all three of them were unfriendly to Zionism. They tried to be "correct." When editorials did appear, they always leaned towards Great Britain, then the Palestine Mandatory Power. Washington also favored the British and the papers naturally mirrored the views of the State Department and the White House. All we could do was to send letters to the editors giving the Jewish viewpoint.

With the outbreak of World War II our position became more difficult. The United States backed England completely and looked with disfavor on all criticism of British policy. Our real work began after the defeat of the Nazis, when the British began to intercept ships carrying survivors of the concentration camps and the crematoria from the European graveyard to a new life in the Holy Land.

The incidents with the refugee ships *Patria* and *Struma* could not be passed over in silence, even by the unfriendly newspapers.

In the spring of 1945, I was elected president of the Zionist Council of Detroit. It thus became my responsibility to lead the Zionist efforts during those stormy years from the end of the war until the day our dream became a reality, when the State of Israel was re-born. It was a time of great struggle for American Jewry. Rabbi Abba Hillel Silver,

Communal Activity; Frustration and Fulfillment

president of the Zionist Emergency Council, was our national leader, giving guidance and direction to the local Zionist councils throughout the country.

Rabbi Silver himself worked like an electrically charged dynamo. He demanded that local councils follow directions without question and without arguments. I do not know what the other councils did but we in Detroit followed instructions to the letter, no matter how difficult.

We sometimes thought a specific action was unnecessary and not worth the great effort that had to go into it but, in the end, after all the discussion, someone would say: "We are like soldiers in a war. We cannot ignore the instructions." With renewed courage and fresh energy we threw ourselves once again into the battle.

I recall on one occasion we received a directive to obtain a letter from the Governor of Michigan to President Truman in favor of the proposal that Great Britain admit 100,000 Jews into Palestine. As it happened, we had gotten just such a letter from the Governor several weeks before. We did it with great difficulty and didn't see the practicability of getting a second such letter. I went to Cleveland to talk to Rabbi Silver. After some introductory amenities I came to the reason for my visit. He knitted his heavy eyebrows over his gloomy countenance and said:

"What? You think it is too much work? I say that to see the Governor twice in two weeks is not too much! We will see every Governor, every Senator, every Congressman every month, every week, every day if necessary. If you are a good Zionist you will do it."

I left his office feeling as if I had just been doused with a pail of ice water, not so much because of what he had said but how he said it. I returned to Detroit and carried through our mission.

Later, when our struggle became more intense, I realized how correct Rabbi Silver had been.

The members of the local Zionist Council divided the work among themselves. Each became a committee of one to carry out a specific task. Each had to recruit into his committee others who could aid in the work. I think it is fitting at this point to mention some individuals who did very good work for the council: Philip Slomovitz, editor of the weekly *Detroit Jewish News,* who had been a close friend of the late Senator Arthur Vandenberg who was a Republican and, for a time, Chairman of the Foreign Relations Committee; Rabbi Leon Fram, Lawrence Crohn and the late Rabbi Morris Adler, who aside from other attributes, was an excellent speaker.

We carried on an intensive propaganda campaign among the Protestant churches, the labor unions, in both Houses of the State Legislature and in the City Council of Detroit. We had people who were close to the Mayor and the Governor and we paid many visits to our Senators and Congressmen.

At first I was astounded at the ignorance of many of our politicians on Zionism and Palestine. With the exception of Senator Vandenberg and Representative Dingel, there were few who knew anything about our problems in the Holy Land. The two men, however, were very helpful.

The Zionist Emergency Council convened national conferences in Washington, D.C. two or three times a year. Delegates representing local councils throughout the country attended. There were speeches and a review of the situation by the late Rabbi Silver. This he followed with instructions on the kind of pleas to bring to our Senators and Representatives. Afterwards we split up and each went to see the Representatives and Senators from his state.

I will never forget how I felt the first time I went on

such a mission. I was terribly nervous and insecure; I shook like a leaf. Thus I was pleasantly surprised at the warm reception I received from Representative Dingel whose district in Detroit was inhabited mainly by Jews, including me. His secretary telephoned him at the House of Representatives and told him I was there. He came immediately. When he heard why I had come, he said that it would be more practical if he were to arrange for all the Michigan House members to convene at his office and I could talk to all of them at once instead of wearing myself out visiting each one separately. I was overjoyed at his suggestion.

Not all the Michigan Congressmen came. Several were too busy. A few were openly opposed to us. But the majority came. They knew nothing about the Palestine question. I made a brief presentation of the issues. This was followed by questions and answers. The outcome was an agreement that all those present would write a letter to President Truman on our behalf. They did so.

Senator Vandenburg had always been a friend of Zionism. I once called on him at a time when the Senate was working night and day to prevent a strike by the railroad workers. He notified me through his son, who was also his secretary, that he wanted to see me and that I should wait until he could leave the Senate floor. I waited around Washington for three days before I was able to see him.

The day came. I was told the Senator would see me at 2 o'clock. Promptly on time he came out and led me to a room reserved for the President on those few occasions when he visits the Senate. We spoke for two hours. He did most of the talking. I soon gathered that he was familiar with all the ramifications of the Palestine question. I could add nothing. I also realized that we had a good friend in him and that he would do everything to help us.

But there was also a disappointment. I learned that he was opposed to the "Biltmore Program" providing for the creation of a Jewish State and felt that the resolution at the Zionist conference in the Biltmore Hotel in New York calling for the creation of a Jewish State was weakening the campaign to annul the British White Paper against Jewish immigration into Palestine.

Senator Vandenberg thought it would be wiser if the American Zionists abandoned the Biltmore program. I tried to explain to him that it was England that had thrown down the challenge. If England had not issued the White Paper, most Zionists would have been satisfied merely to bring the homeless Jews into Palestine and that they would help them to buy land and settle there. But now that Great Britain was enforcing the provisions of the White Paper in so brutal a manner, we could do no less than go all out for a Jewish State! We were prepared to raise the question before a world tribunal at the peace table.

At that moment, I continued, there was no sense in appealing to such a tribunal for increased immigration into Palestine. I also told him that we could no longer rely on England or place any faith in a pact with her. The White Paper was proof of how little England was to be trusted.

So, I argued, we must demand a Jewish State and solve the Jewish problem once and for all.

The Senator did not reply to my arguments. At that point, a page came into the chamber to call him to the floor where a vote was about to be taken. I had the feeling that I did not convince him.

Much different was the meeting with the second Senator from Michigan, Homer Ferguson. He knew little about Zionism or the Palestine question. He was courteous but much too preoccupied with domestic problems. He did not

Communal Activity; Frustration and Fulfillment 241

show much interest in Palestine. Nevertheless he asked me to visit him the following day.

When I arrived at the Senator's office, he sat down and dictated a letter to President Truman in support of our demands. He handed me a copy when it was typed. On another occasion, he was visited by Rabbi Fram, an acquaintance of many years. Rabbi Fram later reported that Senator Ferguson was friendly to the Zionist idea. After that we were able to count Senator Ferguson as one of our friends.

I visited Washington on numerous occasions in connection with my Zionist work. The last time I saw Senator Vandenberg was right after World War II. He was about to leave for a conference in Paris. We thought there was a possibility the Palestine question would come up. A group of six Zioinsts arranged a luncheon in honor of the Senator. We thought he would talk about Palestine but instead he spoke about the Soviet Union and about the world situation in general.

The Senator warned that we must stop the Soviet Union at all costs. To my question whether Palestine was indeed on the agenda, he replied that something of much greater importance was being dealt with and that Palestine was but a tiny dot on the globe. I asked again, what would happen if other delegates would bring up the Palestine question? What plans did the Americans have in such an eventuality? He showed his impatience:

"We have a lot at stake," he said.

To this I replied, "This means that a second Munich can take place in Paris and in this instance the Jews would be offered up for sacrifice."

He rose from his chair and said, "My record as a friend of the Jews is an open book."

"Up to now words sufficed," I said. "But now we must have deeds."

I realized that I was not being very diplomatic and I have had many sleepless nights because of this flaw in my character. I asked myself if I was right to act the way I did. Did I help the cause, or did I, God forbid, injure it?

The liberal Protestant ministers backed us all the way. On several occasions, they invited me to their churches where, incidentally, I did not feel very much at home. But when I was invited to meet at an informal gathering of ten or twelve ministers and their wives at the home of one of the ministers then I felt very much at home and was able to speak easily and freely. We organized many such intimate parlor meetings among the clergy. One of our Zionist workers would give an introductory talk and afterwards the Jewish question in general came up for free and full discussion.

I was surprised at how little they knew about Jews and Jewish problems.

PRESS AND RADIO

AS I HAVE SAID THERE WERE THREE ENGlish daily newspapers, none of them friendly to the Jews. We approached the editors and publishers several times in an attempt to get more objective reports. We agreed that the Zionist Council would issue statements from time to time and that the papers would publish them.

They didn't. And on those few occasions when they did print something, it was usually distorted. In the end we stopped sending them statements.

When two British sergeants were killed in Palestine, the papers carried the story, with photographs, on their front pages, not once but several times. News of British attacks on Jewish villages, on the other hand, were usually reported in a few lines somewhere near the back of the paper.

I went to see the editor-in-chief of one of the newspapers but was not even given the courtesy of an interview. A member of the editorial staff who happened to be Jewish, came out to talk to me. I said to him, "Your paper claims to be impartial. Do you call this impartial reporting of the news, to feature the death of two British sergeants on the front page three days in a row and to bury the story of British attacks on Jewish villages in the back of the paper?"

After a long and heated discussion, it was agreed that the Zionist Council would prepare an article on the situation in Palestine and the paper would publish it in full, without editing. We prepared the article and sent it in.

In the meantime, the situation changed. Other aspects of the Palestine situation had become more urgent. Ten days later, the story appeared, considerably shortened; many of the main points were left out, in spite of their promise.

As for the radio stations, the situation was even worse. One station was owned by a man named Richardson. It was blatantly anti-Jewish. The other two big stations, although not anti-Jewish, were very far from sympathetic to our cause. We could utilize only two small radio stations which carried commercial Jewish programs—and we did so as much as possible.

MASS MEETINGS
AND LABOR ORGANIZATIONS

WE MADE GREAT USE OF MASS MEETINGS. We organized two kinds, one for Jewish audiences and one for the general public, Jewish and non-Jewish. To the latter we would invite prominent non-Jewish speakers. These usually drew fair-sized audiences, about 20 per cent of them non-Jews. We even organized one such mass rally in the open at the foot of City Hall.

The meetings for Jewish audiences were slightly more intimate in character. It was important that we keep the Jewish community informed of developments and keep their interest and support.

The two labor movements, the CIO and the AFL helped us whenever we asked them to. Their leaders were always ready to speak at our meetings and offer their support. But we had trouble with the leftwing groups. They wanted to become involved in Zionist work but we were afraid that their participation would create the impression that the entire Zionist movement was red.

The radicals criticized the Zionist movement charging it was not doing enough. They wanted us to call street demonstrations and take other militant steps. We could not stop them entirely because that would have created dissatisfaction in the community; all the Jews were bitterly anti-British and many were ready to listen to the militant demands of the leftists.

Somehow we managed to satisfy the left wing groups without creating the impression that we were a left wing movement.

THE JEWISH COMMUNITY COUNCIL

ALTHOUGH THE PRESIDENT OF THE JEWish Community Council was an anti-Zionist and the executive director was non-Zionist, the Community Council cooperated fully with the Zionist Council. Without its cooperation we could never have accomplished as much as we did. The Community Council had all the technical resources, the names and addresses of all local Jewish organizations and their representatives and an office staff to do the day to day work.

The continuing battle against the British in Palestine had become sharper. The demands of the Zionist Emergency Council in New York were greater and greater. It called for greater efforts to contact Senators and Congressmen, Governors and state legislators, the Mayors and members of the City Council. We were asked to mobilize the press, the church and the various clubs. In short, we were required to make use of every form of public opinion of whatever value.

I did not do all the work myself but I made sure that anyone who undertook a specific task, should carry it out. This meant meetings every evening, meetings during the day and luncheon meetings. I soon became exhausted. I was tired of pleading with non-Jews to put in a good word for us. I recognized the helplessness and humiliation of our position. Nevertheless I went on with our work. I was constantly aware that in Palestine the Jews endured experiences much worse than mine and that my own labors were as child's play compared with theirs.

I continued to plead for and demand resolutions, letters and telegrams on our behalf to the President, our Senators, Congressmen and to other public officials. I had to tolerate many irksome individuals. I received many anonymous letters and telephone calls from strangers who refused to give their names. Many people called with advice on what the Jews in the Holy Land should do and what the Jewish Agency should do.

When the Arabs attacked the newly born State of Israel, the telephone calls increased in number. One Jew in particular made my life miserable with his insistence that I contact Prime Minister Ben Gurion immediately and persuade him to use airplanes against the Arabs. On one occasion I lost my patience and asked him to stop bothering me. To this he replied, "I am warning you that if Israel loses the war, you will pay with your head."

In the beginning, I would get very angry and hang up on on the callers. After a while, when I had an opportunity to view the situation more calmly, I thought to myself that if we had people who were so concerned with the struggle for a Jewish state, we must surely win.

For me the creation of the State of Israel was almost anti-climactic. I was overcome with emotion—and disbelief. To think that I had lived to see the realization of this dream that we had been working for for so long! I never dreamt throughout the years of work and struggle that I would actually see our work come to fruition.

At the same time, I was concerned lest the proclamation of statehood be somewhat premature. Neither the world nor the Jews had been prepared for such a momentous step. I kept my fears to myself. I said nothing, not even to my wife or children. I was afraid that I might infect others with my doubts. I realized that now was the time for us to redouble our efforts and help the newborn state.

Shortly afterward, a number of Israeli representatives began to appear in our midst, usually at night. They spoke obliquely, not directly, in guarded language in which the meaning was only hinted at. They wanted to contact "someone" who could provide "something." I got on the telephone although I had to awaken people and established contact. The Israelis were in the market to buy everything they needed—but they had no money. Additional people had to be seen to arrange for financing but that too is a separate

Communal Activity; Frustration and Fulfillment 247

chapter. Besides it is not possible to go into detail about those frantic efforts here and now.

On the 14th day of June, 1948, we celebrated Israel's proclamation of statehood. It was an impressive celebration somewhere in the center of Detroit under the open sky. Some 25,000 to 30,000 people were there. The Jewish community of Detroit had never before in its history experienced such a gathering. Up to then our mass meetings were mainly protest demonstrations against unfriendly acts or to bring to the attention of the non-Jewish public certain injustices against the Jewish people.

This time, however, the Jews massed out of happiness, to express their joy, to join their heroic brothers in Israel in a great and glorious celebration. Tears streamed down my cheeks as I sat on the platform, tears of delight and elation to have seen this day and to have been able to play a role, however small, in that historic event! It was a moment of profound, spiritual exhilaration.

Some days later, an acquaintance stopped me on the street and asked, "How come, Laikin, that you were not the chairman of the celebration?"

It led me to think. Really, how did it happen that I was not the chairman? The committee probably felt that my command of the English language was not what it ought to have been, that my accent was too heavy. But my English was good enough when I led our struggle! My accent was not objectionable when I presided at meetings where Senators spoke!

Well, never mind, I have never attached too much importance to honors or publicity in my activities. I was happy enough to see our work crowned with success and gratified that I had been to some extent helpful in achieving it.

A JEWISH COMMUNITY THEATER

A YOUNG MAN, RECENTLY ARRIVED IN the United States, came to our city. I believe the year was 1940. I don't know what brought him to Detroit. In any event, he soon became a frequent visitor in our home. My daughters, too, were happy to see him. He was intelligent and was well informed in Jewish matters. His name was Mark Uveeler. (Mr. Uveeler is now Executive Director of the Memorial Foundation for Jewish Culture).

I must confess though, that I was not at all impressed with Mr. Uveeler at our first meeting. His conversation was full of compliments. The Litvak in me was revolted. It sounded to me like empty flattery. When I got to know him better, however, I realized that he was sincere. The Pole within him was revealed in his tongue. He, poor fellow, happened to meet a cold Litvak!

I began to "examine the bottom of his hay wagon," so to speak, to learn the reason for his presence in Detroit. He placed before me a weighty set of plans to establish a Jewish community theater in Detroit. When he discussed the subject, he became so overcome with enthusiasm that he was hardly able to talk. The words just tumbled out of his mouth, sometimes unintelligibly.

A committee was being formed. I must join the commitee Mr. Uveeler pleaded and demanded. My name and business attainments would add importance to the committee, he said, and without me the committee would come to naught.

I listened and thought to myself, was he really talking about me? Since when had I become such a big shot? Somehow I was not pleased by what he said. I was suspicious of his lavish praise. I tried to wiggle out in a good-humored manner. Later, when I was alone, I thought of it again. The more I thought, the more I agreed that it would be a good thing if we were to have a Jewish theater in Detroit.

The Yiddish theater in America was going from bad to worse. Perhaps there was merit in Uveeler's plan! I would talk about it to others who shared my interest in Yiddish culture. I telephoned Max Holtzman and learned that he was already familiar with the plan. He was enthusiastically in favor and was already looking forward to the staging of the first Yiddish production. I knew that Max was a responsible communal worker, not one to go off half cocked. I put to him a Biblical phrase, "Who are they that shall go?" (Exodus X, 8). He came back with a list of names of Detroit people well known for their interest in cultural activities. I will not list their names here for fear that a lapse of memory may cause me to omit the names of some who were active and whose omission would be a grave injustice.

The next time Uveeler visited our home, I told him that I would serve on his committee. He was overjoyed. After a number of meetings it was decided:

1. To create a fund of $100,000 to assure the existence of a Jewish community theater for several years.

2. To draw people from all sections of the Jewish community into the effort.

The Sholom Aleichem Folk Institute, the Workmen's Circle, the Poale Zion and the Jewish National Worker's Alliance (Farband) were to be the backbone of the project. We also planned to draw into our work, the landsmanshaften, the benefit societies, the Yiddish schools, the B'nai B'rith lodges, and just plain unaffiliated people who were interested in having a Yiddish theater in their city.

Within a few months, we created such a stir as the Jewish people of the city had never seen before. Even rabbis,

Orthodox and Conservative, and plain synagogue members joined the movement. They were active in publicizing the campaign and working for it. In a relatively short time, we managed to collect almost the entire amount—in pledges; about 10 per cent had been paid in and this just about covered operating expenses.

According to the plan, we were to engage eleven actors and pay them a guaranteed salary for 48 weeks a year. They were to perform twice weekly for adults and once a week, on Saturday afternoons, for the children. A committee would choose the plays. In addition, the troupe would perform twice weekly for the landsmanshaft societies. True, many of the landsmanshaften organized their own cultural evenings but in most instances they were not very satisfactory.

We also hoped to establish a dramatic studio for young people. The plans were beautiful but when we opened negotiations with the Hebrew Actors' Union, we were faced with many difficulties. It was impossible to come to an agreement with the Union manager, Reuben Guskin. As a man of the business world, I assumed that Guskin wanted to get higher salaries and better working conditions for his members and that it was only a matter of negotiating an agreement. However, it soon became clear to me that this was not the case.

The salaries we offered to pay were higher than those paid to the Yiddish actors in New York. He was simply opposed to the whole idea of a Yiddish community theater in Detroit. It is difficult to understand how a man of such a reactionary bent could have become the leader and set the policy of the Hebrew Actors' Union. Perhaps it was related to Mark Uveeler. He had been director of the Yiddish Actors' Union in Poland. He was also the initiator of the Detroit theater. In a private chat, Guskin let it drop that he would never permit "greenhorns" to bring new forms and new ideas into the American Yiddish theater.

Guskin was a man of narrow horizons. He looked on the matter strictly from the viewpoint of the union official. Perhaps he was right in demanding that we deposit a full year's pay for the troupe. He did not believe in our idea, had no confidence in it, and wanted to safeguard his members. When we decided to go ahead and do it he threw new barriers in our path. Possibly the worst was his demand to have the last word on which actors we should hire.

Throughout the long months of our negotiations, only one writer, Joel Enteen, a literary and drama critic and an educator, wrote about our plan. With all due respect to the memory of this man, I must say that he did us no favor. He made of the hope an accomplished fact and praised it to the highest heavens. We were not yet sure of our troupe, what we would produce, how often, where—and a number of other unresolved questions had to be answered.

Joel Enteen had cloaked his own dreams and hopes with our plan and transformed it into reality. In the meantime we still had not come to an understanding with Guskin. Our committee decided to send a delegation to New York. We wanted to have a face-to-face discussion with Guskin and we wanted also to have present at the meeting, Shlomo Mendelson, an eminent Socialist writer, and Nahum Nathan Chanin, a leading figure in the Workmen's Circle. Perhaps with their assistance, we would be able to reach an understanding with the evasive Mr. Guskin.

Max Holtzman and I were chosen as the delegation and we had our meeting. We appealed to Chanin to prevail upon Mr. Guskin not to set such harsh demands. We talked for several hours but nothing came of it. It was one of those conversations that went round and round and came out nowhere; it had no beginning and no end.

The very clever Mr. Chanin smiled more than he spoke. Several times he said, "You stubborn fellow, let me say something." But he said virtually nothing, at least nothing that had any value. In the end we accomplished nothing.

Our second task was to see several Yiddish writers, explain our project to them and get them to look into the whole matter and write about it. Where we were right they could say so and where we fell short they could criticize us. We were content to bring the whole matter into open discussion.

We ourselves weren't all that certain our plan would succeed and we were ready to listen to constructive criticism.

We were hopeful that two things would crystalize; what a theater of this kind shoud be, and that public opinion should force Guskin to end his obstruction.

We went to see one of the great Yiddish writers. Holtzman had assured me that he would be sympathetic. He was, after all, a great literary figure and was also a playwright. Like other authors he no doubt wanted to see his plays alive on a stage instead of sleeping between covers on a library shelf.

He was the first of the writers we met. Holtzman explained the problem to him, outlined our plan and asked his advice. We impressed on him that it was not a commercial venture. We were not interested in making money on the project but to stimulate Yiddish culture. On the contrary, we said we were willing to spend thousands of dollars of our own money to make up shortages that were bound to occur in the budget.

The writer asked us, "So, what do you want of me?"

We told him we wanted him to write about our plans

and our difficulties, especially those with the Hebrew Actors' Union. To this the great man replied, "What does it matter to me what the Jews of Detroit wish to do?"

I sprang up from my chair as if I had been stung by a bee. I asked him bitterly, "And when you write a book here in New York, why do you come to Detroit seeking funds to have it published? Why must we alone bear the burden of encouraging Yiddish culture? Are you, the writers, exempt from that responsibility? Since when are there partitions between the Jews of New York and the Jews of Detroit that exempts a New Yorker from being concerned about Yiddish culture in Detroit?"

The writer did not answer my arguments. Instead he abused me. We stood there face to face on the verge of coming to blows. I let out all my frustrations and accumulated anger on him. He replied in kind. Holtzman tried to stop it but failed.

This all happened in the lobby of a big hotel and as our voices grew louder, we drew quite a bit of attention. The hotel manager came over to us and pleaded with us to calm down. Eventually we did.

Many years have elapsed since then. I often think of that incident. I berate myself for having spoken to him so bitterly. He was, after all, a great writer, creative thinker, highly intellectual, ethical, and moral. But when I recall the cruelty of his words, "What does it matter to me what the Jews of Detroit wish to do," I feel my gorge rising again. No! Such words could not be met with silence or polite phrases.

It left such a bitter taste in my mouth that I refused to see any more of our literary luminaries. We returned to Detroit and began to dismantle our project. It was a beautiful dream. I think about it still. True, it would have given us many anxious moments but it would also have given us great pleasure and pride. But the dream faded away. What a shame! What a waste!

BUSINESS—
CAUGHT IN A BUREAUCRATIC MAZE

BUSINESS IN GENERAL WAS GOOD FOR most of the decade and my own business benefited from the general prosperity. But there were problems. It was difficult to get merchandise, so it was easy to make sales—if one had the goods. I didn't always have the goods. Right after the Japanese attack on Pearl Harbor in December, 1941, Detroit was declared a "critical" city as far as the labor force was concerned. This meant a freeze on the number of workers one could hire. He could not employ more workers than he had before the United States was attacked.

I could not hire the additional workers I wanted to open a second shift. To this problem was added the loss of my best workers. They either went into the Army or they took higher paying jobs in other factories. Our industry paid lower wages than those in the automobile plants and many of the workers went there, especially as help became scarce.

After the outbreak of the war, the Government permitted those industries that were engaged in war work to raise their wages. The others were controlled. As a result, I lost still more employees. Every day I had to recruit workers right from the street, mainly the down and outers who had not done a decent day's work in years. My production suffered. I had to do the heaviest work myself. My new employees wouldn't do much work. There were days when I felt I would collapse. My shop suffered. The machines broke down from neglect. No one, with the exception of my foreman, the engineer and one worker, was interested. All three of my loyal employees had been with me for 25 years. They felt like family to me.

The other workers were shirkers. True the wages were not high. I filed an application with the Wages and Hours Board for permission to increase the wages but my request was denied, not once but three times. With the fourth application I was given permission to raise wages by five cents per hour instead of the 15 cents I had requested.

There were times when I seriously considered closing my business altogether. It sapped my strength and I could see no way out of the straits I was in. I could have hired more employees and paid higher salaries illegally, as others were doing. But I had decided when our country became involved in the war that I would not do anything illegal. It was especially sad for me then that I should have been accused of violating the Wages and Hours Law.

This is how it happened. The Wages and Hours Board had issued a ruling that extra wages could be paid for increased production. As a result I negotiated an agreement with the union to pay bonuses to the workers as they achieved higher production levels. The union had assured me that I did not require specific permission from the Board for this arrangement. Three months later I saw a circular issued by the Wages and Hours Board explaining just such a provision. It also stated that permission from the Board was required.

I filed an application immediately. It took ten months for my application to go through channels. Finally I was notified that my application had been approved. At the same time, however, I was charged with having operated under such a plan for 13 months without permission. I was dumbfounded. I was terrified that the newspapers would publish stories about the president of the Detroit Zionist Council violating the Wages and Hours Law. I was afraid also that people would think that I had underpaid my employees instead of the other way around.

If I were found guilty the actual fine would have been small. However, the entire amount I paid out in wages would not have been deductible as a business expense. I was disgusted with the bureaucrats. Why hadn't they specified when they announced the bonus plan that permission was required? Why did they withhold permission for ten months before acting? Why did they grant that permission with one hand and accuse me of violating the law with the other hand?

Their argument was, "You should have asked first before instituting the bonus plan."

I went through months of anxiety. At a hearing of a committee containing representatives of the Government, the workers, and manufacturers, the accusation against me was thrown out. Thus ended my first clash with the bureaucrats.

The fates had decreed that I would meet with many such bureaucrats during the war, but not as one accused, rather as an equal among equals. Often I was the accuser. This I will deal with in later chapters.

A BATTLE AGAINST BUREAUCRACY AND THE BLACK MARKET

I WAS ELECTED PRESIDENT OF THE SANItary Industry of America early in 1943. This was the national association of the wiping cloth industry. Wiping cloths may be either used or new. They are washed out and sterilized, cut to size, and sold to factories. The workers use the cloths to wipe their hands, their machines and the products they work on. Since the United States was deeply involved in a war for its very life and black markets were appearing in many industries, I said in my acceptance speech that I would not permit our industry to develop a black market. I warned that as soon as I would learn that members of our association were charging higher prices than those set by the Government, or if they violated any other law, I would notify the authorities and call for an investigation. I would spare no one.

I ended my address by saying that if they did not like my attitude, they could select another president. I wanted them to know at the outset what they could expect from me. I was re-elected three times and during that period our industry was not once touched with a black market scandal. In addition, we doubled our membership during that period.

That is not to say there were no chiselers, people who were not willing to bend the rules a bit. There were some transactions that weren't strictly kosher but these were the exceptions.

I gained many enemies. At each convention, twice a year, I condemned sharp practices on the line and just over the line of the law. While I did not mention names, those who were guilty knew well enough whom I meant.

Shortly after the United States entered the war, the Government set up regulations for commerce and industry. Otherwise serious shortages and runaway inflation would have ensued. Each industry set up a committee with which the Government officials were to consult on matters relating to that industry.

I was a member of two committees, the Office of Price Administration (OPA) and the War Production Board. Our industry was represented by ten members. I, as president, served as chairman of the committee. Meetings took place in Washington, usually once a month, oftener if necessary.

I had a clash with the Government representatives at one of the meetings. I demanded that both committees meet on the same day, or at least one day after another so that the members would not have to travel to Washington twice when once would suffice.

It was a reasonable request. Yet we had to fight for it. Their argument was that they were two separate committees and that each would have to conduct its business independently. I learned that it was, for them, a matter of prestige. In the end they agreed to our request.

The first session included representatives of the OPA, the War Production Board and the Salvage Department. There were also representatives of other interested Government agencies present; the Navy, Army and Air Force. Each group had its own stenographer, some even their legal advisers. The representative of the U.S. Navy took the floor. He said:

"I don't know why, perhaps it's because the wiping cloth industry belongs to a specific group of people, but it is a fact that this group refuses to help in the war effort."

He said that he had bought millions of pounds of wiping cloth but that he was not getting any shipments. There were sixteen cruisers tied up in various ports unable to sail for important rendez-vous with other warships because they did not have the necessary "wipers," as we called the cloths.

Each cruiser required 16,000 pounds of wipers before it could leave port, and "people belonging to a specific group" were holding the cruisers back by not delivering the necessary wipers. He asked the lawyers to do something about it, to punish those who were guilty.

He spoke at great length, pouring out pitch and sulphur and thundering against us. The anti-Semitic nature of his attack was obvious. I got to my feet. I started calmly and easily. I explained that it was not necessary to go far from the "specific people" to find the guilty parties, that one was right there in the room; it was he himself!

Firstly, I continued, he had "not yet eaten a pound of salt in his lifetime" and so was hardly in a position to make such wild accusations. Secondly, I asked:

"How does it happen that you give orders for millions of pounds of wipers to someone who had never been in the industry and did not even possess the necessary machinery or equipment to produce the wipers? We have many factories with machinery and equipment which operate only eight hours a day but can still produce huge quantities of the cloths but you did not place any orders with their owners.

"Is it outright stupidity, ignorance, or something worse? How is it that when you failed to receive the merchandise from the man you gave the order for a million pounds, you gave him still another order for more than a million pounds? I believe the Senate would be interested in the matter."

The chairman tried to stop me but I stubbornly maintained my right to speak. I pointed out to the chairman that he should have stopped the fleet officer when he made his wild charges but did not. Then at least he could let me defend my industry without interruption. The room was charged with tension. The chairman recessed the meeting for lunch.

In the restaurant, several members of our committee of ten criticized me for having spoken so sharply. A Jew should remain silent and swallow insults. This was what they were counselling. Strangely enough the two non-Jewish members of the committee sided with me.

When the meeting reconvened, I asked for the floor. The chairman thought a while and then recognized me. I changed my tone and said:

"We have come here on behalf of our industry to do everything we possibly can to help the war effort. We would like to hear from the armed forces how many wipers they will need each and every month. We promise that each branch will get all the wipers it needs.

"But we will require certain things, mainly the cooperation of the Government. We would like you to nullify contradictory regulations. For instance, one of the regulations provides that the wipers be washed in caustic soda and another regulation prohibits the use of caustic soda for washing wipers. There have been other instances where one branch of the Government requests an item prohibited by another branch.

"Thus a merchant must face the choice of violating a regulation or pay a fine, possibly go to jail."

The mood of the meeting changed with my statement. We fell to the task and quickly arranged to provide the Government with all the wipers it required. I remained in Washington for two days, calling various merchants in my industry, arranging for shipments. Within five days the Government got half a million pounds of wipers delivered to various ports. I sat at the telephone in the Bureau of the Navy making my calls around the country. I spoke to the dealers and instructed them to ship specified amounts to the ports nearest them or face the alternative of having their factories confiscated as such an order had already been drafted.

I served on the Government committee throughout the war. I met a variety of officials and officers. Most of them had previously been small businessmen or merchants. By and large, they had little or no success in the business world so they grabbed at the Government jobs paying between $6,000 and $8,000. Most of them were devoted to their jobs but were narrow in their thinking. They were also afraid to move without the approval of a higher official. This could be very frustrating. A relatively small and unimportant matter could be tied up for months waiting for a decision.

Some of them were suspicious of the suppliers. They were sure the suppliers were out to cheat them. Some of them simply were lazy and covered their procrastination with bureaucratic hindrances. Worst were the young pups, the very young bureaucrats who were eager enough but managed to do everything topsy-turvy. They were the young lawyers and so-called experts who thought they knew everything when, in fact, they knew very little about the industry. They were difficult to get along with. It was difficult to convince them that what they wanted was either impossible or impractical, both for the industry and for the Government. The hindrances, obstructions and difficulties placed in our path by the Government and their well-meaning and ill-meaning bureaucrats were unbelievable.

To regulate an industry, it may be necessary to restrict it, but certainly not to strangle it. The industry should continue to function and produce at a maximum level while, at the same time, using smaller quantities of material and less manpower. It was also important that no advantages be given to one industry in favor of another.

I was convinced that the Government, despite some shortcomings, carried through the gigantic task satisfactorily. When the definitive history of World War II is written, most of the credit for the American victory will, of course, go to the soldiers, the young men from the farms and factories and offices who never dreamt they would become soldiers, let alone heroes.

Second in line for credit come the generals, the officers who planned and carried the war through to a successful conclusion. In the early years they thought mainly in terms of defense. Later, however, they were to carry through massive invasions that will remain in world history as wonders of military art.

Third in line are the big industries which managed, in a miraculously short time, to make the changeover from civilian to war production. How this was accomplished, very few outsiders can comprehend, but it was done, and without seriously dislocating civilian production.

Fourth came the small businessmen, those whose names will appear nowhere in the annals of World War II. But they too contributed their share. Had the small businessmen broken down, they would have seriously impeded the war effort. In this category are the grocers, cleaners, repair men and other merchants of many and diverse kinds. Most of them were not organized and not recognized by the Government. They had trouble getting gasoline, tires, workers, materials, etc. Their wives had to take the place of workers, putting in extra long hours to fill the community needs. Thanks to these unsung heroes, our daily lives continued on a more or less even keel.

A dark page in this history—if it is written honestly—

will deal with the role of the unionized worker, not all, but a substantial number. I am referring to those who took advantage of the war situation and the shortage of help by failing to do an honest day's work.

I saw them in the automobile factories. There were instances where two or three men had to be hired for the very same job. One of the men would take care of the machine and the other two would be in the smoking room, either smoking or playing dice. Absenteeism was extremely high. No one knew how many workers would show up the next day. Production planning was almost impossible. To assure production, many employers had to hire twice the number of workers he needed.

True, the manufacturers did not lose by this arrangement, the Government did. The manufacturers received Government contracts on a cost plus basis, that is, the Government paid them approximately 10 per cent above their costs of production. On this basis, the manufacturer could not lose. The greater the costs, the greater the profit.

This meant expenditures for the Government but no one worried about that. However, this waste of manpower created, or aggravated a shortage of manpower. Many industries suffered as a result. I visited many factories and could see for myself the problems created by material and manpower shortages. I saw things no Government agency or investigator could possibly see.

There were other distractions, other pin pricks to disturb. One such was a failure, deliberate or accidental, of a non-Jewish official to comment on the fate of the Jews in Nazi-occupied Europe.

At a convention of our industry, in Cleveland in 1944, Mayor Lausche, the future Governor and then Senator of Ohio, delivered an address on the importance of industries to cooperate with other industries to help the war effort. He called on individuals to ignore their personal interests and concentrate on only one thing, the winning of the war.

To impress on us the character of the war and the nature of Nazism, Mr. Lausche, of Czech descent, referred only to the Lidice massacre. He said not a single word about the Nazi crimes against the Jews although it was quite well known by then that the Nazis were annihilating millions of them. I resented this omission bitterly. Mr. Lausche was well aware that fully 90 per cent of the people in the audience were Jews, yet he remained stone silent about the Nazi depravities against the Jewish people.

As president of the industry association, I thanked him for having come to address us. In my speech of thanks, I described some of the grim events that were being described more and more fully in the press. I observed that we Jews knew quite well who and what the Nazis were but that it was important for the non-Jewish Americans to know about the sufferings of the Jewish people.

After the meeting several of my Jewish colleagues criticized me for being tactless.

MY DAUGHTERS

AS I MENTIONED PREVIOUSLY, WE HAVE four daughters, Pnina, Beth-Sheva, Judith and Shulamith. Although they were born of the same parents, brought up in the same household, in an almost identical cultural environment, they are four very different people, with different characters and differing views on life.

Pnina is a dreamer, with an artistic bent. She was not very diligent as a student but possessed a great desire for knowledge and had a great love for music. She is tall and slender, with black hair. She is beautiful. Incidentally, all of my daughters are beautiful so if I do not repeat the adjective with each one of them, do not think I am stingy with praise.

Pnina spent only one year at the University of Wisconsin in Madison, and then left to get married. She chose a fine young man, a graduate of the university but not versed in Jewish subjects or traditions. That is not to say he was opposed to Jewish studies, it was just that his parents did not stress Jewish studies when he was growing up.

I took the young man into my business where he stayed for two and a half years. It did not work out. He did not like the business. Also, his parents lived in Baltimore and his mother was anxious to have her son near her. I suspect that this played a large part in his negative attitude toward my business.

His mother promised him great fortunes from the family business which they would transfer to him. Nothing came of it, of course, but the young couple moved there. Pnina had to live with her in-laws. My daughter is not quarrelsome but there was scarcely a moment of peace between Pnina and her mother-in-law. Pnina became ill, so much so that I was frightened.

It was impossible to get an apartment in Baltimore so Pnina and her husband moved into a small town nearby where they were the only Jewish family. My wife and I were heartsick at our daughter's difficulties but we didn't intervene. We were confident that since Pnina and her husband loved each other, they would find their own way.

In the meantime, my son-in-law and a cousin of his bought a store in another small town. Half the purchase price came from his father and the other half from me even though I was generally opposed to the venture. I did not see any great future in it. My share was supposedly a loan.

My son-in-law could earn a modest living in the business. It certainly would not make him a wealthy man. So he opened an automobile agency. Once again his father and I put up the money. This was successful and now his earnings are substantial.

Pnina and her husband lived in a small town for over three years. There the education she had received stood her in good stead. Her books, music and the Zionist ideals helped her through the difficult days. They were a refuge when life became too bitter. She was now the mother of three children, Moshe, the eldest, Deborah, the middle child, and Abigail, the youngest.

Their home is strictly traditional. Moshe studies in a Talmud Torah. Pnina is a leading member of the local chapter of Hadassah, the Women's Zionist Organization, and is also chairman of its Committee on Cultural Activities. My son-in-law is proud of his wife's Jewishness. Although his mother's home is non-kosher, he wants his own home to be traditionally Jewish. After years of disappointment and aggravation, we now derive great pleasure and satisfaction from Pnina's life.

Beth-Sheva, a university graduate, won a $1,000 scholarship in dramatic art. She spent a year at the University of Indiana and another year at New York University where she earned a Master's Degree in Dramatics. My wife and I were unhappy over her choice of studies but we did not interfere. She remained in New York for a year after school, then returned to Detroit where she conducted a drama class at a Jewish center and also gave private lessons.

But the theater had magical powers and when she was offered a position on the stage in Ann Arbor, the university town, she accepted. Beth-Sheva, like her sister, Pnina, studied in a Jewish school for twelve years. She is familiar with Jewish life. She visited Israel and returned full of enthusiasm. However, her Judaism is secular rather than religious. She has a national awareness but is anti-religious. I keep hoping that her attitude will change in due time and that she too will keep a traditional Jewish home.

Judith is also a university graduate. She won the Avery Hopwood Award for poetry and prose. All her poems and short stories are on Jewish themes. She is the most Jewishly conscious of my daughters. For twelve years she studied at the Labor Zionist Yiddish Farband School. At the university, she and Beth-Sheva took a course in Biblical Hebrew together. They were the only ones who still remained in class at the end of the semester, all the others had dropped out.

During the period of the struggle against England as the mandatory power in Palestine, Judith was very active in "Izfa," (Intercollegiate Zionist Federation of America). She spread the message especially among women's church groups. Judith speaks Yiddish well but can speak Hebrew even better. She often writes to me in Yiddish.

After graduating from the University of Michigan, Judith left for New York to continue her studies at Columbia University. In two years she earned her master's degree in International Affairs. She subsequently got a position with the State Department. She was sent to India where her job was to collect everything published in India, Pakistan, Ceylon and Afghanistan. This took her to most of the cities of those countries.

Judith has a strong character and has a faculty for bending circumstances to her will. She has a great thirst to learn, to know, to see things for herself. It sometimes frightens me. It seems similar to that of a person who fears he does not have too much time and tries to accomplish everything while he can.

In her personal life Judith is very modest, has no desire for fancy clothes, does not use cosmetics and has simple tastes in food. She has a deep love for music and plays the piano quite well. Her friends, Jewish and non-Jewish, and we too, especially love the way she sings Israeli folk songs with the Sephardic pronunciation.

Judith returned from India in 1954. Naturally we missed her very much but realized that we could not hold her back. Twice in her young life, we almost lost her. The first time when she was only a few weeks old. She had an obstruction in her digestive system and was saved by surgery. The second time was when she was seventeen. She fell ill and developed a fever that went up to 108 degrees. My wife and I always felt that her survival at that time was a gift to us.

When it came time to enroll our youngest, Shulamith, in school, my wife was opposed to my entering her in the Farband School. I fought against her but, in the end, she won out. Shulamith studied for ten years in the Sunday School of a Conservative synagogue and four times a week she attended classes in one of the schools of the United Hebrew Schools, a central religious school organization subsidized by the Detroit Federation.

Shulamith did not learn much at the Hebrew school. The subjects were taught in a very dull and unimaginative way. The teacher would ask questions and then supply the answers herself. She lectured incessantly. This, incidentally, was also a shortcoming in the Farband School. English was the language of instruction in the Sunday School. This allowed more time for the teacher to instill in the students a romanticized Judaism rather than Jewishness. The Bible was not taught. The children read Bible stories instead. Thus she gained an

Communal Activity; Frustration and Fulfillment

acquaintance with Jewish legends rather than tradition. Even so the amount of Hebrew she did learn was more than is generally acquired by Jewish girls in America. Shulamith does not know Yiddish at all.

She managed to keep up with her studies, but with difficulty. By the time she reached high school, we had decided that she would not be going to college. However, she changed completely in high school. She suddenly blossomed into a good student. Shulamith enrolled at the University of Michigan to study law, a course that would take seven years to complete.

The most Americanized of my daughters, Shulamith loves baseball. She reads a lot but is not overly fond of music. Amusements play a greater role in her life than they did for her sisters at comparable ages.

My wife, Chana Leah, was always drawn to the General Zionists. She had become a member of Poale Zion because of me. If she had followed her own bent, she would have joined the Mizrachi (religious Zionists). Always inclined toward traditional Judaism, she became even more pious in later years. Her chief activities were in Hadassah (Women's Zionist Organization) and the Jewish National Fund. In addition, she belonged to the women's club of the Yiddish School, the Talmud Torah, the Jewish Home for the Aged and the Hebrew Free Loan Society.

Generally, we were gratified and pleased that all of us, we and our four daughters, were walking the same path. There were no sharp ideological differences among us. Where we did differ, it was only a question of shades of opinion, perhaps more liberal, more conservative, but essentially we agreed. In cultural matters, my wife was more inclined towards music while I showed a preference for my books. That is not to say that she did not read. She read many good books both in Yiddish and in English. On the other hand, my love of books did not keep me from attending concerts with my wife.

There was never a sharp controversy between me and my wife. When it was necessary to come to an important decision, we were almost always able to do so together. But in matters of lesser importance, often very small matters, we frequently reached the point of heated words. Contradictory character traits in each of us collided and this sometimes caused needless heartaches. But in matters of importance, our characters were in complete harmony.

HOW THE WAR AND ITS OUTCOME AFFECTED ME

MANY PEOPLE REALIZED THAT THE FATE of the Jews would be desperate when Hitler came to power but no one ever dreamed that the Nazis would actually annihilate them. Although I always felt that the Germans were capable of launching pogroms against the Jews, I never really believed that the Nazis would carry out the threats they made before they came into power.

I read two Yiddish dailies and many of the more important Yiddish and American-Jewish periodicals. I devoured everything ever written about the Jews in Germany long before the outbreak of the war in 1939. When the Nazis intensified their pogroms and burning of synagogues I felt the ground tremble under my feet, as if the earth itself was beginning to crumble.

I was deeply troubled. The White Paper issued by the British Government restricting Jewish immigration into Palestine was equally depressing. It closed the trap on the Jews and destroyed the last hope of escape. The world looked on and kept silent. Once when I opened my heart to a Christian friend, he tried to reassure me.

"Calm down," he said. "The situation is not as bad as you think. Most of the news stories are only propaganda."

I felt like hitting my head against the wall. Even the good Gentiles refused to face the truth, perhaps because they didn't want to. To accept the situation at its face would mean they would have to do something about it.

The war had begun. The Nazis scored victory after victory. And wherever they came they destroyed the Jewish population. I used to receive letters from my mother who was living at that time with my sister in Mogilev-on-the-Dnieper. Another sister and a brother still lived in Bobruisk. The letters came to me via Japan.

From their letters I realized that they were completely unaware of what the Nazis were doing to the Jews in areas they captured. I did not know what to do. I was afraid to write them about it because it was the time of the Nazi-Soviet pact. If I wrote them it might very well cause them trouble, perhaps even bring accusations of espionage. To remain silent was also bad. At least if they know they could seek relatively greater safety by going deeper into the interior of the Soviet Union.

I could no longer restrain myself. I wrote to my mother urging her to flee and get everyone else in the family to seek safety in the interior, even if it meant going to Siberia. Anything but not to remain in White Russia. To this day I do not know if my warning ever reached her. I heard not a word from them during or after the war. I tried various ways to learn their fate, the Red Cross, the Quakers, the American Jewish Congress and others. One day I received a post card from my older sister, with whom my mother lived. The card bore only my name and the city, Detroit. It had no street address but somehow it came to my door.

My sister wrote that she had returned to Mogilev. From subsequent letters, I learned that my brother Sholem, his wife Rebecca, and their two little children had escaped from Bobruisk to Mogilev and when the Nazis approached Mogilev my sister fled beyond the Ural Mountains. My mother and my brother and his family remained in Mogilev. They could not or did not want to leave the city.

The Nazis occupied Mogilev on Rosh Hashanah, the Jewish New Year, in 1941; they slaughtered the entire Jewish population. Thus did my mother, an elderly woman of 74, my brother, his wife and their daughter and son, perish for the sanctification of God's name. May their memory be blessed. My brother's older son fell in battle. Thus was an entire family obliterated.

My sister lost her older son during the war. Her daughter had no wish to return from the Ural Mountains after the war and married a non-Jew. My sister remained with her younger son and husband. My younger sister in Leningrad with one child, also lost her husband in the war. Through our correspondence, I gathered that they were desperately poor. They had nothing. They did not say so openly. On the contrary, they claimed they had enough food and clothing and were well off. However, they added, "a pair of shoes and an overcoat would be useful."

I was happy that I was in a position to send them things and ease their difficult life. Every one of their letters contained expressions of praise for the "great father," Joseph Stalin, who worries over them and takes care of all the people in the great land. I understood that these words of flattery were the price they had to pay to get their letters through the censors.

At the end of 1948, I wrote them of the outstanding role played by the Soviet delegate to the United Nations in the creation of the State of Israel. In reply my sister wrote that they did not need a Jewish state, that they live well in Russia and that Stalin was their father. She also asked me not to send any more packages since they had all the good things they needed. She ended by saying she wanted no further dealings with me and asked me to stop writing to them.

I was heartbroken but I had to honor her wishes, if they were indeed hers. In any event, I stopped writing and heard from my sister no more. I contribute thousands of dollars to charity each year but there I was, unable to help my own family. I feel in my heart that they needed my help and would have welcomed it. The worst of it was that I might have jeopardized their lives and liberty with my letters. It gives me no rest. God knows what difficulties my carelessness may have caused them.

The news that my mother and my brother Sholem and his family had perished was a severe blow. I had read much in these days about the atrocities committed by the Nazis. I thought I had become hardened to their bestiality. But when I learned of my mother's death, and my brother's and his family's the pain was almost more than I could bear. I am still reading about our martyrs, drawn to them like a drunkard to whiskey even though he knows it will do him harm. Even now when my strength has ebbed (my illness does not permit me to become upset or excited), still I continue to read about the holocaust, the Third Destruction.

I tried to push those morbid thoughts from my mind by plunging deeper into my business and into community activity. I drove myself relentlessly, not stopping to take a vacation, and devoting long hours to my work. Still I felt I was not doing enough for my people. I walked around with a deep and unshakable feeling of guilt. It was only by a quirk of fate that it was I who was walking around alive and reasonably well, and not my brother, Sholem. Did he not have as much right to live as I?

No matter how much I did, how many checks I wrote, how many causes I worked for, I could not escape the feeling that it was not enough. This depression continued until the 14th of May, 1948, when we Jews of Detroit celebrated the proclamation of the State or Israel. It was a grand demonstration. Tears of joy streamed down my face. At last I was able to shake the feeling of guilt. I had contributed to that glorious day, the fulfillment of an age-old dream. Even though my contribution did not matter much in the overall total, still in the life of one man, it was a significant amount and meant quite a lot to me. I felt that my efforts had borne fruit, and my labors were rewarded.

After the 5th of Iyar, the Hebrew date of the creation of the Jewish State, I began to feel spiritually and physically let down. I thought to myself, "Enough!" For over 30 years I had been active in Jewish life. "Dayenu," it was enough! Now it was time for the younger people to take over.

Two weeks later, I suffered a breakdown. My body became swollen and was covered with blisters. It was a weird illness. The swelling was not uniform but in local areas, some parts of my body were normal and some were swollen. My face looked monstrous. For seventeen days I lay thus, swollen, in bed, unable to move. My mind, however, was clear and sharp. I emerged from the illness with weakened limbs, my fingers were numb, wooden. In time they improved but I never did recover fully from the illness.

I resumed activity in the business but it was no longer

with the same energy as before. I seemed to have lost my drive as well as my energy. I began to look for a younger man to take into the business with me, to relieve me of much of the responsibility and the physical work. I was willing to offer such a man fifty per cent of the income without having to invest a single penny of his own. But such a man was not easy to find; one who was both experienced in my line and was honest. So I decided to sell part or all of my business. Again I was not successful. I could not find a buyer.

I also had to curtail my communal activities. I accepted no offices but I did remain on various executive boards. I attended meetings and participated as much as my strength would allow.

CREATION OF THE STATE OF ISRAEL

AFTER THE CREATION OF THE STATE OF Israel, some Zionists began to agitate for an end to the Zionist Organization of America. I claimed it would be a grievous error. Israel would be in great need of our financial assistance and also our political help for many years, I told my colleagues. The argument that this should be the responsibility of all the Jewish people seemed childish to me. Who are the Jewish people? How does one reach them. No, there must be an organized group of people committed to a specific program, a goal. So, I reasoned, why break up existing Zionist organizations and start building new ones from the ground up, not knowing what, if anything, would ever come of it? Such talk, I maintained, was weakening the Jewish State.

I felt that I could not withdraw from Jewish community activity; that there would always be something to do, and that there would always be a need for people who had the ability to think for themselves and the courage to express those opinions when they had to be aired and even if they were not the most popular at the moment.

But my health did not permit it. This posed a psychological problem. Throughout the years I never thought about myself or my health in my work. There were things that had to be done and that was that. Good or bad health just didn't enter into my thinking. If it was necessary to work 18 or 20 hours a day in business or some communal activity, I did it. Whether it was physical labor or sitting through endless meetings in rooms filled with suffocating smoke, it did not matter, I stayed as long as necessary.

Now, suddenly, I must take care of my own needs. Often I felt nausea and dizziness. Sometimes my heartbeat became erratic and I was unable to move my legs. It was no use, I finally resigned myself to the fact that one must adjust his activities to his capabilities, and that included the state of his health.

I began to read more. And here I suffered another disappointment. Many Yiddish writers had divorced themselves from Jewish life in this country. The life and times of five and a half million Jews in America is sadly missing from Yiddish literature. There are many complaints of the lack of readers of Yiddish books. This is a bitter truth. But is there a decent Yiddish book of Jewish life in America? Alas, the Yiddish writers fled from the field and left the subject for the American-Jewish writers. As a result I began to read books written in English.

The state of my health worsened. I decided to give up my business. Perhaps that would ease the pressures on me and permit me to rest more. Since it was impossible to sell the business lock, stock and barrel, there was no choice but to sell it piece-meal. Of course I would lose money this way, but I felt there was no alternative.

At the end of 1951, I sold my building and the machinery. I left a small jobbing business for myself, content with whatever profits came in. For the balance of my living expenses, I would have to dip into my life savings but I felt my health warranted it. However, before I could put my new program into operation, I came down with pneumonia. This weakened me even more and naturally I neglected my business.

In the spring, when the weather turned warm, I felt the strength return to my body. In the beginning of June, 1952, I suffered a heart attack, a coronary thrombosis. Whiling away the weeks in the hospital, I took an accounting of my life. My years numbered 56, not many, but I did live a full life, living not for myself alone nor for my wife and children alone. I had helped many people and did as much as one Jew could do for the entire Jewish people.

Naturally, I thought, I would like to live longer. I would like to see all my daughters happily married. But if it was not to be, then I was ready to face my destiny. Only one thing I prayed for, that I should not remain an invalid. I should not become dependent on others.

A week later, while lying quietly in bed I suffered another heart attack. I was unable to move for about twelve hours, not even a finger. Nor was I able to utter a sound. I wanted desperately to say something. I wanted to say something about my daughter Judith who was then in India. When I recovered, I experienced an opposite psychological reaction. I revolted against death. I wanted to live! After all, before I did not live for myself. Until now I worked for others, for causes, for Israel, for friends and associates, for wife and children, for the good of the community. Now I wanted to live and enjoy life's bounties for myself as well.

I left the hospital with instructions from the doctor to live normally, whatever that means, not to walk quickly and not to climb stairs. "Don't get excited," he warned me, "Don't eat too much and cut out smoking." Little by little I became accustomed to my new way of life. Never before did I pamper myself and now, suddenly, I must watch out not to walk too fast. And the doctor warned me, "Live normally."

In the beginning, I found the regime difficult to accept. Gradually I became adjusted to it. I accepted the fact that by and large it could not be otherwise. My protest at being pampered as if I were someone's spoiled child would not help me. Millions of others have to live a restricted life, why not I? Why was I so special? I was forced not only to accustom myself to the realities of the situation but to accept it more or less as a normal way of life. This is how it must be and there's no use complaining about it.

In September of that year, 1952, I began to get pains in my back and shoulders. The doctor turned me one way, then the other. They squeezed and prodded but could find no apparent reason for the pains. They decided on X-ray. So I was X-rayed. Every part of my body was photographed. After six weeks of X-rays and examinations, the doctors concluded that all my organs were in good health. But the pains became worse. I couldn't dress or undress myself. At night I could not turn in bed.

I was referred to a specialist on skin and bone tissue. The specialist twisted my hand and legs, poked and prodded and decided—X-rays. The whole story was repeated. The specialist wrinkled his forehead and wrote out a prescription, which was of value only to the druggist. Then he decided on X-ray treatments. They did help somewhat but I still had difficulty sitting down and when I was sitting down, I had difficulty getting up. I walked with the gait of an old man, taking small, timid steps.

My legs were wooden. I could hardly drag them along after me. To get them into an automobile when we had to go somewhere was torture. It distressed me deeply to be in need of help from others, although in this instance the other persons were my wife at home and my secretary in the office. I felt betrayed by my body which had stood me in such good stead throughout the years. I was afraid to become dependent on others. It would mean a yielding of control over myself. And so I felt both betrayed by my body and punished by my destiny.

Naturally my illness affected my business adversely. My competitors, some of whom I had helped on numerous occasions, threw themselves on my business like vultures swooping down on a carcass. They told my customers that I was finished, that I was liquidating the business and that I was not long for this world.

As long as I lived, I did not want to give up the entire business. I had to do something. To sit home and do nothing would be worse. In addition, I still needed an income for my wife and daughters. I could have managed with the money I saved but that would have meant cutting out many things, charity included. My contributions came to about $10,000 a year. That I could not continue from savings. If one does not have, he cannot give. This may be true but it means nothing to the fund raisers and accounters of charity. If I should stop giving, they would skin me alive.

Everyone thinks his institution is the most important one in the world and each demands a contribution greater than the year before. If I should say I could not give, they would simply not believe me and press their demands. And, if you did not give they would come again, this time a committee of two and the struggle would be re-enacted.

Two paths were open to me. One was to say, "No!" firmly to everyone and refrain from lengthy explanations. For this one must have a heart of stone and this I do not possess. The second path was to leave Detroit, settle down in a small town and tear myself away from Jewish life. This I did not wish to do. So actually, I had no choice but to remain in business and earn enough to take care of all my charity commitments.

With this in mind, I went into partnership with one of my former competitors who had a small business. I realized that I would not earn as much as before, but I felt that if I were forced to lie in bed or go to the hospital, at least there would be someone to look after the business. Perhaps I would even be able to travel to a warmer climate for some months and perhaps restore my health.

Our agreement was to go into effect on January 1, 1953, at a time when I was in ill health. I did not do it with a light heart. For 32 years I had been in business by myself—without partners. Suddenly I had to accustom myself to a partner. I realized it would be a difficult adjustment but it had to be made. For months I could not hold a pen in my hand. The doctors finally diagnosed my illness as arthritis. My body was bent over. I could neither dress nor undress. Later my condition showed some improvement. I could walk erect and although I did not have much strength in my hands, they improved enough to let me do some things for myself.

THE HOSPITAL

FOR SEVERAL YEARS THE DETROIT JEWISH community was engaged in building a hospital of its own, with a capacity of 216 beds. The cost was estimated to be between $6,500,000 and $7,000,000. The community raised $2,500,000 in the spring of 1942. Since the Allied Jewish Appeal was combined with the Community Chest in the fall of 1942, it was unable to raise additional funds. Some time later the city of Detroit launched a $20 million campaign for general hospital construction. Out of this fund, the Jewish hospital received $2,500,000. That raised the total to $5,000,000. Another million dollars was borrowed from the bank and the remaining $500,000 was raised by special contributions.

Before construction could get under way, a controversy arose over kashrut. The hospital committee decided that the kitchen would be non-kosher. The Orthodox and Conservative rabbis and all religious members of the community, as well as many non-religious members protested and demanded that the hospital maintain only a kosher kitchen.

Protest meetings were held, resolutions were adopted and statements were issued to the American-Jewish and English press by the kashrut committee. The hospital committee and the executive committee of the Federation ignored the protests as if the hospital were their own private concern. They did not even deem it necessary to summon a meeting to give both sides an opportunity to express their views.

When the protests became louder, too loud even for our Federation, the chairman of the hospital committee agreed to compromise and sent a letter to the kashrut committee assuring the members that those who wished to observe the dietary laws while in the hospital, would be able to do so and that there would be a separate kitchen for this purpose.

And so it remained, a kosher kitchen and a "trayfeh" kitchen in a hospital named "Sinai," after the mountain on which the Jews received the original command to observe the dietary laws!

I saw in this both a tragedy and a comedy. Many Jews I spoke to were all in favor of a "trayfeh" kitchen because the hospital would accommodate non-jews as well. We should not impose our own practices on them, they argued. I argued back that Catholic hospitals also have non-Catholic patients but on Fridays they never serve meat. In addition, they have icons in all the rooms. To this they replied that the Catholics were different.

If a vote were to be taken among the Jews of Detroit, I am convinced that those who advocated a "trayfeh" kitchen with separate kosher facilities, would have won.

The comedy was something else. I knew personally all the members of the hospital committee as well as those of the Federation Board of Directors. Almost all were good men, amiable and respected. But as soon as they become members of a body that has a degree of power, a change seems to come over them. A Russian bureaucrat in Czarist times was but an underling compared with some of our "leaders." Democracy flies out the window. They consider themselves smarter than the others, better informed and know best what is good for the community. Often they become autocratic, even despotic. It was easier to get a hearing before a Senate Committee than before the Federation Board.

Looking back over several decades, I realize that we have come a long way in achieving democracy in community life. But it is difficult indeed to fortell how much longer we must go before achieving our ideal of democracy in Jewish communal life.

It is appropriate at this point to describe another incident, a meeting organized by the Shaarey Zedek Synagogue. The discussion centered around the future of the building. It had been erected only 20 years before and prior to that the congregation had given up a building in use for only sixteen years. It is a curse in America that population groups, Jews especially, do not stay long in a neighborhood but pick themselves up and move elsewhere, community and all. The neighborhood changes. The Jews move out and non-Jews, mostly blacks, take their place.

It was decided to purchase a tract of land, about twenty acres, some twelve to fifteen miles distant from the original site. It might well be that in another five or ten years the new building would also be given up. Millions of dollars are thus wasted. Even worse, Jewish life cannot be established; the community is always in flux, constantly changing, on the run. In its wake are abandoned synagogues, deserted community centers and other institutions, edifices that required large sums of money and a great deal of community effort.

The same holds true for private homes. My house, built with great care, toil, worry and money, is in a neighborhood that is no longer Jewish. It is mostly black. Almost all the Jews fled with the arrival of the first few Negro families. I remained alone among the blacks. I was the last Jew to leave the neighborhood. It was not a question of color. It was for me a question of cultural and communal relationships. I like to think of myself as being unprejudiced. I had no objection to Negroes buying homes in my neighborhood. They tried to keep them in good order, but unfortunately most of them had to double up to pay off the mortgage and keep up the expenses. So several families occupied each house and many took in boarders besides.

Thus it was inevitable that many of the houses would begin to deteriorate and soon the inevitable signs of a slum began to develop. I would have opposed this if whites moved into the neighborhood and doubled up. And I must admit there are whites with whom I would not care to sit at the same table. There are many whites of this sort in Detroit, particularly those coming from the hinterlands and the south to seek employment in Detroit's factories. By and large they board with families or stay in furnished rooms. Their interests seem limited to their jobs and the local saloons.

Why was it necessary to purchase fifteen or twenty acres for a synagogue? Mainly for the parking lot. With suburban spread, most Jews must necessarily live a distance from the synagogue and if they want to attend services, they must drive over, even on the Sabbath. An area of eight to ten acres is required to accommodate 1,000 or 1,200 automobiles.

I was at the meeting at Shaarey Zedek when the matter was discussed but I did not participate. I felt uncomfortable discussing the erection of a synagogue in terms of a parking lot. But these are new times, with a new kind of Judaism.

ISRAEL BONDS

EVERYONE WHO ATTENDED THE MEETING was given a list of 30 names and telephone numbers. The object was to sell these people Israel bonds. As an added inducement, every one who purchased at least one bond, was to receive a ticket to a concert featuring the noted violinist, Yehudi Menuhin.

After telephoning the first fifteen people on my list, I

had to go out for a breath of fresh air and to calm my nerves. The excuses some of them gave for not buying were beyond comprehension. "I am going to Florida so I have no money to buy bonds," one of them told me. "I have already bought bonds and cannot afford to buy any more." I had this man's card in my hand and knew that he had not yet bought a single bond.

And so it went from one prospect to another. Despite the refusals, we did manage to sell a sizable number of bonds. There were people who bought and bought again, many of them several times. The others tried to excuse their refusals with sighs of regret and expressions of sympathy. It was enough to make me sick.

A SUMMING UP

THESE TEN YEARS WERE THE MOST FRUITful of my life, in all directions, communal, social and personal. I devoted my time, my energy beyond my strength to the public good. No task was too small or beneath my dignity. If I believed it would be useful to the community, I would undertake any assignment. In fact, I always felt I was not doing enough for my people.

I served my country honestly and with devotion during World War II, not seeking personal gain or glory. On the contrary, my business suffered because I was always bending over backwards to make sure I was not violating the law. I was more pious than the rabbi, as it were. I was always fearful that I might do something that could be interpreted by the Government and the members of my business association as being in violation of the law, that I was using my position for personal gain.

I received letters of thanks and plaques from the War Production Board and the U.S. Treasury Department for my work. I am proud of those letters as I am also of the plaque I received from my association.

When I reached the age of 57, I was broken in health and dispirited. I lost all ambition. I no longer derived any pleasure from my communal work. I cut down my business and turned it into a small operation, and with a partner at that! The normal pleasures of life no longer enticed me. For a time I even lost the desire to read a book.

I hoped that it was a passing feeling and that I would one day regain my zest for life and my desire to work for the community. In my despair, I wrote the following: "I cannot accept the feeling that my life of activity, of struggles and the spirit of enterprise that marked my life has passed and that I am entering a period of vegetation. I realize it all depends on me. I have to strengthen myself and find within me the will and the power to wish to do things, to undertake new projects, the wish to live!

"I know that it depends on me alone. No one else can help me. I hope I can find the way to this revitalization."

PERSONAL AND BUSINESS PROBLEMS

AFTER AN INTERRUPTION OF FIFTEEN years, I resume my reminiscences. It is with some difficulty that I gather my thoughts. At the age of 72, my memory is not as reliable as it was a decade or two ago. Nevertheless, I will record some of the events I consider notable. I'm afraid that some of the experiences I wrote about previously will be out of harmony with some of the things I will write about

Communal Activity; Frustration and Fulfillment

now. Much time has passed. Many changes have taken place and my views on several matters have changed with them.

My partnership was not very successful. My partner had a son in his thirties and I had hoped to be able to teach him the business. That would have given me more leisure time. I would have been able to come to the plant for several hours and still have time for myself. But my partner's son was something of a playboy. He was often absent. He knew very little and made no effort to learn. He never called on customers and took no interest in the day to day functioning of the business.

Since my partner did very little himself, all the work fell on my shoulders. My partner told me at the start that he, personally, would do nothing. He did not know anything about our business and he said he was not suited for such an undertaking. The business still prospered, so I put up with it.

Some three years later, my wife and I took a three-month trip to Israel and Europe. When we returned, I was appalled to find how my business had suffered. We did not gain a single new customer. Even worse, we lost many of the old ones. I wanted to give up the business altogether but my partner refused to release me. In the interim, I became ill and had to undergo surgery. The operation was not entirely successful. I developed an infection and had to remain in the hospital for three weeks. Then I had to stay at home for an entire month. Even after that, I moved around with an open wound for several months before it healed.

A year later, the wound opened again and I had to undergo surgery a second time. This time I stayed only ten days at the hospital. Several months later I suffered a heart attack. With this succession of illnesses, my business suffered more and more. I was determined to get out once and for all. My partner still refused to end the partnership. I warned him that if he persisted in his refusal, I would take legal action.

That threat reached him. He did not want court proceedings. Toward the end of 1959, I sold him my share of the business and granted him a two-year period to pay me the sum agreed on. The sum was very low. It had to be, otherwise the only way I could have been able to get out of the plant would have been to be carried out.

The negotiations were friendly. There were no quarrels. My partner did not haggle about the price because I asked so little. He had to admit then and there that it was indeed a bargain. He paid off his obligation within the first year, not waiting for the two years to elapse. We have remained friends through the years.

Emotionally it was difficult for me to give up a business with which I had been connected for thirty years. The concern was on the verge of bankruptcy when I took it over. I nursed it back to health and worked it up to a thriving business, one that became one of the foremost in the field and one that gave me a very comfortable living. It may not have been the largest cloth business in the country, but it was the strongest financially and enjoyed an excellent reputation among the dealers, among my customers and in the banks.

It wrenched my heart to see what had become of the business. In the summer of 1968, the firm went into bankruptcy without the possibility of paying anything to the creditors.

Having rid myself of one affliction, I took steps to shed a second. Years before, I teamed up with a partner to form a financial corporation, using my money and his experience. During World War II, I was too occupied with my own business and with communal activities to pay much attention to the financial corporation. I happened to look into the books on one occasion and everything turned black in front of my eyes. I saw a loss of over $100,000. The bookkeeper had falsified the books. I had an accountant but apparently he failed to notice it. My financial wizard of a partner received his check every month and did not know what the bookkeeper was doing. During all this, I was receiving monthly reports from the accountant which showed the corporation making a profit.

My financial partner had invested only a few thousand in the financial corporation. He is an extraordinary person with special talents, a lawyer who did not practice his profession. He loved to philosophize and was not much interested in anything but someone else's money. He caused me much heartache. It took me 18 years to clean up all my debts and then to begin to pay myself the sum of money I had put into the financial corporation.

As soon as I had recouped most of the money I had invested, I sold my share of the financial corporation to my philosopher partner for one dollar. I did not care a bit what he collected from the corporation just so long as I was rid of the headache. In the 18 years that the corporation was functioning my partner earned $136,000. I did not earn two cents on my investment, or for my time and effort.

Throwing off my business responsibilities gave me more time to think. I wondered how it was that since 1914 I had had fourteen different partners in eleven different ventures and with the exception of one, every one of them caused me trouble and heartache. Several of my partners swindled me, others were outright thieves, several outsmarted me, and others simply used me for their own gain.

I asked myself of what was I guilty? I did not quarrel with any of my partners. I never stole a penny from anyone. And I remained on friendly terms with all of them. Nevertheless, I must say, I made many serious mistakes. Why did I blunder so in choosing partners? I see others who have had partners, for many years. Perhaps they too have had difficulty.

I would like to add only that the partner who was decent and aboveboard did not live long. He was an elderly man and our partnership lasted only a year and a half. But his heirs paid me doubly. They cheated me and caused me great anguish. Yet they were counted among the elite of the community. They were also well known for their piety.

When I resumed my memoirs, I had already been out of business for nine years. I invested small sums in real estate and several of these investments bring me a modest income each month. In some ventures I lost money. I do not have to manage the property personally, a management corporation takes care of it for me. And thus ends my business activity.

A TRIP TO ISRAEL AND EUROPE

THE TRIP TO ISRAEL WAS THE REALIZAtion of a dream that my wife and I had cherished ever since the proclamation of the State in 1948. We sailed to France on the *Queen Mary* and spent ten days in Paris. From there we went by train to Naples in Italy. In Naples, we embarked on the *Negbah* for Israel. The *Queen Mary* was a ship of some 80,000 tons. The *Negbah* was a mere 5,400 tons. The *Negbah* was an old ship, lacking in modern accommodations. Even so, we were all happier on the *Negbah* than on the *Queen Mary,* happier than in the first class on the *Queen Mary*. We were among Jews. The service was excellent,

Communal Activity; Frustration and Fulfillment

much better than we had expected. We were especially happy that we were en route to Israel.

We toured the Jewish state and visited the many institutions that were of such great interest to us. We enjoyed it immensely but the tour was not without its share of aggravation. Throughout our lives, each year at the end of the Passover service, we said, "Next year in Jerusalem." What could be more appropriate then, to celebrate the Passover Seder in Jerusalem? We made reservations at the President Hotel which was holding a Seder for tourists.

Instead of a festive Seder night, it turned out to be a nightmare. There was no recitation of the Hagaddah. There were three bottles of wine for over 300 people. The Seder got under way about ten o'clock at night. The guests were hungry and tense. They began to pound on the tables. The manager could not be found and there was no one else to talk to.

We later learned that the Seder was delayed in the hope that additional tourists would arrive. If they had, God only knows what they would have had to eat; we had very little to eat and what there was, was cold. We were still hungry when the Seder ended. And for this, we were charged $45.00.

The central office of the Jewish National Fund also caused us some grief. Mendel Fischer, then the national director of the Jewish National Fund in America, had written to the office in Jerusalem on our behalf, praising us for our work on behalf of the JNF; that we had worked for the organization for many years, and that I had been president of the JNF chapter in Detroit for a number of years. Fischer asked that we be greeted in a friendly manner by the local officials and be shown the courtesies due good friends and faithful supporters. He also informed them that we wished to plant a forest of 10,00 trees to be named, "Yaar Laikin."

When we arrived at the central headquarters of the JNF, we asked where and when the Yaar Laikin was to be planted. We were anxious to be there on time. We were told rather brusquely, "We will let you know." When two weeks passed without a word, we telephoned the JNF. We were in Tel Aviv at the time and planned to visit Haifa, Safed and the Galilee. Naturally we had to have some advance notice of the planting so we could arrange our itinerary accordingly.

In reply to our phone call, we received the same answer, "We will let you know." Three days later, we telephoned Jerusalem again. At that time, it sometimes took a whole day to get a line through from Tel Aviv to Jerusalem. Again we got the same answer. This time however, I lost my temper and let them have it, but good. It was only then that they gave me a date and told us where the planting would take place.

As a member of the Poale Zion movement for forty years, I invited a number of leading party members to be present when my wife and I planted the first trees of Yaar Laikin. I knew them well for many years. Most had been guests in my home when they came to Detroit on party business. Several promised to attend but not one of them showed up. It was, so to speak, "a poor wedding."

Not one of my many friends invited us to their homes for as much as a cup of coffee—with the exception of Golda Meir (at that time she still called herself Meyerson). And in her house I was deeply insulted. It came about this way.

In Detroit we had had difficulty selling Israel bonds. The director of the Jewish Federation was opposed to the sale of Israel bonds in Detroit and did everything he could to hinder the campaign. I imagine he was afraid that the bond campaign would hurt the Allied Jewish Campaign. Or, perhaps he was against it because he couldn't control the local Israel

Bond Organization as he did every other Jewish organization in Detroit.

Israel bonds were sold by all the Zionist groups. A Zionist committee was established to organize the sale. The committee entered into an agreement with the Federation to conduct bond sales during January and February. The period from March 1 to May was reserved for the Allied Jewish Campaign.

At the beginning of 1955, our Israel Bond Committee decided to hold a banquet as a means of selling bonds. The banquet was to take place the last week in February. However, we had to postpone the date because several organizers and several major purchasers could not be in the city at the time. We postponed the banquet just one week—to March 1st. At this, the director of the Federation raised the cry that we were interfering with the Allied Jewish Campaign.

The director managed to win over to his side the anti-Zionists of the city. It was as if "the Phillistines were upon us." Some of the Bond Committee members fought against the Federation director, charging that he was a dictator and worse. Some of the adjectives were stronger and less complimentary.

Two opposing groups were formed, one siding with the Federation and the other with us. Our group maintained that the banquet must go through as planned, to sell bonds and also to show the Federation director that he could not dictate what Detroit Jewry should or should not do, especially since the whole problem hinged on a single day.

Henry Montor, then the national director of the Israel Bond Organization, urged us to hold the banquet, not to weaken. Telegrams were dispatched to Israel and others came back. Apparently Eliezar Kaplan, the Finance Minister at the time, did not want to take a stand in order not to antagonize a section of the Detroit community. The committee decided to postpone the dinner until June. They reasoned that a split in the Jewish community must be avoided because both the Allied Jewish Campaign and the Israel bond drive would suffer.

It is easy to start a quarrel but difficult to bring peace. Both campaigns were dear to us, the Zionists. When Montor heard of our decision, he sent a directive that the banquet must take place on March 1. At that point, all of us resigned from the committee. Even so, Montor won out and the dinner took place as scheduled. It was a miserable fiasco although Moshe Sharett was the guest speaker.

Golda Meir had sided with Henry Montor. In Israel, she picked up the matter and spoke bitterly about the Jewish Federation of Detroit and its director. When I tried to persuade her that we Zionists were anxious to avoid a split in the Detroit community, she called me a traitor. I told her that Israel would have suffered if the quarrel had gone further. To no avail, Mrs. Meir still claimed that I was a traitor, that I had betrayed the interests of Zionism.

There were in her house, at the time, about a dozen other American Jewish leaders from various cities. I was terribly insulted. Then suddenly, there came to my mind the words of Rabbi Ishmael: "This is the Torah and this is its reward."

But such incidents are but warts on the countenance of Israel. When we saw the green fields, the lush orchards, the booming factories, the hospitals, the cultural institutions, the homes for the aged and the nurseries, our hearts filled with joy and pride.

We witnessed the celebration of the seventh Independence Day with tears in our eyes. We also attended the May 1st parade. The red flags were a bit too abundant for us. We knew that this had nothing to do with communism or the

Communal Activity; Frustration and Fulfillment

Soviet Union, but even so, it was difficult to digest so many red flags.

From Israel, we flew to Italy where we were satiated with art, especially church art. From Italy, we traveled to Holland where an uncle and cousin of my wife's lived. We spent ten days there, visiting different parts of the country, the museums, and the tulip fields. We were most enthusiastic about the Dutch people. Nowhere did we see such tall people, both men and women. Alongside them, I looked like a dwarf.

The Dutch were so sedate, poised, modest and friendly. However, the Jewish community made a very poor impression on us. Few Jews remained in Holland after the Nazis, may their names be blotted out forever, were driven out. In addition, there were many mixed marriages and many conversions, further weakening the Jewish community. Many who had survived the concentration camps "exchanged their ticket," as we said in Yiddish of a Jew who converted to another faith.

There is no anti-Semitism in Holland, neither in the government nor among the people. So why did the Jews convert? I spoke to several Jews who had converted and asked them why. They replied that they did not want their children or their grandchildren to suffer the ordeals they had had to endure. I wondered if they were serious! Were they trying to fool me, or possibly themselves? The Nazis considered as Jews all those who had even a single Jewish ancestor as far back as the fourth generation. It was my opinion that financial advantages played an important role in their conversions—and it sickened me.

In Holland, everyone must belong to a community. If he is a Jew, he joins the Jewish communal organization. The community taxes each member for communal programs and the Government collects the tax just as it collects its own taxes. The money is transmitted to the community by the Government.

The Jewish community organizations faced extraordinary problems after World War II with the return of survivors from the concentration camps and those who emerged from hiding. To enable the community to begin to function again, the communal leaders decided to tax each returning Jew for the time he was absent, in some instances for five or six years. Many, who valued their money more than their Judaism, converted rather than pay the back taxes.

I met with the vice-president of the Jewish community and asked him if thus a Jew without funds was not driven to conversion by the community. He replied that the Dutch Government compensated everyone for property confiscated or destroyed by the Nazis so that every returning Jew had the funds to pay taxes. He said that the community was in dire need of money and those who refused to pay could leave. His reply sounded rather harsh and unbending to me.

We traveled by ship from Holland to England. Our daughter Judith was in London, working for the State Department as a vice-consul. Judith rented a car and took us through a number of cities and small towns. I was struck by the way the British were working to rebuild their cities to make them look as they did before the war.

Just as it came time to return home, the dock workers declared a strike and shortly afterward the railroad engineers went on strike. Interestingly enough, the railroad engineers were striking for a raise of four shillings a week, about 56c. They had been working 44 hours a week for a wage amounting to about $28. Their working time was not continuous. They had to work part time during the day and part at night. Unfortunately the engineers lost their strike.

Life in London suffered little as a result of the strike. On the day we had to leave, all passengers were transported to the pier in buses. There we boarded small boats which took us to the *Queen Elizabeth* which was anchored outside British territorial waters.

COMMUNITY ACTIVITY

THE JEWISH COMMUNITY COUNCIL WAS functioning very well, and independently. The Federation tried for many years to gain control of the Council. It sent some of its people into the Council as delegates of various organizations but even this disguise didn't work. Failing in its attempt to gain control, the Federation tried another trick, to reduce the budget of the Council and refuse to allocate funds for cultural activities.

For years the Council had asked for a $500 allocation for a lecture series in Yiddish. The Federation would never approve the allocation. Each item in the budget refers to a specific activity and if the funds are not used for that activity, they cannot be used for any other activity without a special appropriation. Unspent funds go back to the Federation.

One time the Council and the Jewish Center agreed on a series of Yiddish lectures. The series came to an end when the Center backed out, offering the lame excuse that Yiddish speaking Jews were not interested in Yiddish lectures. And this despite the fact that each of the lectures that did take place drew an audience of 400 to 500 people.

The Jewish Community Council has a clause in its bylaws providing that meetings were to be conducted in both English and Yiddish. Several delegates, of whom I was one, spoke in Yiddish. However, over the past twenty years many younger people came onto the executive committee and among them were a number who did not understand Yiddish. Yiddish was still permitted in discussion, but now the president translates the remarks into English. Often the presidents themselves were insufficiently familiar with Yiddish and the translations would distort the remarks of the Yiddish speaking member. As a result, all of us, myself included, were forced to speak English only at the meetings.

Twelve years before the Federation had launched a campaign to induce the Council to come into the Federation and carry on its activities as a Federation committee. Some of the members of the executive committee were in favor, but they were unaware of the pitfalls. In many cities just such "mergers" took place and it usually spelled the end of the Council. There remained only a committee, with no power and no independence. It had only the right to recommend, it did not even have voting rights.

Our Council appointed a committee to negotiate with the Federation. The negotiations dragged on for years without results. The older members, those who led the work in the early years of the Council, were on the alert to assure that the Council would remain democratic and that it would represent the Jews of all shades in the community, with the possible exception of political organizations, business associations and labor unions. They naturally opposed the unification plan.

Gradually the plan faded into oblivion. The Federation gave up its attempt to take over the Council and peaceful relations were restored, especially when a new executive director, William Avrunin, took over the Federation. Mr. Avrunin had no desire to dominate the Council or to control the Detroit Jewish community institutions.

As I write these lines, in 1970, the Council is still func-

Communal Activity; Frustration and Fulfillment 299

tioning very well. It has a budget of about $150,000 annually. Its permanent officers are a president, three vice-presidents, a secretary, a treasurer, an executive committee of 48 members, and the following committees: For External Affairs, 52 members; For Internal Affairs, 63 members; Cultural Committee, 33 members; Committee on the Acceptance of New Organizations, 5 members; Radio and Television, 22 members; Church and State Affairs, 5 members; Planning Committee for Quarterly Delegates Meetings, 12 members; United Committee of the Council and the Council of Orthodox Rabbis, 8 members; United Committee of the Council and the Zionist Council, 2 members plus the presidents of both organizations; Committee on Mass Meetings, 5 members; Equal Rights, 3 members; and Local Affairs, 14 members.

There are also two sub-committees, one on Soviet-Jewish Affairs and the other to mediate disputes in the community.

As can be seen from the number of committees, the activity of the Council has been expanded to include almost the whole spectrum of Jewish life in Detroit. I served on the executive committee for thirty years, until my health compelled me to withdraw.

The Council president is elected each year. He may serve for three terms in succession and then must give up the post to another. Members of the Executive Committee are elected for three-year terms; they can be elected for an additional term and then must withdraw for one year before being elected for another two terms. All decisions of the executive committee must be ratified by the delegates at their quarterly meetings.

At the time I record this chapter of my memoirs, the Council consists of 349 member organizations. The majority of members are from 33 synagogues representing all three branches of Judaism; Orthodox, Conservative and Reform. They brought with them to the Council their men's clubs and their sisterhoods. The second largest group consists of the Zionist organizations, 43 in all. The third largest number of members were from 38 B'nai B'rith lodges. Also included in the Council are the suburbs of Detroit. In 1966 it was estimated that the Jewish population of Detroit and its suburbs was 84,500.

A FORMER NAZI

THROUGHOUT MY THIRTY YEARS OF ACtivity in the Detroit Jewish Community Council, I was known for my insistence on defending Jewish rights. The Council was established mainly by Yiddish-speaking Jews but through the years, by death and by aging, many of the Yiddish-speaking Jews dropped out and were replaced by younger, mainly English-speaking Jews. Most of them knew very little about Judaism. Many are liberals. I call them fuzzy liberals, befuddled in their thinking.

The liberals started a campaign to invite the blacks to settle in Jewish neighborhoods. Ironically, it was they, the befuddled liberals, who were the first to run when a black family moved into their neighborhoods.

Most of the meetings during that period were taken up with Negro questions and problems. Jewish matters were forgotten. On one occasion, I exploded from frustration and called them hypocrites. Not a single member of the executive committee lived in a neighborhood that had Negro families, I was the only one. And I remained in my neighborhood, the only Jew, until my isolation from the Jewish community was too great.

Communal Activity; Frustration and Fulfillment 301

No one answered my accusation. I got the feeling, though, that I was not exactly welcome at the executive committee meetings any longer. At the next election, my name was not entered in nomination.

At this point, I would like to relate another incident, that of the discovery of a former Nazi, a woman, who had come to the United States after the revolt in Hungary in 1956.

It was the late nineteen-fifties. A Jewish woman, walking in the street, suddenly came face to face with a woman she immediately recognized as a Nazi activist who had mistreated her and other Jews in Budapest. The Jewish woman became hysterical and a commotion ensued. The Jewish Community Council heard about the incident and launched an investigation.

The Jewish woman told the Council officers that during the Nazi occupation in Budapest, she and other Jews were driven from their homes and herded into a ghetto. The woman she had seen in the streets, her sister and mother were installed as overseers by the Nazis of a building into which many Jewish families were crowded. Every night, at midnight, the mother and her daughters drove the Jews out of their rooms and made them assemble in the courtyard, ostensibly to check that no one had escaped. They were forced to stand there motionless for hours. Those who moved, or fell, were beaten. The three witches robbed the Jews of their jewelry, clothes and other valuables and subjected them to horrible indignities.

The Jewish Council contacted the national organizations and asked them to investigate. I do not recall if it was the American Jewish Committee or the American Jewish Congress but one of them contacted the chief rabbi of Hungary who verified the report of the Jewish woman. He testified that the mother and daughters were all Nazis and that the mother's son had been the head of a concentration camp in the vicinity of Budapest. After Hungary was liberated, the Nazi women were arrested, tried, and sentenced to two years in prison each.

In Detroit, there lived an Italian who owned a restaurant patronized largely by Jews. He met the former Nazi when she came to America after the brief revolt in Hungary in 1956 and married her. The Italian always enjoyed good relations with the Jews. He was in no way anti-Semitic. I have no way of knowing if he knew of his wife's Nazi past.

The Jewish Community Council kept the story under wraps but rumors began to leak out that the woman behind the cash register at the Italian restaurant was a former Nazi activist. The Jews stayed away and business fell off sharply.

The Italian complained bitterly to his Jewish friends. He said he always enjoyed good business relations with Jews and welcomed their patronage in his restaurant. He could not possibly be accused of anti-Semitism. Why then, he asked, did the Jews boycott his restaurant?

A campaign was launched by elements of the Jewish Community Council to issue a statement denying the whole story. A delegation of the fuzzy liberals showed up at a meeting of the executive committee and argued that it should issue a statement that the restaurant was, so to speak, "kosher for the strictest observer," and that the restaurant should not be boycotted.

It was at that point that I found out about the matter. Before, the Council had kept a tight lid on the story. Not even the executive committee, of which I was a member, was aware of the problem, only the president, the director of the Council and perhaps one or two other persons.

The executive committee held several meetings on the

Communal Activity; Frustration and Fulfillment

question and the discussion became more and more heated. The liberals argued: "It is no fault of the Italian, and besides, the whole story is a fabrication. Even if it is true, we Jews must forgive and forget."

I argued that the Council must put the matter before the entire membership honestly and let the delegates decide on a proper course. Most of the executive committee members, with the president in the lead, were eager to give the Italian a clean bill of health and get his restaurant off the hook financially.

But what do we do with the letter of the Chief Rabbi in which he stated clearly that the woman had been a Nazi collaborator, a very willing one?

The president had a brillant idea. He would call a general meeting. Whoever wished, could attend. At the meeting the whole matter would be discussed and a decision made on how to proceed.

The meeting took place. Present were mainly those who sought to protect the Italian restaurateur. They spoke heatedly. I also expressed myself forcefully. I stressed that the Council could act only one way, to present the facts before the members and let them decide.

At this point, a Reform Rabbi rose and delivered himself of a sermonette, the gist of which follows: "The previous speaker (meaning me) is emotional because he feels guilty that he remained alive while other members of his family were annihilated. The letter of the Hungarian rabbi cannot be given credence because he may have been under compulsion to write as he did."

His words stabbed into me as if they were little knives. I did not wait until the chairman recognized me but rose to my feet as soon as the rabbi finished. I asked him, as I did all of the fuzzy liberals, if being emotional was a sin. How long did he think, I continued, that his wife would remain with him if he had no emotions? As for not believing the Chief Rabbi of Hungary, I told him not to measure the European rabbi with his own yardstick. A commotion ensued and the chairman ended the meeting.

The next meeting of the executive, the one at which the matter was finally to be voted on, was a painful one for me. Another rabbi, this time Orthodox, took the floor. He spoke calmly and reasonably. However, he too was of the opinion that the Chief Rabbi of Hungary might have erred in his statement. The speakers that followed repeated his recommendation that the Jewish Community Council issue a statement clearing the woman, that the story of her Nazi activities was "unsubstantiated." Along with this was the recommendation that any boycott activity against the Italian restaurant be called off.

A young man took the floor, the son of a wealthy Orthodox Jew, very pious. His words also stabbed at my heart. "Why should I care about something that happened 7,000 miles from here?" he said. "Whether Hitler murdered one million or six million Jews makes little difference to me. We are living here in America."

I leaped to my feet and pointing my finger at the speaker, said angrily, "If I did not know who your father was, I would have thought you were a Nazi. What are you doing in a Jewish organization?"

Everyone present was astounded, both by the young man's remarks and by my strong reaction. And to the rabbi I said, "You too, Brutus? How do you explain such an attitude?" He apologized and confessed that he had been mistaken.

I surmised from the tenor of the meeting that my motion to publicize the whole affair would fail. I was also afraid that the motion to exonerate the woman might pass. I therefore made a motion that the Council do nothing, that it rid itself of the problem by not taking any stand, one way or the other.

The president appointed a committee to formulate a resolution on the question. This it did, in many words that said nothing. I abstained from voting. When the president transmitted the resolution to the affiliated members, he added the phrase, "No boycott should be conducted against the restaurant."

All this happened when the president's term was expiring and what he did was done. I never raised the question again.

POALE ZION,
THE LABOR ZIONISTS

I HAVE BEEN AN ACTIVE MEMBER OF THE Poale Zion, the Labor Zionists, for five decades. Lately my activity has slackened off—for a number of reasons. For one, I have not been on very good terms with the central office for some time. I do not attend meetings at the party headquarters in New York. The officials believe that they possess all the wisdom in the world and pay little attention to the opinions of outlanders, those who came from outside of New York City.

Even at conventions, when a non-New Yorker asks for permission to speak, he may request it at the first session and, if he is lucky, he will be recognized at the closing session. The chairmen are invariably New Yorkers. When speakers are limited to two minutes each and one is on the floor formulating an opinion, the chairman cuts him off in mid-sentence if his time is up.

Our organizations preach democracy but are highly dictatorial. In Detroit several of the leading members conducted themselves in less than a democratic manner. If one disagreed with them, they would simply refuse to discuss the matter. If this did not end it, abuse would follow. If this didn't work, the questioner would be villified and treated as if he were an enemy of the Jewish people.

An example is the camp of the Farband Labor Zionist Order in our area. A number of years ago I complained that the camp was not being managed properly. There were too many employees and a number of them were incompetent. To add to the overhead, every employee brought his family to the camp with him, at the camp's expense. There were sloppy purchasing procedures and inadequate controls.

When I raised these issues, I was first criticized and then abused. Realizing that my efforts were of no avail, I withdrew from activity in the camp program. Naturally our camp operated at a deficit; all other Jewish camps in the region showed a profit. Many of these camps were able to pay up their mortgages and had no difficulty managing all year round on the income they received from their summer seasons.

I restricted my work with the Poale Zion to branch number three, one I helped to establish in 1934. For many years it was the most active branch in the city. Throughout it remained a Yiddish-speaking branch. As the years passed many founders moved away, others died. There are nine founders left. Many new members came in. Some remained for only a short time, few are still members.

At present the situation is not good. Because of the language problem, we have not been getting any of the

Communal Activity; Frustration and Fulfillment

younger people. Branches 1 and 3 have only a few members each. The younger generation preferred to join the English-speaking branches. Several members of the Poale Zion are playing important roles in the Jewish Community Council. However, the party itself and the Farband Labor Zionist Order have lost their leading roles they held in previous years in the Community Council. However, they continue to play a leading role in the Histadrut campaign on behalf of the trade unions in Israel.

The reason for the decline in our leadership can be traced to the decline in the number of "landsmanshaften." These are societies that are organized by groups according to the cities or towns in Europe they came from. The "landsmanshaften" members were always supporting the Labor Zionist movement. There are not many "landsmanshaften" left but those that do exist support the Labor Zionists. They sell Israel bonds, contribute to the Histadrut campaigns and are active in the annual Federation campaigns.

Branch 3, whose members are few and well along in years, now plays a minor role in the community. Even so we manage to collect several thousand dollars each year for various Israel campaigns and helped to maintain a Yiddish school. We also support the weekly *Yiddish Kempfer* and the monthly *Jewish Frontier.* Both are organs of the Labor Zionist movement.

In August of 1968, the three Yiddish schools, the Hayim Greenberg School of the Farband Labor Zionists, the school of the Workmen's Circle, and the Sholom Aleichem School, were merged into the "United Hebrew-Yiddish Culture School." It became federated with the United Hebrew School system of the Detroit community that is supported by the Federation. A unified curriculum was prepared and the move, long overdue, proved a blessing to the school.

I might add that in 1969 the Labor Zionist Organization sold the building which we had put up only about 12 to 14 years before, and of which we were all so proud. We undertook to build a new home for we realized that without a central headquarters for our movement the various branches, meeting in different places, would inevitably begin to fall apart.

A few old timers decided that we must have our own home, one in which the Poale Zion, Farband, Pioneer Women and Histadrut would all be under one roof. We were also determined that our merged Yiddish-Hebrew School should have a permanent home with plenty of classrooms, airy and spacious, and enough meeting rooms for the Habonim (Labor Zionist Youth).

Because of the high construction costs today the building will come to half a million dollars. It is due mainly to half a dozen "haverim" (members) all "akshonem" (stubborn) that before 1971 is out the building will be ready for occupancy. It is being built in Farmington, a suburb of Detroit, an area which has experienced a sharp increase in Jewish population in recent years.

The whole movement is happy about the new building, especially since the mortgage will pose no problem. We will have to borrow only a small sum to tide us over until all the pledges come in.

THE AMERICAN JEWISH CONGRESS

I WAS ALWAYS A STRONG ADVOCATE OF the idea of an American Jewish Congress to speak in a unified voice for American Jewry and worked to establish such a body. Since I was a member of the Labor Zionist Party I automatically became a member of the American Jewish Congress when the party affiliated with the Congress in 1918 or 1919. And when the Congress began to enroll individuals as members I joined a second time.

I remained in the Congress until it opened its doors to those who joined it as part of a Communist infiltration. I tried as best I could to stop them. When I found that my efforts were of no avail, that the Congress was permitting them to join and occupy leading positions, I resigned. I did not rejoin it even when the Congress withdrew the Detroit charter and organized a new chapter in the city. I was offered the presidency but I turned it down.

The new branch of the Congress would consider such questions as the hungry masses of India and China and problems of oppressed people generally. But not Jewish matters! That was my main objection. I told them if they really wanted to do something for the oppressed, they should not call themselves "Jewish" Congress, but rather they should become part of the general civil rights movement. As long as they kept the name "Jewish" in American Jewish Congress, I maintained, they should devote themselves to Jewish questions.

I stressed that if they wanted to take up general problems, or those relating to other than Jewish matters, they should join organizations set up for those purposes. Thus, after many years of activity in the American Jewish Congress, I severed my relations with it.

BELONGING TO A SYNAGOGUE

WE CAME TO DETROIT IN 1929. WE WENT to synagogue from time to time but did not belong to any one congregation. My wife, Chana, was more pious than I and went more often. After some years we felt it was time to join a congregation. We thought that it was not right for others to support a synagogue from which we benefited and to which we had little or no responsibility.

We wanted to belong somewhere. The children were growing up and we wanted to give them an intimate feeling of the synagogue. The Conservative synagogue did not appeal to my wife, nor to me for that matter. We were both raised in Orthodox homes and although in America we went to synagogue services only on special occasions, a nostalgia for the old country prayer house still smoldered in our hearts.

It seemed strange to me in the Conservative synagogue to see the rabbi walk over to the microphone from time to time and announce the page on which the prayer could be found. Or the form of saying "Kaddish" by the mourners. The rabbi recited the "Kaddish" and the mourners repeated after him. I was especially shocked when at the time of the "Hakofot," during the Simchas Torah Festival, when the congregation marches around the synagogue with the Torah Scrolls, the president announced the honors of holding the Torah by calling out "William Jones, step up and take a Scroll." Instead, he should have called everyone by his first name and his patronymic, thus: "Reb Hayim Ben Reb Abraham, Tayen Koved Le' Torah," (give honor to the Torah).

It is quite a distance from "Tayn Koved Le' Torah" to "take a Scroll." So, we hesitated. We weren't sure the Conservative synagogue was the proper place for us. We attended several Orthodox synagogues in our neighborhood and felt even less comfortable there. Some worshippers were saying their prayers aloud. Others prayed in hushed tones. Still others shouted their devotions. The mourners "Kaddish" was recited aloud, not in unison but each speeding along at his own pace, some ending earlier, some later.

During the services, several of the congregants could be seen chattering. It was quiet but the whisperings carried a long way and they disturbed the service. My wife objected strongly to the practice of separating the women from the men in the Orthodox prayer house. The women were usually seated in the balcony, or, if downstairs, then their section was separated from the men's section by a curtain.

In the end, we joined the Shaarey Zedek Synagogue, the largest Conservative congregation in Detroit. The synagogue was only twelve blocks from our home and it was no great achievement to walk to services on the Sabbath and on holidays. We could not get ourselves to ride to services on the Sabbath, although, truth to tell, we did use the car on Saturdays, but not to "shul."

I was never involved in synagogue activities although there were times when I did make attempts to become active. I believe that with my views on life and on Judaism I was a bit too much of a maverick to be a synagogue worker. I did attend the annual and semi-annual meetings to hear reports of activities past and future. I saw right from the outset that the synagogue was not exactly managed along democratic lines.

A committee chairman delivers a report. As soon as he's finished, someone moves to accept the report. Another member jumps up to second the motion and the report is approved. There is never time for questions or discussion. Everything moves at high speed, I believe steamroller might be a fitting word. For someone like me, who got his schooling at meetings of the Workmen's Circle and, even more so, at the Poale Zion, where each little item might well become a controversy taking hours to resolve, the synagogue meetings seemed strangely mild and well ordered. I often wondered why the members sat so passively and did not complain or object, or do something.

In recent years, committee reports have no longer been presented. The synagogue issues a bulletin, entitled *The Recorder*. The bulletin contains news of all congregation activities. The semi-annual meetings have been abolished. Instead, several weeks before the annual meetings, short reports of committee activities are published. At the annual meeting, the president remarks in his opening speech:

"You have probably read in *The Recorder* the reports of the committees. If anyone wishes to have additional information, let him ask the director in the office. He will provide a more complete report."

Let me make it clear that I am not charging that the officers and the directors failed to conduct congregation affairs properly. On the contrary, they all gave up much of their time and energy to lead an institution of such varied activities quite well but they did it as if it were their own kingdom.

The synagogue has a men's club, a sisterhood, a junior congregation and a large library. Unfortunately the Yiddish books are stored in crates in the cellar on the pretext that no one asks for Yiddish books. The synagogue also has a school ranging from kindergarten to high school level, with an enrollment of 1,400 pupils.

Of the 1,800 members, only a few hundred show up at the annual meetings. At one meeting only 65 members attended. Those who come sit by passively, accepting the reports without comment. As a result, the leaders are under the impression that whatever they do is correct and acceptable. If someone should ask a question and the question leads to a debate then the leaders take it as a personal affront and the opponent is considered a trouble-maker. I have myself been cast in such a role on a number of occasions.

In the nineteen fifties I heard it said "from behind the scenes" that some of the leaders were toying with the idea of adopting the ideas and philosophy of Dr. Mordecai Kaplan, the Reconstructionist, and that Rabbi Ira Eisenstein was coming to Detroit to lecture on Reconstructionism.

I had read several books written by Mordecai Kaplan and, truthfully speaking, I did not understand his philosophy at all. There is a God but there is no God, meaning that there is a God but He is the universe, in nature. He is not a personalized God cast in the image of man. Prayers are recited not to the Almighty but to one's self. I realize I may be doing Mr. Kaplan's views an injustice but that is the way I understood them.

I went to the lecture, curious and anxious to understand. I had heard Dr. Kaplan speak several times but not about his theories. Usually he poked fun at the Orthodox rabbis and this offended me. However, Dr. Eisenstein was scheduled to speak on Reconstructionism and so I went with eagerness and great expectations.

The chairman introduced Dr. Eisenstein with words of great praise, as if he were a new Isaiah. Dr. Eisenstein spoke for about 50 minutes and used most of that time to ridicule Orthodox rabbis and some of the traditional prayers. He singled out for special derision, the prayer, "Because of our transgressions we have been exiled from our land."

He turned to the rabbi and said, "Not so long ago you prayed (it was several weeks after Passover) 'Because of our transgressions. . . .' I ask you, is this not nonsensical?

Do you know why Judea lost its Jerusalem and why the Holy Temple was destroyed? Because the Roman army was stronger than the Jewish army." He said this with a contemptuous laugh. In a similar vein he continued, "You pray to God. You ask Him to help you. But such a God does not exist. There is no one there to help you."

When he finished, the chairman called for questions. I was the first to ask for the floor, but not to ask a question. I wished to make a statement. I said I had come to listen and to learn what Reconstructionism was all about but instead I had to listen to a diatribe against God and against Hebrew prayers. We had heard the same thing at the end of the nineteenth century from the heretic Socialist writer, Benjamin Feigenbaum, I continued. What the speaker said was not new. The only thing that might be new was that while Feigenbaum had said his piece on the sidewalks of New York's East Side, here we heard the same thing from a rabbi speaking from a pulpit in a synagogue.

Those present, some six or seven hundred, broke out in laughter.

A young lady asked the speaker whether according to his brand of Judaism, a Jew might eat pork. He replied that he did not know why if a Jew wanted to eat pork he should not do so. He himself, the speaker added, did not eat pork because he did not like it.

I asked Dr. Eisenstein how he knew he did not like pork. The audience laughed and applauded the question. We never heard about Reconstructionism after that evening. However, as a result of my comments and pointed questions, I was branded by several of the leaders as a trouble maker.

I rarely missed a lecture on Judaism or on various phases of Jewish life and communal activity. Unfortunately they were not always uplifting experiences. Several grave disappointments are still fresh in my memory. I'll mention two of them. One was a rabbi of the Reconstructionist movement who harangued the audience for almost an hour and a half, ridiculing the Orthodox and Conservative wings of Judaism. His concepts of religious belief in general were outright heresy.

The second, a Conservative rabbi, lectured on Jewish ethics in relation to the Christian tradition. He distorted Judaism completely and climaxed his talk with the statement that the Jews themselves were to blame for the holocaust because they "neglected to teach the Gentiles the ethics and morality of Judaism as ways of life."

I do not wish to convey the impression that all rabbis are of the caliber of the above-mentioned lecturers. On the contrary, by far the greatest majority of rabbis are highly learned men, steeped in Jewish values and tradition.

Also in the middle nineteen fifties the question of moving the synagogue arose. Many Jewish families were leaving the neighborhood and it appeared to be only a matter of time before most of the congregation would melt away. I was against the move although I did not express myself thus at the annual meeting. I sat and listened. I was against Jewish families fleeing the neighborhood as soon as a few black families moved in. It was my feeling that the Negro families that moved into a Jewish section would make good neighbors.

However, if the Jews would start to run, then we would soon be forced to sell our homes and our community institutions at a fraction of their cost or value. The neighborhood would turn completely black and the buildings would quickly deteriorate. But if the Jews remained, there would be no room for other black families and the neighborhood would achieve a workable balance.

However, the annual meeting passed a resolution authorizing the purchase of land for a new building. In this, the leaders of the synagogue proved to be right and I wrong. The number of Jews leaving the neighborhood grew from month to month. And as they left, the blacks moved in. No power on earth could keep them back. It was a veritable Niagara Falls.

Shaarey Zedek Congregation bought forty acres of land and built a beautiful five million dollar synagogue on the site. In 1969, as I write these lines, the membership has climbed to 1,800 families. There are 25 committees functioning with 529 committee members to conduct the congregation's many activities. In addition there is a committee of the sisterhood with 48 representatives and a committee of young married couples consisting of 23 members. The annual budget amounts to over $900,000 and the mortgage to about a million dollars.

WOMEN'S RIGHTS

ANOTHER EVENT WORTH NOTING OCCURred at the synagogue, one in which I took an active part. At one of the annual meetings someone introduced a resolution to change the constitution to provide that "Women should have the same responsibilities and enjoy the same privileges as the men."

According to the constitution, no one could introduce a resolution to alter the constitution. Such a proposal must first be submitted to the Board of Directors. If the Board accepts the proposal the resolution is presented for consideration at the annual meeting. However, on this occasion, the president presented the resolution to the annual meeting. No one took the floor to question it. Instead, one of the directors immediately voiced a second to the motion.

I didn't want to be a "wise guy" and so waited to see if someone else would speak. No one did. The president was ready to take the question to a vote. I am certain that the resolution would have been adopted. At that point I rose to my feet and asked, "What does the motion actually mean? Will a woman have the right to be called to the Torah? Will she be able to lead the congregation in prayer? Will she be able to sound the Shofar on Rosh Hashonah?"

The president replied, "No, it does not mean that."

I asked again, "Then what does it mean? If the resolution appears in the by-laws then a woman will certainly have the right to demand all those privileges. And if they are not given to her then she would be able to take the matter to court and a judge would certainly rule in her favor."

I said I was not for or against giving women equal rights but I wanted to know and I wanted the membership to know exactly what it was we were voting on. I said it was not honest to affect such a radical change through the back door, as it were. "Tell us openly what you wish to accomplish by your motion," I demanded.

With that, several of the older members began to voice objections to the motion in general. When the vote was taken the majority voted against it but those who were in favor shouted their "ayes" very loudly. The president said he wasn't sure whether the motion had passed or not and decided that a secret vote would be taken. He instructed everyone to record his vote for or against on a slip of paper.

However, during the balloting the president spoke in favor of the resolution. He did not explain the implications or the purpose of the resolution but stated that if the motion was defeated it would be an insult to the officers and the Board of Directors.

I felt I had to intervene. I said that at the time a vote is taken it was not proper for the president to try to persuade the members to vote one way or the other. Despite the presidents remarks the overwhelming majority voted against the motion. I would like to add here that according to the synagogue by-laws a woman is allowed to vote if her husband was not present, or if she had no husband.

I thought the matter was settled but such was not the case. The same resolution was introduced at three suceeding meetings and on each occasion the synagogue leaders stubbornly refused to explain why they were introducing the resolution. On each occasion I led the opposition until the question was finally removed from the agenda.

On another occasion it again fell to me to upset the applecart, so to speak. An announcement of an annual meeting contained a notice that there would be several matters presented for amendments to the constitution. They were mainly legal technicalities made necessary because the synagogue was no longer in Detroit, but in Southfield, a suburb which was situated in another county. However, one of the amendments provided that the Board of Directors, among its various duties, should have the power to determine the salaries of the rabbi and the cantor.

I wondered why, after a hundred years, it suddenly became necessary for the procedure to be changed. I read the constitution carefully to learn who determined the salaries of the synagogue officials. The constitution was explicit on this score. It stated that the Board of Directors determined the salaries but that they had to be approved by the membership.

The amendment would deprive the membership of a

Communal Activity; Frustration and Fulfillment

voice in the salaries to be paid to the rabbi and cantor. It would also have the effect of giving the Board of Directors the power to dismiss the rabbi or cantor against the wishes of the congregation, for if the Board were to reduce the salaries of either the rabbi or the cantor they would be obliged to resign their position.

I telephoned a number of members to ask how they felt about the question. Twenty-two were definitely opposed to the amendment. I asked each of them if they would attend the meeting and help me defeat it. Each of them replied in the same vein: "Is it really worth it to come and fight? It is no use, you can't fight City Hall."

I was deeply annoyed by such an attitude for it meant that the members were reluctant to vote against a motion presented by the Board of Directors, even if they opposed it. I argued with them but to no avail. Most of them said they did not intend to come to the meeting. A few promised to come and take the floor in opposition to the motion.

I began to have doubts myself. I wondered what I would gain by battling against directors who wanted to usurp the rights of the membership in deciding such an important matter. I telephoned the president and asked him outright what the officers and directors actually wanted in placing such a motion on the agenda.

The president informed me that it was actually the wish of the cantor. It was incredible. The cantor himself was willing to give the directors the right to set his salary scale without recourse to the membership! Nevertheless, I informed the president that I and other members were opposed to the motion and would fight against it at the meeting.

I was on generally friendly terms with the officers and was afraid that in the heat of the discussion I might say something that would offend them. To avoid this I prepared my statement in writing and was very careful to add nothing that could hurt anyone's feelings.

Four hundred members turned out for the meeting. When the motion was presented and seconded, I asked for the floor, the first to speak. I read from my paper in a quiet, measured voice, listing my objections and the dangers of such a motion. I praised the officers and directors for their devotion to the congregation and for their day-to-day fulfillment of their many responsibilities.

For this, I continued, they needed the assistance of the entire membership. By withdrawing from the membership the right to vote on important matters they, the officers, would estrange them. This would further widen the gulf that already existed between those who carry the burden of leading such a large institution and the masses of members who are content to let them do so.

I assured them that I and all of us had the greatest confidence in the officers and directors but who could foretell what would happen in the future? Who would replace them and what different set of circumstances would confront the congregation that would make it inadvisable, even dangerous to give them such powers?

I related my telephone conversations with the twenty-two members who were opposed to the motion. None of them showed up at the meeting to voice their disapproval. In conclusion, I urged them to remember that what was written by the pen, could not be chopped away by an axe.

Three others followed me, all supporting my viewpoint. When the vote was taken all but two voted against the motion. The vote was followed by a burst of applause in my honor. After the meeting a number of people came up to congratulate me on my presentation and for the courage I had shown in opposing the motion. But there was a price for my victory. My friends among the Board of Directors stopped coming to my house and when we met in the streets or the synagogue, they acted as if they didn't know me.

My wife, Chana, may she rest in peace, supported me all the way. She was convinced of the correctness of my stand and encouraged me to place the truth above everything else. All of my public addresses I first discussed with my wife. She helped me with her sage advice and her suggestions. She had a rare talent for finding just the right word, the most telling phrase, both in Yiddish and in English. She was my editor and censor.

My experience unnerved me enough to persuade me to let others carry on the struggle for a while. And if things developed along certain lines not to my liking it would not mean the end of the world. I had created enough enemies.

There is a man in my circle who has many friends. He is chummy with everyone and everyone held him in high esteem. Once, after a stormy session at a meeting of the Jewish Community Council, he put his arm around my shoulder, as he did with everyone, and told me that my arguments were sound and that my position was correct. I asked him why, if he agreed with me, did he not take the floor to express himself? He replied, "Who, me? Why should I make enemies for myself?"

I understood why everyone liked this person. Thank God I am not like him.

A YIDDISH WRITER AND HIS DISTORTED CHARACTERS

I BECAME INVOLVED IN STILL ANOTHER matter; I am still involved. With me, it is like with the Persian poet Omar Khayam who wrote: "In true repentance I have sworn, but was I sober when I swore?"

I had decided, this I firmly believed, that I would no longer overreact when I witnessed an injustice or something not to my liking in our social-communal life. But how to avoid it, that is quite another matter.

For many years past I have been deeply distressed by a host of Jewish writers writing in English and describing Jewish life in very negative terms; how money-mad the Jews were, how unscrupulous, domineering, etc. Non-Jews reading these books get a not very elevating impression of Jews and Jewish life.

For centuries Christianity has portrayed the Jew as a devil, with horns and a forked tail. In recent times this has almost stopped but our so-called Jewish writers seem to have taken over the burden of denigrating the Jews, just as Gentile writers had done before. It is not now considered "respectable" to read the anti-Semitic ravings of writers like the Nazi Julius Streicher or the Ukranian Troyfim Kitchko. Instead, it is now fashionable to read books by Jewish authors who portray Jews in a most unfavorable light. These books are read in the hundreds of thousands by Jews and Gentiles alike.

What is worse is that many Jews, particularly Jewish women, eager to keep up with the latest in literary fashions, buy the books, if only because they are on the best seller lists. If they are best sellers how can they be bad? They know as much about Judaism as the chicken who gazes at the atonement text in the prayerbook. But they have to be able to say they have read the book that everyone is talking about and to praise it highly. Other women, not wishing to be left behind in the intellectual swim, rush out to buy the book and soon they too are singing its praises.

One Yiddish writer who knows Jewish life and is familiar with Jewish culture, history and traditions, took it upon himself to write in this vein about his people. In his books he portrays his Jewish characters in a manner that must bring joy to the worst anti-Semites. It is almost impossible to find in his writings one character who is normal. Almost all are scoundrels, oversexed and lacking in basic decency. Why must he depict Jewish women as wanton sluts who will go to bed with any man they happen to meet?

He writes the same drivel about our mothers and grandmothers in the shtetlach. The anti-Semites must lick their chops at these juicy morsels of Jewish self defamation. Before a book of his is printed in the original Yiddish it is already being translated for publication in English. When it comes to debauchery he is a specialist; his words drool with lewdness.

He blackens our names but there is little we can do to convince him to change his style, or at least to include some decent Jews in his stories. It's no use, there's more money to be made in sensationalism.

Of late he has become a sought-after speaker. Even synagogues have invited him to lecture at their cultural evenings. This disturbed me greatly. How can this detractor of the Jewish people be a lecturer in a synagogue? In time he was invited by my congregation, Shaarey Zedek, to address a cultural gathering. I went, hoping to hear some sort of explanation of the way he wrote or an analysis of one of his recent novels. I heard neither. He spoke only about himself.

The writer spoke generally about books he had read and people he had met. He said not a word about his treatment of Jews here in America or in Europe where his roots were. He said not a single word about Yiddish literature. Neither did he utter a word about Jewish culture, present or past. Just as he was a capable writer, so was he an accomplished speaker. He knew well how to amuse the audience with a joke or a light comment, how to talk a lot and say very little.

I spoke to several people who had heard him speak at other synagogues and at Wayne State University. It turned out that he delivers the same studied lecture wherever he goes.

I sent a letter of protest to the rabbi and to the synagogue officers for having invited him to speak at the synagogue. Almost three weeks passed and I had still not received a reply. I sent a copy of my letter to the *Jewish News*, a Detroit Anglo-Jewish weekly newspaper. Part of my letter was published but the name of the synagogue was omitted. Subsequently I received a letter from the rabbi rebuking me for having sent my letter to the paper. He wrote that the synagogue had acted correctly in inviting a well known author to address a cultural meeting. He said further that he, as a rabbi, failed to find anything malicious in the author's books.

I corresponded further with the rabbi but failed to convince him that a writer of this sort should not be invited by any synagogue since such an invitation would imply approval of his negative portrayal of Jews. The rabbi's response was that he was not familiar with Yiddish literature but that the writer in question was a good writer. I wrote him that never in the history of book writing were bad books written as well as they are now. And thus the matter rested.

Many friends telephoned me and congratulated me for taking a stand against the writer. Again, when I asked them why they did not write to Shaarey Zedek or to the *Jewish News,* they fell silent. The same happened at a meeting of the Jewish Community Council. Scores of people praised me for my opposition to providing a forum for this anti-Semitic Jewish writer. But when I asked why they did not express their views openly, they failed to reply. This caused me great sadness.

ACTIVITIES AND STRUGGLES

AS I WRITE THESE LINES, AT THE AGE OF 73, I feel a need to sum up my communal activities to this point.

I became a Zionist after hearing the gifted orator, Shmaryahu Levin, in 1915 or 1916 when I lived in Gardner, Massachusetts. I did not participate in Jewish communal life in Gardner. There was a synagogue and also a B'rith Sholem Lodge but I belonged to neither.

Shortly afterward, in 1918, I moved to Springfield, also in the state of Massachusetts. There I joined the Poale Zion, the Zionist Labor Party. I also became interested in the idea of an American Jewish Congress and on two occasions made public speeches advocating such an organization. Once was at a meeting of the Independent Workmen's Circle and the second time was on a street corner. I did not have any success. I remained in Springfield for only six months.

I came to Baltimore toward the end of 1918. I related earlier in my reminiscences how I had participated in the founding of a Yiddish school for children in Baltimore. Later we established a second school, in another part of the city.

I would now like to describe what happened to both schools, which were opened with so much effort and so much difficulty.

The two schools did not last too long. There was a political struggle in the Workmen's Circle. Communist members or sympathizers tried to capture the leadership. I was a traveling salesman at the time and was rarely home. Other very active members, for a variety of reasons, were also unable to attend meetings. I pleaded with the leaders of the Communist group not to disturb the schools, not to use the children in their battle against the "Old Guard." They promised me that they would enlarge the schools and improve them after they had gained control.

I did not believe them but I was powerless to resist since I was away so much of the time. It came to pass as I had feared. As soon as the Communists gained control of the leadership positions, the first victims were the two Yiddish schools.

I settled in Detroit in 1929 and some time later became active once again in the Poale Zion. I also became very active in the American Jewish Congress and remained active until it opened its doors to Communist elements. At that point I withdrew from activities and later resigned.

I did not join the Poale Zion right away because there was a personality struggle taking place within the party and I did not wish to become involved in it. I attended its meetings, contributed to all its campaigns, but not as a member.

My wife and I joined the Parents' Club of the Yiddish school and were very active in its work.

In 1934 the Central Bureau of the Poale Zion suddenly became interested in the work of its Detroit section. A delegation came from New York to review its programs and activities. Included in the delegation were David Wertheim,

Communal Activity; Frustration and Fulfillment

General Secretary of the Party; Joseph Sprinzak, later to become the first Speaker of Israel's Knesseth; and Golda Meyerson, later to become known as Golda Meir, Israel's Prime Minister.

The delegation remained for an entire week but was unable to effect a reconciliation between the quarrelling groups. They decided, instead, to establish a new Poale Zion branch, persuaded me to become president of the new branch, especially since I was not involved in the dispute.

The new branch, Number 3, was organized in March of 1934. It has been in continuous existence ever since but at present is small and ineffective. Of the founders only a few are still around. In the early days it was the most active branch in the city and did excellent work both for the Jewish homeland and for Detroit Jewry.

In 1935 a movement got under way to establish Jewish Community Councils in all American cities with a fair-sized Jewish population. The idea appealed to me greatly. Dr. Samuel Margoshes, then editor-in-chief and English columnist of *Der Tog (The Day)*, popular New York Yiddish daily, came to Detroit to speak in favor of such councils. I agreed with him fully and became active in efforts to organize a Detroit Jewish Community Council. The Council was established in 1937.

I made the rounds of the Landsmanshaften drumming up support for the council, convincing them of the importance of such an organization with representation from local organizations which was responsible to its affiliated organizations for programs and activities.

I was a member of our local Council's Executive Committee for 29 years. I also played an active part in the work of many of its committees. I am still a member of several committees that are still functioning.

In 1947 the struggle to establish a Jewish State reached a new high. The Zionist Council of Detroit by itself was not strong enough to undertake the greatly increased tasks. We did not have sufficient funds and we lacked manpower, especially those capable of developing and implementing the programs the new times demanded of us.

We had no paid employees. The mail and the publicity releases were sent out from my business office. Another shortcoming was the lack of speakers, especially those who could go before non-Jewish groups to explain our cause and to approach local and state officials.

At the time I was president of the Detroit Zionist Council. On thinking the matter over it occurred to me that what we needed was a unified council including the Zionist groups, the Community Council and the local Jewish organizations. The Jewish Community Council had a budget of some $90,000, which was covered by the Jewish Federation. The Council had a large staff of paid workers who could do the technical work. Perhaps the Council leaders could also recruit capable speakers.

I was not disappointed. The Jewish Community Council agreed with the idea. However, it was to be understood that the Community Council would not be engaged in Zionist work on its own initiative but only at the request of the Zionist Council. In other words, the Zionist Council would initiate the actions and the Community Council would help.

I would like to add at this point that Dr. Shmaryahu Kleinman, a member of the anti-Zionist Jewish Labor Bund, was at that time president of the Community Council. That didn't prevent him from supporting the idea as strongly as any of the active Zionists, thus behaving in accordance with his Jewish heart.

I had the great privilege of being a delegate to the his-

Communal Activity; Frustration and Fulfillment

toric "Biltmore Conference" named for the hotel in New York in which it took place. It was at that Zionist conference that the resolution was adopted calling for the creation of a Jewish State in what was then Palestine.

Detroit was always good to the Jewish National Fund. The JNF, as it is popularly known, was established to buy land in Palestine for the settlement of pioneers and builders. For years the JNF had an active Ladies Auxiliary. The women collected more money than the men. The men of the Poale Zion and the Zionist organizations campaigned for the JNF but on a small scale.

Soon after Branch 3 of the Poale Zion was established my wife, Chana, who had been active in JNF work since she was a young girl, began to agitate for greater efforts on behalf of the JNF. She took the entire movement to task for neglecting this worthy cause. The party branch appointed three representatives to the JNF Council in Detroit, my wife Chana, Nathan Linden and William Hordes. All three of them have since passed to the world beyond. Linden, Hordes and Chana remained active on behalf of the JNF to the last days of their lives. Mr. Hordes even became known as "Mr. National Fund."

At my wife's urging I was gradually drawn into the work of the JNF and in the early 1950's I was elected president of the Jewish National Fund Council of Detroit.

The Ladies Auxiliary of the JNF arranged cultural gatherings every month. Once a year there was a special campaign which always produced many thousands of dollars. The campaign ended with a large cultural gathering to which all the contributors were invited.

For many years my wife carried on a personal campaign to keep these monthly meetings and annual gatherings Jewish and spiritual in nature. She wanted the program to include Yiddish and Hebrew songs and the guest speakers to talk on Jewish themes. This general policy was understood but was not honored in actual practice. It took years of persuasion but in the end she won out. When Chana was very ill I took over the task of telephoning the women who had given her contributions over the years. She checked with me repeatedly to make sure that I covered all the cards and omitted nobody. She herself had become a life member of the Women's Auxiliary years before.

On the occasion of my 60th birthday the Poale Zion, together with the local JNF Council, planted a "Laikin Forest" in Israel in honor of my wife and me. We contributed $10,000 toward the forest. The rest of the money came from members of the Poale Zion, the JNF Council and the local Hadassah organization, in which my wife was also very active. Friends and acquaintance also added to the total and in a few months time there was enough to plant a forest of some 12,000 trees. A tree costs 2 dollars.

OTHER CAMPAIGNS

ISRAEL BONDS! VERY SOON AFTER THE Israel Bond campaign was organized a committee was formed in Detroit to sell bonds. The director of the Jewish Federation, afraid it would interfere with the Allied Jewish Campaign, placed all kinds of obstacles in our way. At one point he argued that those buying Israel bonds would reduce their contributions to the Allied campaign. I had the impression that the director was trying to get to the entire committee through me. I am happy and I hope he, too, is happy that his dark forebodings did not materialize.

Community Activity; Frustration and Fulfillment   331

I would like to relate one episode of that period. An Israeli representative, Mr. Pree-Har, the first Postmaster General of Israel, came to Detroit to help in the sale of bonds. I visited him at his hotel daily, bringing with me prospects who were likely to purchase Israel bonds. I took him to my home for dinner almost daily and afterwards to a meeting where he described how the bonds were helping to build Israel. After the meeting I brought him back to his hotel.

He remained in Detroit for more than a week. On Friday night he was a guest at our Shabbas table along with others whom I wanted Mr. Pree-Har to meet. Suddenly, he burst forth with, "I'm glad I'll soon be returning home, I hate American Jews." It came so suddenly I was dumbfounded. My wife recovered first and said to him, "We did not beg you to come to us. We did not send for you."

We were all terribly depressed for the rest of the evening. When he left he did not even bother to say "Good-Bye." We never saw him after that.

The sale of Israel bonds increased in Detroit from year to year. At present Detroit buys over $1,000,000 in Israel bonds every year.

The story of the early Israeli representatives and their attitude towards American Jews is a chapter in itself, a chapter that would be best left unwritten. Later the situation changed for the better, thank God.

YIVO: YIVO, the Yiddish Scientific Institute, was established in Vilno, then under Polish rule, and soon an emissary came seeking funds. I became a contributor immediately. Later, when it re-established itself in New York, after fleeing from the Nazis, I became even more interested in its work of Jewish research and gathering of archives and helped to raise funds for it.

I was especially active when Mendel Elkin became its chief librarian. He was a "landsman," a countryman, hailing from my home town in the old country. When he came to Detroit to conduct fund raising campaigns for YIVO I took him to visit everyone he wished to see. He stayed in a hotel but most of his work was done in my home. He ate at our house and was a treasured and honored guest. He was a true gentleman, a wonderful story teller and was possessed of a rare sense of humor.

I have been a member of the YIVO national Board of Directors for many years and have represented it at the Detroit Federation. Regretfully I am no longer able to attend its annual conferences. I attended two such meetings and found them most interesting and stimulating.

Jewish Teachers Seminary: I have been a regular contributor to the Jewish Teachers Seminary in New York since the early 1920's. Whenever the late Joel Enteen came to Detroit on behalf of the Seminary, I took him around to visit his prospects. In his company I witnessed many tragic and comic scenes as he succeeded or failed to persuade his prospect to contribute to the Seminary, or to prevent them from reducing their gifts.

Enteen was a fanatically devout and sincere man and like all fanatics he lacked a sense of humor. I once told him that he had to widen the circle of the Seminary's supporters because it would be unable to expand to meet its growing needs with only those contributors he had then. Misunderstanding my motive entirely, he assailed me.

"Why?" he asked. "Have you perhaps grown tired of contributing to the Seminary? You would like others to contribute instead?"

I had too much respect for him to argue. I never raised the point again.

I was a member of the Seminary's Board of Directors for many years. When the Seminary was given a charter as an accredited college, I was, naturally, one of the founders.

I still make my annual contribution but since the Seminary merged with the Hebrew Teachers Seminary Herzliyah, I have grown apart from the educational institution.

Congress for Jewish Culture: I have also been a regular contributor to the Congress for Jewish Culture since it was established. And before the Congress came into being I contributed funds to its predecessor, the Central Yiddish Culture Organization (CYCO), now the publishing department of the Congress for Jewish culture.

A MEETING WITH SHOLEM ASCH

I HAVE ALWAYS HELPED YIDDISH WRITERS get their books published and helped them sell their books afterwards. Naturally, the size of my contribution depended on my estimate of the author and his works.

In recent years I have cut down considerably on this aspect of my philanthropy. Books are still mailed to me right after publication with a bill for payment. To tell the truth, I am not always happy with the books I have been receiving. Too often it is enough only to leaf through some of the pages to realize that there is nothing in the book for me. I have more important books to devote myself to.

On such occasions my first impulse is to return the book. Several days later, however, my anger evaporates and I rationalize: "After all, how can I insult the writer? He is sure that what he has written is important, a valuable contribution to Jewish culture. And also, who should be more aware than I of the difficulty facing Yiddish writers in getting their books into print?"

Instead of returning the book I send off a check for the amount billed me. A more irritating problem is presented by the author who sends his book with no indication of the price. This adds the further burden of having to estimte the worth of a book and this is not an easy task.

I have a large house but unfortunately American homes are not built to include large libraries. As a result I am being crowded out by all the books that keep arriving. I no longer know where to put them. Once I returned two books. This was when my wife was lying deathly sick and I was in no mood for reading. Now, years later, I regret having done so.

It was only natural that I should meet many Yiddish authors. One of the most prominent authors I became acquainted with was Sholem Asch, the prominent Yiddish novelist.

My wife and I met Sholem Asch in the home of a good friend in Florida. It was shortly before he left the United States. Asch was in a depressed mood and hardly uttered a word. It was a few days after a particularly ugly incident in which some people had called him "meshumed" (apostate, a renegade from Judaism.) It is one of the worst insults that can be levelled against a Jew.

In addition to my wife and me, the guests included the late Lesowoder and his wife. He had been a popular figure in Jewish literary and cultural circles. The conversation was stilted and strained. It hardly moved. It was a beautiful day. We were all in the garden sitting under the fruit trees on hard wooden benches and orange crates. Asch came over to me, squeezed my shoulder affectionately and said, "Come, let's take a walk."

After walking a while he pointed to my friend's garden and said, "I know that he is thankful to you for all this."

(This was partly true.) He continued, "He is a very fine person but he is terribly insecure. He is worried because he has a mortgage of $6,000 on his house. Pay it for him. Then he will be able to live in peace. He is a good person." He removed his hand from my shoulder and fell silent.

We walked on for several minutes without a word. Then he turned to me and said, "It is not good. It is very sad."

"Yes," I answered. "As one gets older one becomes even sadder."

I knew why Asch was so depressed. The insult he had experienced some days before must have pained him deeply.

When we returned to the garden, my friend's wife complained that her toaster was broken. She repeated it several times as though it was a terrible calamity. Asch told her that he had several toasters at home and that he would give her one. The poor woman was overjoyed. When we all entered Lesowoder's car for the trip home she reminded Asch, in Heaven's name, not to forget the toaster.

Arriving at Asch's house, which stood on an island in Biscayne Bay, I was immediately captivated by the magnificent view. He had a beautiful home, with a separate building for his library and his workroom. I admired his large garden with its many fruit trees and all kinds of other trees and bushes as well as many beds of flowers. Everything was neatly arranged. Everything was in perfect harmony. I felt that it was as beautiful as this in Paradise.

In the shade of the trees were groups of chairs, two, four or six together. As far as the eye could see there were chairs grouped around small tables. I knew that Asch was planning to sell his estate and thought that if he gave some of his chairs to my friend, it would not lower the price of the estate and my friend would be overjoyed.

We waited for about fifteen minutes before Asch came out but without the toaster. He motioned with his hand and said, "Well, let it be so," and with another wave of his hand returned to the house. Not even a "good-bye."

None of us uttered a word as we continued our way back to where we were staying.

THE GREAT DICTIONARY OF THE YIDDISH LANGUAGE

I WAS CONVINCED FROM THE OUTSET that the compilation and publication of so vast a project as the *Great Dictionary of the Yiddish Language* was a mistake. Important as such a work would be it was still necessary to consider the practical problems of completing a dictionary that would run into so many volumes. We did not have a sufficient number of experts nor the financial means for such an undertaking.

I told this to the editor-in-chief, Yudel Mark. I also expressed my doubts in a letter to the monthly magazine, *Die Zukunft (The Future.)* I was assured that my letter would be published, but it wasn't.

I had in mind a bitter experience of trying to publish a general Yiddish encyclopedia. Yiddish-speaking Jews who would use such an encyclopedia, are usually proficient in a second language. They could just as easily refer to encylopedias in that language for information on general subjects. However, those encyclopedias were generally lacking in information on Jewish subjects and we do need a Jewish encyclopedia. Several enterprising and ambitious Yiddish scholars undertook to prepare a general encyclopedia in Yiddish.

Unfortunately, both the impetus and the funds for the project petered out right in the middle. I was very much afraid that the same fate would overtake the *Great Dictionary of the Yiddish Language*. Despite my reservations I promised to contribute $500 to the project, $100 for each of the first five volumes. According to Mr. Mark there would be a new volume published each year until the dictionary would be complete.

I felt that this was an impossible task. Only two volumes have appeared; there would have been four if the schedule had been kept. I paid in $400 of the $500 I had pledged. I received a strong letter from Mr. Mark stating that I had not kept my promise. I had sent only $400. I replied that I had indeed kept my promise since I had pledged $100 for each new volume of the dictionary. I had paid in for four volumes but had received only two.

I received another letter from Mr. Mark, this one milder in tone. In my reply, I wrote that I envied him. He had only one love, the dictionary. But I was involved in a number of love affairs—the State of Israel and its many funds; Jewish education in all its shades; Jewish culture in all its forms, and, my first love, my wife and family to whom I also had obligations. I had been retired, I was not earning any money and had to support myself and my family from my savings.

God would some day decide, I continued, that He was in need of advice from me on how to rule the world and He could invite me to be near Him. This might provide the answer to all problems. But what would happen if God decided that He could well do without my advice, or if He forgot about me completely, especially when I became old and sick? Illness in these times is a luxury that only people with lots of money can afford. And if one has no money then he must turn to his children or to charity. I pray constantly that I should never come to such a state.

Several days later, my wife suffered a stroke. The two months she spent in the hospital incurred costs of $16,000. No wonder our sages warned us "not to open our mouths to Satan."

As if I was not already convinced of the futility of my act, I mailed off the remaining $100 to Yudel Mark. I have since learned that he has settled in Jerusalem and has resumed his work on his *Great Dictionary of the Yiddish Language*. Another staff carries on the work in New York. I hope that Jerusalem's spiritual climate will enhance his work on the dictionary and effect its ultimate and successful completion.

I was pleasantly surprised some time later, in 1969, when I received the *Modern English-Yiddish-English Dictionary* compiled by Uriel Weinreich who had been a professor of Yiddish at Columbia University. The dictionary is beautifully printed and very well organized. The reader can find his translations easily, from Yiddish into English and from English into Yiddish. It is a joy to use this splendid reference book. I was glad that the dictionary had not been published before. Someone from the University of Michigan came to me some years before and actually showed me proof sheets of this dictionary but it was not a finished product. He asked for my help to get it published. Weinreich devoted more time and effort to his dictionary and it was worth it. It gives me a feeling of pride to own it.

A COMMENT ON
JEWISH LIBERALS AND RADICALS

HERE I WOULD LIKE TO COMMENT ON liberals and radicals in Jewish life. In the 1920's and 1930's, we had them in various hues and shades from light pink to bright red. They all possessed one thing in common despite their differences in coloration; they were liberal in their utterances but not in their deeds. They spoke constantly of making the world a better place, but to carry their idealism into real life was not in their minds. Also, they hated Zionism as a religious Jew hates idolatry.

Now, in the 1960's, we find these liberals active in the Jewish organizations. Some have become influential even in Hassidic circles. We also have them in branches of the Poale Zion.

I realize that people do change their opinions and their philosophy. I am aware of the statement of our sages that where a penitent person stands, not even a very righteous man can displace him.

Nevertheless I pray to God not to punish me for not wishing to be in the company of such penitents for no spiritual pleasures emanate from them.

Early in the 1930's, I was present at a meeting where one of those liberals held forth loftily: "Why do people make such a commotion about the Jews? There are only sixteen million Jews throughout the world. Even if all of them were annihilated, would it be such a calamity? More people die in one day of hunger in China or India. So of what importance are sixteen million Jews?"

Of course the man was an idiot. But no one challenged his idiocy and no one left the meeting in protest.

During the past ten or fifteen years our liberals have

taken upon themselves the problems of the blacks. So much so that they feel they must defend even those guilty of robbery, arson and even murder. More recently some of the fuzzy liberals have awakened from their self-deception but there are others who not only continue to defend the rowdies among the blacks but even go so far as to incite them to riot.

I have been dealing with such befuddled liberals since 1921 when the Poale Zion Party split into right and left wing factions. I took no part in that struggle. The empty phrases of the left filled me with disgust. I was always suspicious of those who used beautiful phrases and who acted as though they represented the Almighty Himself in the struggle against injustice. I always have the feeling that they act so, consciously or unconsciously, to cover up their own evil inclinations.

A VISIT TO ISRAEL

IN OCTOBER OF 1968, I VISITED ISRAEL ACcompanied by my daughter Pnina and her husband. Since Pnina was the only one of my daughters who had not been to Israel, we decided to make the trip together, especially after her middle daughter returned from a seven-week visit with glowing reports of all she had seen in the Jewish homeland. I wanted once again to see how the country looked and how its people had progressed. I had read everything I could get about the Jewish State and thought I knew all there was to know about it. It wasn't so. One has to be there in person, to see with his own eyes and get a taste, yes a taste, of the land.

Communal Activity; Frustration and Fulfillment

We visited almost all the cities in the country. We also visited many communal villages and kibbutzim. We went deep into the Sinai Desert, going as far west as the Suez Canal. We went up north to the Golan Heights and across the country from Ashdod to the Dead Sea.

Wherever we went we were amazed to see all that had been accomplished in so short a time by so few people. When other people built their lands it took centuries. Israel accomplished this phenomenal growth in just two decades. Only thirteen years before, Ashdod was just the name of a site where once stood a historic city of the Philistines. When I saw it the first time it was nothing more than long stretches of desert.

Now, in 1968, I beheld a modern city boasting a large port with big ships taking on and discharging cargoes. It has tall buildings, a bustling market with many stores, large ones too. There was a section for small industries and a bit farther away a section for larger industrial plants. The city has wide, smoothly paved streets and housing developments surrounded by trees and flower beds.

All this had been accomplished actually in eight years. I marveled at the way the Israelis had pushed the desert back. We could see where the construction of buildings ended and the desert began.

All the cities have expanded, grown both in size and in population. Haifa sprawls over Mt. Carmel. There are beautiful and spacious homes on the city's hills. Every town has convenient hotel facilities. The many stores, both large and small, are well stocked with merchandise. One can get almost anything money can buy.

The largest city, Tel Aviv, sometimes looks a bit neglected. Some of its streets are narrow and some of its buildings are faded and drooping. The new sections are much prettier.

Transportation, mostly by bus, is very good. There is a local airline for inland flights, mainly to Elath in the south. Taxicabs are also plentiful. There are all material things but of great importance not only to the visitor but also to the local population.

We naturally visited many shrines and historic sites: Bethlehem, Hebron, Tiberias, Safed and many other places. We stood in awe before the tombs of our patriarchs Abraham, Isaac and Jacob and the matriarchs Sarah, Rebecca and Leah; at the graves of our Talmudic sages and codifiers of Jewish law Rabbi Yohanan Ben Zakai, Rabbi Akiba and Maimonides.

At each gravesite I stood for a long time with bowed head. I was deeply moved, my whole body tingled. I was standing on holy ground. I didn't feel quite the same at the educational institutions, the Weizmann Institute in Rehovot, the Hebrew University in Jerusalem, and the Haifa Technion, Israel's equivalent of M.I.T. in the United States. There, I experienced an overpowering feeling of pride. There were other universities in Tel Aviv, Haifa and Beersheba but time did not permit us to visit them all. And the yeshivoth! Where else does a country of some two and a half million people have so many educational institutions?

During my visit to Jerusalem I spent some time with an old friend, Professor Sol Liptzin, who told me that soon there would be an American College in Jerusalem especially for American students. The language of instruction would be English. Later I was notified by Professor Liptzin that the college had opened its doors and had enrolled its first group of students.

I had an entirely different feeling when I visited Acco, the city built by the Phoenecians some 3,700 years ago. We wandered through and around the ancient fortress city that

Communal Activity; Frustration and Fulfillment

held the history of many peoples. The fortress included a lodging house for travelers and Maimonides himself is said to have spent a night within its walls. The British Mandatory Power turned the fortress into a prison and kept locked in its cells the Sternists and other opponents of British control. A number of Jewish fighters for national liberation were hanged there.

Now the fortress contains a museum which describes the turbulent events of the fight against the British. It includes newspaper accounts, photographs and other display material. One can see the cells in which the captives were held and even the names of the inhabitants. There was no furniture in the cells. The prisoners had to sit and sleep on straw mats spread on the cement floors.

The room where the Jewish martyrs were executed remained unchanged.

I spent half a day wandering through the prison and left only when one of the watchmen told me it was time to close up. I carried away with me a feeling of shock that followed me throughout the prison. It was almost as if I myself had been there as an inmate, not a visitor.

As I walked around the yard surrounding the fortress I noticed many people, young and old, dressed in green uniforms. All were sitting or walking quietly, deeply absorbed. I asked the guard who those people were. He told me they were mentally ill patients. Some of them were victims of the wars with the Arabs but most of them were survivors of the Nazi concentration camps.

Our first act in Jerusalem was a visit to the Western Wall which I had never before seen except in photographs. It was mid-day and only a few people were there, most likely tourists like myself. Several stood close to the Wall touching it with their hands and moving their lips in prayer.

Others stood quietly facing the Wall, lost in their thoughts.

I approached the Wall and touched its massive stones. Tears came to my eyes. How long I remained standing there I do not know. My daughter finally came to me, took me by the arm and led me away.

Several days later, it was a Friday afternoon, Professor Liptzin telephoned and asked if I would like to go with him to the Western Wall for Sabbath services. "But how would I return?" I asked. We would walk together, he said. It was not too far from the hotel where we were staying. I was overjoyed.

It was still daylight when we hailed a taxicab and were driven to the Wall. Scores of Jews were already there. Soon more began to stream toward the Wall from every direction. Several hundred had assembled there by the time Mincha prayers were said and still they came. At the time of the evening prayers to "Receive the Sabbath Queen," the plaza in front of the Wall was filled.

I looked around at my fellow worshippers. There were Jews with long earlocks, with short earlocks, with beards and without beards; Jews in caftans and others in short jackets, dark-skinned and light-skinned, their faces aglow with a spiritual light.

Suddenly groups began to form in accordance with their appearance and mode of dress, the size of their beards or their earlocks. Each group began to recite the Sabbath prayers separately, with their own cantors leading them. I walked from group to group listening to them intone the traditional chants, each in its own way.

One man came to me and asked me to join his group which needed a tenth man to complete a minyan. I went. Soon others joined us and our minyan became a whole community. When we came to the hymn, "Come my friend to meet the Sabbath," several groups began to dance. It was truly an inspiring and never-to-be-forgotten experience.

We returned on foot through a narrow street with hundreds of steps leading up. Stores owned by Christian Arabs lined both sides of the street.

Never during my stay in Israel did I grow tired. I walked long distances, climbed mountains, bathed in the waters of Elath and the Dead Sea, climbed to the top of David's Tower, things I would not have dared to do at home. And I never felt better! I enjoyed walking through the streets and talking to people. I admired their courage and their calm acceptance of the difficulties they were facing. I was particularly impressed by their confidence. Come what may they would endure.

Many told me, "We in Israel are not afraid. Only the American Jews are fearful."

I got a taste of what it was like to be an Israeli one Saturday evening in Tel Aviv. We took a walk along Diezengoff Street, the principal thoroughfare of the city and saw thousands of people, young and old, promenading. Wide as the side-walks were it was difficult sometimes to pass by. All appeared happy and self-assured. Boys and girls walked along arm in arm. The coffee shops were crowded, all the tables and chairs were occupied. After a while we were able to get a table and ordered coffee which we sipped as we watched the passing parade of fellow Jews from all parts of the world.

I have visited many cities in the United States and in Europe. Nowhere did I see such untroubled people, not even in Paris. It pays to visit Israel, if only to walk along Diezengoff Street on a Saturday night.

We stopped at fine hotels. The service was good but the dining rooms could have stood some improvement. So could the food. Apparently the Israeli chefs are anxious to emulate their French colleagues. They act as if water was impure. Wine they served in a minute, but a glass of water is another matter. The diner might as well be eating in the middle of the desert. I asked for water several times but to no avail. Even an appeal to the head waiter failed to bring the precious liquid. When one begins to raise his voice and show some anger then the glass of water is finally brought.

When we were in Nablus, as the Biblical city of Sechem is called by the non-Jews, we visited the Samaritans and went into their prayer house. The high priest spoke Hebrew with the Ashkenazi accent of the Western Jew. He also spoke English. They showed me their Torah scroll which they said was 3,700 years old. They said it was inscribed by an ancestor of the high priest, by a great grandson of Aaron, brother of Moses. The high priest claims he is descended from the Tribe of Levy. The high priesthood is not inherited. Only the oldest member in the priestly family inherts religious leadership. Other Samaritans claim descent from other ancient Hebrew tribes, one family from the tribe of Menasseh and several families from the tribe of Ephraim.

All the families combined total some 400 souls. About half of them live in Nablus and the other half in the Israeli city of Holon, near Jaffa, which is now part of Tel Aviv. The high priest said the Samaritans were very poor and that they had difficulty in maintaining their school. There are so few of them that it is sometimes difficult for the young people to find mates. Sometimes there are more girls than boys and at other times the reverse is true.

I was happy to find, on this trip, a change for the better in the attitude of the Israelis towards American Jewry and towards the Yiddish language. When we visited Israel in

1955, most people showed little regard for American Jews and they refused to converse in Yiddish.

An example. We stopped at a store one hot day to buy a glass of seltzer. The woman who owned the store spoke to us in German. I noticed that she had a number tatooed on her arm which meant that she had been in a Nazi concentration camp. I asked her the name of her home town. She replied that she was from the Eastern European city of Byalostok. I asked her angrily if she spoke German or Yiddish when she lived in Byalostok. She remained silent.

When I went into a bank or a post office no one answered me in Yiddish. This time, however, in 1968, wherever I went, to the Finance Ministry, the bank, the stores, everywhere I found people able and willing to converse with me in Yiddish, even though we could have spoken in English. I even found a Moroccan store-keeper who was able to carry on a conversation in Yiddish.

FAMILY, HEALTH AND CHILDREN

AS I MENTIONED IN AN EARLIER CHAPTER, only two sisters survived the war. They were all that remained of my family. The Nazis murdered my mother, my brother, his wife, and their two children. In 1948 my sisters wrote to me from the Soviet Union asking me to stop corresponding with them; they said they no longer wished to hear from me. However, I continue to write, three or four times a year, only a few lines. I inquire about their health and report on the state of my health, nothing else.

I do not receive any replies to these letters and the letters are not returned. I do not know what to make of it. If I received even the briefest reply I would make the trip to the Soviet Union to visit them. But I do not hear from them and so I refrain from visiting them lest I make things worse for them.

I have been feeling much better in recent years. My heart is more relaxed; I do not do any physical work. I have some pain and the slightest physical exertion leaves me tired. But these are the ravages of age and I can put up with them. I still drive my own car but I avoid driving at night. Outside of the city I do not drive at all. In the suburb where I now live, there is virtually no public transportation and without a car one cannot go anywhere.

Pnina, my oldest daughter, manages a traditional Jewish home. She is the president of a local Hadassah chapter and is active in the sale of Israel bonds. She is an avid reader and is well versed in Judaism and Jewish history. She is a competent pianist and loves art. Her son, the oldest of four children, is married. He attended the Hebrew School of a Conservative Synagogue and was a good student. Unfortunately, he did not go very far in his Jewish studies. The school was not a very good one. There were no qualified teachers. Often classes were taught by women members of the school board.

On my visit to Baltimore, where my daughter lived at the time, I went to see the director of the school. He blamed all the shortcomings on the rabbi. My grandson can read the prayers in Hebrew but that's about all. He was a good student at the university. Now he is in his father's business.

The oldest daughter is studying at the university. She attended a congregation school but her knowledge of Judaism is also limited. Both children play the piano.

Pnina's middle daughter also attended a congregation school but she knows even less about Judaism than her sister.

The youngest daughter attends a Jewish day school and loves Hebrew more than English.

After many years of ups and downs, they are now well off financially. My son-in-law has an automobile agency and is doing very well.

My second daughter, Beth-Sheva, is married to a psychoanalyst. He is of the Freudian school and is quite successful.

Although Beth-Sheva and her husband are not religious they follow many of the ancient Jewish traditions. They light candles every Friday night and they celebrate the Jewish holidays—but in their own way. They are very much concerned about Israel and are interested in Jewish life in America. They visited Israel and were enthused with what they saw. They were determined to go again the following summer and take the children with them.

Beth-Sheva received her B.A. from the University of Michigan and a Master's from New York University. She has devoted a great deal of time to recording for the blind and to the Art Museum where she compiled a bibliography of the definitive books on each artist who has worked in the graphic arts. But her first love is still the theater. She performs with various local dramatic groups. She also directs the dramatic group at the Jewish Community Center.

They have two children, a boy a bit over ten and a girl about nine. They attend the Sunday School of a Reform Temple. The boy is proficient in Hebrew and will undoubtedly acquire a greater knowledge of Jewish religion and history by the time he reaches Bar Mitzvah age. The girl is a beginning student.

For general education they attend a private school. Both are very bright and are a full year ahead in their classes. The boy reads a lot, especially American history. In this he knows more than his grandfather.

Judith, the third of my daughters, got her B.A. at the University of Michigan and her Master's at Columbia. She reads and speaks Yiddish and has a good command of Hebrew. She worked for the State Department in the United States and then in India and later in London. After returning home she wrote articles for a Detroit newspaper and for a number of magazines. In 1962 she wrote a book for children entitled *Understanding Israel.* Public schools all over the country have been buying the book.

For a while Judith was the representative of the American Jewish Congress in Detroit and Cleveland. Later she became an assistant professor at Wayne State University. At present, she is an assistant professor at Albion College. Judith's husband, a Ph.D., was associated with the Detroit school system, in later years as principal of a high school. He is now a full professor and also Dean of the Education Department at Albion College.

Albion is a smallish town about 100 miles from Detroit, with a population of some 12,000. Judith and her husband have two little girls. When they lived in Detroit, the older of the two went to a Yiddish-Hebrew Farband School. Now, living in a town that has only half a dozen Jewish families, it is no longer possible for either of the children to attend Jewish school on a regular basis. Instead, they take the children to Jackson, a town some 18 miles distant, every Sunday to attend Sunday School. Jackson has a sizable Jewish Community but has only one synagogue which serves all three denominations, Orthodox, Conservative and Reform. Judith teaches the advanced classes.

Shulamith attended a Talmud Torah as a child but learned very little there. She disliked her teacher intensely. I spoke to the principal several times and suggested that he transfer her to a different class. Each time I received the same reply; according to her age and educational level, there was no other class for her. Finally we had to transfer her to the Shaarey Zedek Sunday School where the language of instruction was English instead of Hebrew. She was the best in her class and graduated with honors.

Shulamith is a graduate of the University of Michigan with a Master's from Wayne State University. She taught for a while in a junior high school in a mixed neighborhood; blacks, Puerto Ricans and whites. The white children were mainly from former farm families. In that school she learned things about life completely new and strange to her; pupils of 12 and 13 who had become pregnant; violence, often accompanied by knifings; and other manifestations of deprivation and ghetto existence.

After a year she gave up her post and took a position in the department of general studies in the Day School of the Academy Beth Yehudah. She was delighted with her new pupils, their conduct and their capacity for learning. Homework was never a problem. They brought their assignments in on time and complete. She also admired their interest in topics outside the classroom. For several years her class took part in a quiz show sponsored by a local newspaper and competed with teams from other schools, including non-Jewish private schools.

The questions ranged far and wide, from films through sports and politics. Shulamith's class invariably won. She couldn't understand how her pupils found time to do so much added reading since their school hours were almost double those of the regular schools. In addition, they had enough homework to keep them busy for whatever hours were left in the day.

Shulamith based the dissertation for her Master's degree

on "The Rise and Development of Yeshivah Beth Yehudah," a theme she wrote with love and understanding.

Shulamith is married to an engineer and is the mother of three children, two girls and a boy. They make their home in Los Angeles. Her husband was born in Germany and was taken by his parents to Palestine when he was one year old. He took part in Israel's War for Independence as a volunteer; he was too young to be drafted. After the war, he came to the United States to study and remained here. He still dreams of returning to Israel. I wonder if it will ever come to pass?

Two of my four sons-in-law lost their fathers before they married. The father of the third died a year after his son's marriage. Thus I have only one "mechutin," the father of a son-in-law. He lives in Baltimore and is a fine man but his interests and mine do not run along similar lines. With the exception of our grandchildren, we do not have much in common. For the past few years, he has been partially paralyzed and his mind is not always clear.

I have no relatives in America with the exception of one cousin in Los Angeles. My wife, Chana Leah, had a large family but none of them live in Detroit. I have many acquaintances; my wife had many more. But acquaintances and relatives are two different things. I had a good friend of many years but he passed away. I miss him and often feel lonesome. I have several friends, highly educated and interesting people. But I am much older than they. We meet occasionally but I tend to avoid them when I feel sad or lonesome. I do not want to impose on them and I do not want people to keep me company out of pity.

CHANA LEAH, MAY SHE REST IN PEACE

I WAS MARRIED TO CHANA LEAH FOR over 45 years. She passed on to the True World on the 28th of February, 1968.

She had suffered a stroke. Her brain was severely damaged and soon she became completely paralyzed. During the 54 days she remained in the hospital she did not regain consciousness for a moment. There were times when I spoke to her that I thought she heard me. But she gave no sign.

I summoned brain specialists and asked if perhaps surgery could prolong her life. They were not at all encouraging. They said that even if my wife survived an operation she would still be paralyzed. They performed several tests and examined her very carefully but in the end decided that they could not operate.

It was frightful to watch her agony. The doctors assured me that she felt no pain but I didn't believe them. I felt they were just trying to make it easier for me and our daughters.

And so she passed away, at the age of 72. Now I would like to describe what kind of a person she was so that her grandchildren and the great grandchildren and others to come shall know something about her.

Outwardly she looked like a woman of grandeur. She gave the impression of being tall but was actually only five feet three inches in height. She held herself erect and walked proudly. Chana was a very beautiful woman and commanded respect from everyone, even other women. She read widely, both in Yiddish and in English and was a lover of good music. In her youth she had a beautiful voice and often sang as she went about her household tasks. She knew many English and Yiddish songs and even included Negro spirituals in her repertoire.

Chana loved the truth. She could not stand sham or dishonesty in anyone. She could not tolerate empty phrases or people who said one thing and did the opposite. She disliked vulgarity and smutty stories. She indulged her love for art by frequent visits to museums and art galleries. At home she surrounded herself with scores of art objects.

My wife's taste in clothes was quite original. In her younger years, when our finances did not allow her to purchase fancy clothes, she sewed for herself and the children. Often she remodeled old clothes, turning them into new and fashionable garments. This does not mean that she slavishly followed the latest in fashions. She bought or made her clothes to suit herself. She was not one to run with the herd, as it were.

Our home was kosher. My wife managed a traditional home with family observances on the Sabbath and on the holidays. She never objected to my contributions to various causes or to my communal activities, even when it meant neglecting her.

Although she was a woman of many virtues, my wife was, after all, human, and not without some shortcomings. She was not the soul of diplomacy. She was outspoken and often said things she might have left unsaid, usually at just the critical moment. Her knowledge of English was far better than mine. Thus, if in conversation, I would use the wrong word or phrase, she would correct me immediately, breaking my train of thought. I pleaded with her frequently to let me at least finish what I was saying before correcting me. It was no use.

This was really quite unimportant. Even so, we sometimes had some pretty sharp arguments because of it.

Chana was never really satisfied with herself. She wanted to have a college education. She also wanted to be a polished public speaker. She had a keen mind but did not express her thoughts very well. She wanted to be a painter and attended art school for a year. Actually she did show some talent but more in the field of design. She also wanted to be a pianist. Although she sang well and was a lover of music, she was never able to pursue her musical education.

There were external problems and inner conflicts. She was quite young when her father died. The oldest of six children, my wife had to stop school and become a shop worker at the age of fourteen. She had to stifle her thirst for learning and help her widowed mother care for her family.

We were very poor when we married. Such a simple matter as getting a piece of bread was often a serious problem. When the children came she had to postpone once again her dreams of furthering her education. By the time my earnings began to approach more satisfactory levels, we were both in our forties. Later she tried to resume her oft-interrupted education, but without too much success.

The children were growing up. It was time to see to their education, both Jewish and general. There were also piano lessons and dancing school. And so the years flew by with her dreams unfulfilled. This made her feel inadequate, an incomplete person. It was tragic. She had every reason to be happy; beautiful and gifted daughters, all married in due time and to fine intelligent young men, all leading a satisfying, productive life. She had eleven beautiful grandchildren whom she loved dearly. Financially we were well situated. We had a beautiful home and were respected in the community. It would appear to be enough to satisfy anyone.

Still my wife was not happy. That I could see without too much difficulty. When I asked her why she was at a loss to explain her deep feelings of discontent. Now that she is gone I have a deep feeling of emptiness in my heart.

Late in 1966 we sold our house, which we loved, and moved into a big house in Southfield, a suburb of Detroit. We both wanted a large house to be able to continue to entertain guests on Sabbath eve and to receive visitors from other cities as had been our custom for many years. But it was not destined to be, for Chana became ill. She had to undergo eye surgery and still suffered from a bad fall years before from which she had never completely recovered. She was afraid she would fall again and hesitated to take a step without holding on to me. Assurances from the eye doctor and our family doctor that she could walk without assistance were of no avail.

In her later years my wife was pretty much of an invalid. She kept close to the house and refused to go to meetings even when I offered to drive her there and call for her afterward. Perhaps she didn't want to impose on me.

Gradually she lost interest in the household and let our housekeeper take over more and more. We have had the same housekeeper, a black woman, devoted and capable, for over 20 years. My wife taught her to cook and to keep a kosher home. She took care of all the housework and I did the shopping.

I did not realize how ill Chana was. When she argued with me over some trivial matter, I became annoyed. But soon I realized that she was sicker than I or the doctors had thought. I no longer became annoyed with her demands. I gave in and didn't argue. Now, it is all over.

I have changed nothing in the house since her death. Our housekeeper is still with me and as long as she takes care of the house and prepares the meals I continue to invite guests for Friday evenings. If my daughters are unable to

Communal Activity; Frustration and Fulfillment

visit me over the week-end my housekeeper sees to it that there is plenty of food for me while she enjoys her two days off. I intend to continue this routine as long as my health permits. What will be later, when my health begins to fail, I cannot foretell.

I have no desire to live with any of my children. Although all of them have invited me to do so, I prefer to lead my own life and live in my own house.

The year 1968 was for me a difficult and tragic year. I lost my beloved wife, Chana, after forty-five years of life together. Two weeks later I lost a very dear friend whom I had known for over fifty years. That same year the business that I had built up so painstakingly over the years and watched over like a fragile child, went into bankruptcy. Although I had not been associated with it for some years, its good name was still precious to me. Finally, Branch no. 3 of the Poale Zion, which I helped organize and over which I presided for many years, was dissolved after 34 years of active service because the few members who remained were too old and frail to carry on.

I am fortunate indeed in having four devoted daughters and eleven grandchildren so I can share their joys and their hardships, to keep my life occupied with their problems and their achievements. Nor have I removed myself from communal activities. I continue to be as active as my strength permits—for the state of Israel and for Jewry in general.

I have no regrets or apologies for my activities over the years. If I had to live my life over again, I would, with perhaps a few minor exceptions, repeat my life exactly as I have lived it. I am certain that my dear wife, Chana, now in the True World, agrees with me.

Completed this first day of Nissan, Tashkat, 1969. English translation concluded the first day of Nissan, Tashla (March 27), 1971.

Last photograph of my wife and me, at Grossinger's, October, 1967.

My daughters Judith, Pnina, Beth-Sheva, and Shulamith. My home, 1968.

My daughters left to right sitting, Judith, Pnina, Beth-Sheva, Shulamith.
Standing, their husbands,
Dr. Sol Elkin, Stanley Wilkins, Dr. Harold Davidson, Israel Tuchman.